P9-BZO-764

Jackson & Perkins®
Selecting, Growing, and Combining
OUTSTANDING PERENNIALS

• MIDWESTERN EDITION •

TERI DUNN & MELINDA MYERS

COOL SPRINGS PRESS
A Division of Thomas Nelson Publishers
Since 1798

www.thomasnelson.com

Acknowledgements

Many thanks to: Jenny Andrews, Hank McBride, Billie Brownell, and Ramona Wilkes at Cool Springs Press; Donna Mello; and the 2003 Boston Red Sox...*y los tres amigos.*

—Teri Dunn

Jackson & Perkins®

Selecting, Growing, and Combining

OUTSTANDING PERENNIALS

Copyright 2003 Teri Dunn and Melinda Myers

All rights reserved. No part of this book may be reproduced or transmitted in any form, or by any means, electronic or mechanical, including photocopying, recording, or by any information storage and retrieval system, without permission in writing from the publisher.

Published by Cool Springs Press, a Division of Thomas Nelson, Inc.
P.O. Box 141000, Nashville, Tennessee 37214.

Library of Congress Cataloging-in-Publication Data is available.
ISBN 1-591860-88-1

First printing 2004
Printed in the United States of America
10 9 8 7 6 5 4 3 2 1

Managing Editor: Jenny Andrews
Designer: Bruce Gore
Production Artists: S.E. Anderson and Bill Kersey

Visit the Thomas Nelson website at www.ThomasNelson.com

TABLE OF CONTENTS

INTRODUCTION

The Promise of Perennials

Standing outside on a gentle early-spring day, the heady scent of good soil in the air, and a freshly planted bed of young perennials before me, I survey my work proudly. The plants look small and vulnerable, with little tufts of foliage and small nametags by their sides. And yet...they look so promising. I vividly imagine this same spot in midsummer, and feel a surge of hope and excitement.

A perennial is indeed a promise—that the young plant will grow larger and stronger, a delightful sight not only in its first season, but even more so in the years to come. For unlike an annual, a perennial does not have a single year of glory and then need to be replaced. Planting day is an investment. There are beautiful flowers and attractive leaves to look forward to. And more—watching a young plant take hold and prosper, making a bigger and better show with each passing year. Along the way, the perennial gardener is also granted pleasures of the moment, such as a butterfly alighting on a purple coneflower, or the perfume of a white-flowered summer phlox greeting you when you return home in the evening.

And a perennial garden delivers on the promise of its many plants in combination. Flowers surge upward and outward, forming living bouquets. Leaves of different colors and textures intertwine and overlap. As the garden fills in, pictures you envisioned become reality—blue veronica looking enchanting with lemon-yellow coreopsis; an exciting combination of Indian blanket, crocosmia, and black-eyed susan, with their hot-colored red, yellow, and orange flowers; or the sweet, soft appeal of silvery, felted lamb's ears with pink dianthus. Spontaneous pictures also happen, as when a trailing salvia cascades beside bright purple verbena, making an unexpectedly handsome pairing.

Once started, the show further improves. And that is why so many gardeners turn to perennials—they live up to their promise.

Getting Started

Installing a perennial garden, or even just adding a few perennials to your landscape at a time, is not a mysterious project. It takes common sense, and it takes some planning.

Like so many other purchases for your home or yard, you get what you pay for with perennials. Quality plants yield quality results. Choosing perennials, then, becomes a two-part process.

Black-eyed Susan, *Rudbeckia fulgida* var. *sullivantii*

A lush perennial shade garden with ferns, astilbe, Japanese primrose, and Solomon's seal.

Good Varieties

First shop for the varieties you want. This is a lot of fun. There are so many great ones to choose from, and more coming onto the market every year. Thumb through those dreamy catalogs that arrive in your mailbox in late winter and flag your favorites. Peruse gardening magazines and gardening books for more ideas and options.

In a later chapter of this book, you will find a gallery of 100 excellent perennials, including important details about their needs

The love of gardening is a seed that once sown never dies.

Gertrude Jekyll

and habits as well as recommendations for tried-and-true cultivars. This directory is a good place to start, particularly if you are new to perennial gardening and overwhelmed by the huge variety available these days.

How do you know if a variety that's captured your fancy is a good one? Award-winners are solid choices, but unlike annuals or roses, the perennial world doesn't abound in beauty contests; you'll mainly see the occasional Perennial Plant Association winner, honored because it proved to be widely adaptable and very reliable. Varieties identified as new are, generally speaking, superior, simply because plant breeders are constantly making improvements. Classic choices and old favorites may have familiar-sounding names—they may appear repeatedly in reference books, catalogs, or gardens you've admired.

But in the end, your own garden's unique conditions (soil type, sun or shade, etc.) and your own approach to gardening (total devotion or laissez-faire, or somewhere in the middle) will dictate which perennials are best.

Japanese Iris, *Iris ensata* 'Caprician Butterfly'

Good Plants

Savvy shopping and high standards will get you good perennials for your garden. Basically, you want to get quality plants from reputable sources. The second chapter will arm you with the information you need to discern whether a plant is in good health.

The company, nursery, or garden center from which you purchase should also inspire confidence. Their staff should be available to answer your questions knowledgably, and they should have a policy of standing by their wares. If they are able to help you with garden design a bit, with interesting groupings of compatible plants or even pre-planned gardens, even a rank beginner can taste early success!

A Perennial Garden You Can Be Proud Of

It's such a thrill to watch a perennial garden take hold and become better, fuller, and more beautiful with each passing year. This dream is completely attainable. And—to paraphrase the old adage—the journey is as good as the destination. Every step of the way yields its own rewards and delights.

The journey really begins when you imagine the colors and textures you want to see mix and harmonize (or even startle or surprise) from one season to the next. Your picture will be made from a living palette. This presents its unique challenges—plants are more dynamic, willful, *and* whimsical than, say, paints! But you can still aim for certain effects, and tweak the picture later, by changing varieties within a species or changing plant choices altogether. Perennials, as a

group, are adaptable and forgiving. If you offer them good soil and good care, they won't mind if you tinker.

So make a plan, as specific or vague as you wish, and plunge in. And when you install your perennials, bear in mind these basic principles (explained in more detail in the coming chapters):

- Good soil leads to happy, healthy plants. If you do nothing else for your perennials, good-quality, prepared soil is a must.

- Proper planting—including attention to proper spacing—leads to happy, healthy plants.

- Well-cared-for plants show their appreciation by developing into a gorgeous garden.

A mixed border with a wide variety of plants, including peonies, alumroot, buttercups, and roses.

PERENNIALS PAST, PRESENT, AND FUTURE

IN THIS CHAPTER:

- **History of perennial gardening**
- **What is a perennial?**
- **A little botany**
- **Where do perennials come from?**
- **Trends in perennial gardening**

History of Perennials and Perennial Gardening

While perennials have appeared in gardens for hundreds of years, either for their beauty or their usefulness, gardening specifically with perennials is a fairly recent development. In nineteenth century England estate gardens were typically divided into "rooms" and the "border" was an important part, combining a variety of plants such as bulbs, annuals, perennials, and shrubs. As gardening moved into the twentieth century, designers began to see the merits, including longevity and ease of maintenance, of growing perennials and some gardens began to be planted primarily with perennial plants.

In the U.S., gardeners seeing gorgeous images of English gardens longed to have the same thing in their own backyards. And the trend of perennial gardening began to take hold in this country as well. Unfortunately, many plants that thrive in England are not well adapted to some regions of the U.S. In more recent years there has been a strong push to utilize plants that are well suited to local conditions.

In the past twenty years perennials have made great strides in popularity, leading to a wealth of plant possibilities and garden styles utilizing perennials. The Perennial Plant Association is a national organization devoted to promoting perennials. Local societies also exist in many areas. Plant societies that focus on particular genera have also developed and there are groups devoted specifically to hostas, daylilies, irises, as well as other plants.

Aster × frikartii 'Jungfrau'

Herbaceous plants can be annual, biennial, or perennial. The annual *Cleome hassleriana* (left) grows to maturity, produces seed, and then dies in the course of one year or one growing season. The biennial black-eyed susan species *Rudbeckia hirta* (middle) takes two years to complete this cycle, though it often reseeds in the garden and thus might appear to be perennial. Perennials can live for several to many years. *Helleborus orientalis*, Lenten rose (right), is a very long-lived perennial plant.

What Is a Perennial?

A perennial is a plant that continues to grow (and reproduce, via seeds, root expansion, or both), year after year—often for many years. In contrast, annuals grow from seed and hurtle through their entire life cycle in a single season, going from flowers to fruit to decline. Biennials take two years to complete the cycle.

It is no wonder, then, that more and more gardeners are flocking to perennial gardening. After the initial investment of time and money, choosing and planting, gardeners are finding that perennials ask little and give a lot. They make a long-lasting garden—one that gets better and better as time goes by.

What qualifies as a perennial can also depend on your climate. Because of its cold hardiness, a plant might be an annual in one part of the country, but perennial in another; sometimes these are referred to as "tender" perennials. In warmer zones even some tropical and sub-tropical plants can be perennial. In addition to cold hardiness issues, plants can be restricted by the heat of a region, particularly night temperatures. High-altitude and cooler climate areas can accommodate a different group of perennials, including those called alpine plants, which melt in hot, humid climates. Learn about your particular region to know what your range of perennial possibilities might be.

PERENNIAL HERBS

Santolina and lavender with daylilies.

Herbs have been grown in gardens for centuries for medicinal uses, flavorings, and other purposes. Many attractive herbs are now included in perennial plantings, such as bee balm, yarrow, artemisia, sage, thyme, lavender, lamb's ears, and rosemary.

A Little Botany

Perennials represent many different plant families, which is one reason there is such wonderful variety among perennial plants. Some families are fairly small, but some are quite large and many perennials are cousins. The aster family, Asteraceae, is one large group, including asters, daisies, sneezeweed, Joe-Pye weed, goldenrod, chrysanthemum, and sunflowers. Under the family category, plants are further defined by their genus and species, which make up their botanical name.

Worldwide a particular plant has the same botanical name, though it might have a wide variety of common names. Common names can also be confusing if different plants have the same or similar names. Sweet William is a common name for *Dianthus barbatus,* but wild sweet William refers to *Phlox divaricata,* which isn't even in the same plant family. So, to really know what you have, what you want, and what you're buying from a nursery, pay some attention to the botanical name.

The first part of the botanical name designates the genus. The second word is technically the "specific epithet" (shortened by the lay-person to "species"). For *Monarda didyma,* or bee balm, *Monarda* is the genus and *didyma* is the species name. A plant that is listed with just its genus and specific epithet is called a species, and is typical of how that plant looks in the wild.

Some wild species are popular and beautiful garden plants just as they are, such as butterfly weed and bluestar. But many perennials also have numerous forms that differ from the wild species in growth habit, flower or foliage color, or some other trait. These forms, varieties, or cultivars are natural mutations. Hybrids are crosses between two different plants, meaning the pollen of one has been introduced to the other plant's flower and seed has formed. The plants grown from this seed will combine traits of both parent plants. A hybrid is designated with an "X" in the name, such as *Astilbe × arendsii.*

What Is a "Cultivar?"

"Cultivar" is short for "cultivated variety," and means that the variety was developed in cultivation. Cultivars bring in a new or better color, or a better plant in terms of growth

Plants are categorized by family, genus, and species. Some plant families are quite large. Jerusalem sage, *Phlomis fruticosa* (left); obedient plant, *Physostegia virginiana* (middle); and autumn sage, *Salvia greggii* (right), are all in the mint family, Lamiaceae.

Aquilegia caerulea 'Crimson Star' is a red-flowered cultivar of a blue-flowered species of columbine, *caerulea* meaning "blue."

habit, bloom period, hardiness, and longevity, providing us with an amazing range of choices.

Cultivar names are in single quotation marks and follow the genus and species. For example: The yarrow cultivar 'Fanal' is written *Achillea millefolium* 'Fanal'.

Generally speaking, a cultivar comes into being in one of two ways. A horticulturist or amateur hybridizer develops it by crossing two or more "parent" varieties in search of worthy "children." Or a sharp-eyed gardener or horticulturist may cull it from a public or private display or a nursery, the only pink sedum in a group of dark purple ones, for instance. A new type of plant becomes a cultivar when it is separated out and given a name.

Where Do Perennials Come From?

Perennials come from all over the world, and plant explorers, breeders, nursery propagators, and gardeners continue to find and introduce new species and forms. Hostas are originally native to Asia, flax lily hails from New Zealand, coreopsis is from North America, and ice plant is from Africa. Though many perennials are adaptable as to their soil, light, water, and nutrient requirements, the habitat of the original species can give some indication of what suits a plant best.

The reason so many plants from around the world can be used in gardens in the U.S. is that there are great similarities between habitats in different countries. The Temperate Zone encompasses several continents and plants found under certain conditions in one place are often well suited to similar conditions even across thousands of miles of land and ocean.

A note of caution, though: Some plants have natural controls in their native land that might be absent in another place and some species have entered the country whose ram-

The species Chinese silver grass, *Miscanthus sinensis*, has become a nuisance in parts of the Southeast, seeding itself prolifically and threatening to overwhelm native species. However, its cultivars, such as 'Gracillimus' and 'Morning Light', have thus far been well behaved and continue to be popular garden plants.

Species hostas, such as *Hosta plantaginea*, are native to Japan, Korea, and China. Because there are similarities in climate and soils throughout the Temperate Zone, many perennials from Europe and Asia are well suited to U.S. gardens.

pant growth threatens to overwhelm native species in the wild. Educate yourself about plants considered "invasive" for your area and be aware of the consequences of planting aggressive species. A plant that is considered invasive can potentially be a problem in your garden, though every garden is a bit different and a plant that is invasive in one place might be fine in another location. The issue of "invasive exotic" plants, which is the term used for aggressive species from other countries, is still a subject of debate among gardeners, naturalists, state agencies, and nursery owners.

The Great Traits of Perennials

What is it about perennials that makes them so attractive to gardeners? First, they come back year after year and create a stable but ever-changing presence in the garden. Second, there are a wide variety of choices, in flower, form, and foliage, making them beautiful and interesting from season to season. And there are perennials suited to every landscape situation. Third, many of them are generally low maintenance once they are established.

Flowers
Perennial flowers come in all shapes and sizes. Some are daisy-like, some are small and line flowering stalks, some are shaped like bells, some are fluffy—the diversity is astounding. Equally thrilling is the rainbow of colors available. A huge range of bloom periods occur,

The leaves of many perennials are quite beautiful. Wormwood, *Artemisia arborescens* 'Powis Castle', has feathery, silvery foliage, adding an attractive texture and color to the garden, and serving as a good contrast to bolder, brighter colored plants.

too, so you can plan to have something in bloom literally from earliest spring all the way into fall's cooler weather. No matter what they look like or when they appear, perennial flowers bring excitement and character to your garden.

Foliage
Often upstaged by showy flowers, the leaves of perennial plants have sometimes been overlooked. But when the flowers are not open yet or have already faded, inevitably the foliage takes the stage. Many perennials have attractive foliage.

Intriguing contrasts of foliage texture are possible and prolong the beauty of your displays. From bold and glossy to fine and

PERENNIAL WILDFLOWERS

Many gardeners might not realize it, but several outstanding and often-used perennials are native to the U.S., which can make them more adaptable to local conditions than exotic species might be. While the trend toward using wildflowers is fairly recent in this country, our native plants have been popular in Europe for many years, where a number of excellent cultivars have been developed. Popular wildflowers for perennial gardens include:

- **Alumroot** (*Heuchera americana*)
- **Bee balm** (*Monarda didyma*)
- **Beard-tongue** (*Penstemon* species)
- **Black-eyed susan** (*Rudbeckia fulgida*)
- **Coreopsis** (*Coreopsis* species)
- **Foamflower** (*Tiarella cordifolia*)
- **Goldenrod** (*Solidago* species)
- **Joe-Pye Weed** (*Eupatorium purpureum*)
- **New England Aster** (*Aster novae-angliae*)
- **Summer Phlox** (*Phlox paniculata*)

feathery, leaves can create a tapestry. Leaf color can also be taken into account: Some perennials have reddish leaves (and even stems), while others have white or yellow markings. And there are many variations on green itself, from deep, dark minty green to crisp, bright lime green to gray-green and nearly blue.

The flowers of perennials come in many shapes, colors, and sizes. Daylilies have large trumpet-shaped blooms with six petals (actually a combination of petals and sepals called "tepals"), while purple coneflowers have bristly clusters of orange disc flowers encircled by a ruff of pink or white ray flowers.

Seeds and Roots

Because perennials last more than one season, you'll witness their growth and reproduction habits. Flowers go to seed and—unless you clip them off beforehand—shed their bounty in your garden. Some of these may germinate the following year, effectively creating a larger grouping, which expands your display for free and with no effort from you. (If there are too many, you can always pull them out, or dig them up and move them somewhere else or give them away.)

Many perennials spread out via their roots. You cannot observe what's going on underground, of course, but you'll see the results in ensuing years when new shoots pop up nearby. Again, you get free plants in this expansion plan. If the new sprouts are too close to the mother plant, simply dig them up and carefully replant them elsewhere.

Trends in Perennials and Perennial Gardening

This is an exciting time to get involved in perennial gardening. Never before have there

In recent years there has been a dramatic increase in the variety of flower colors available for some types of perennials, including daylilies, poppies, irises, yarrows, and summer phlox.

Daylily, *Hemerocallis* hybrids

been so many excellent and interesting choices. It is also easier than ever, partly because of the many improved plant varieties, but also because suppliers—mail-order catalogs as well as local garden centers—are much more knowledgeable and willing and able to help you.

Plant exploration has paid exciting dividends, too. From Australia to China, from Appalachia to the tropics, enterprising botanists and horticulturists have brought new plants into cultivation, contributing all sorts of new possibilities—new colors, new forms, and exotically beautiful foliage, as well as durability and improved cold-hardiness. Genuinely different and improved plants are available like never before.

Flowers

Where once there were a few classic favorites, now an explosion of choices exists. Familiar categories have expanded tremendously—daylilies, in solids and bicolors, now come in nearly every color of the rainbow. The same is true for beautiful bearded irises, and Oriental poppies aren't far behind. The boundless curiosity and creativity of perennial gardeners have inspired these expansions, but horticultural science is keeping up. Plant breeding and propagating techniques are more sophisticated than ever. Information and fresh ideas are spread and exchanged far and wide.

Longer bloom periods are another advance. Where a wild species may bloom briefly, gardeners demand longer seasonal interest. Cultivars that keep on producing flowers are now commonplace, with more arriving on the scene every year as horticulturists continue the hunt or develop improved plants. Longer-

lasting blooms, ones that are slow to fade and fall off the plant, are also available.

Low-maintenance Gardening

Perennials that require less fussing but still look great are valuable indeed. Some of these are improved selections of naturally tough, durable wild plants, such as the many exciting new kinds of purple coneflowers. Others are plants that growers have selected after testing and proving that they don't need constant pruning, watering, or fertilizing to look their best. If an easier-to-care-for garden is your wish, seek out and grow the newer cultivars of perennials.

And there has been a trend toward smaller lawns since lawns can be lot of work! Not just mowing, but watering, fertilizing, and weeding. Some studies assert that no other garden element hogs as many resources and takes as much maintenance (time and effort) as a lawn. Add that to the fact that gardeners excited about growing perennials want to try more or expand the displays . . . and it's easy to see why lawns are shrinking. If you are a beginning perennial gardener, steal land from your lawn for your displays in increments, so you can decide over time how much grass you

Dwarf versions of popular garden plants, such as cheddar pink, *Dianthus gratianopolitanus* 'Tiny Rubies', are perfect for today's smaller landscapes.

For a full season garden, consider not only the bloom periods but the leaves, seedheads, and fall colors of perennials. Arkansas blue-star, *Amsonia hubrechtii*, is grown as much for its beautiful yellow foliage color in autumn as it is for its sky-blue spring flowers.

really want in your yard. In the end, you will enjoy much more beauty for much less effort.

Smaller Plants for Smaller Gardens

Gardeners these days have smaller properties—huge, sprawling gardens are a thing of the past. It might be a suburban half-acre, or it might be a deck or patio on condominium or apartment, but any small space can be a fabulous perennial garden. To accommodate this trend, nurseries have been seeking out and promoting more compact plants. Some are naturally smaller in size, while others are dwarf cultivars of traditionally bigger plants (for example, the perky yellow 'Stella d'Oro' daylily).

The Full Season Garden

Today's gardeners seem to want more than just fabulous summertime flower gardens. Springtime still features glorious bulb displays, but increasingly early-blooming perennials are joining the mix. And the pleasures of rich and varied colors in the fall—from perennials, not just from tree foliage—are now well within reach. Even "winter interest" in the form of attractive foliage or intriguing seedheads is being touted. For a garden you can enjoy in every season, seek out a range of bloom times. A constant parade of color is one of the great joys of perennial gardening!

The Rise of Foliage

One of the most thrilling and innovative trends in perennial gardening in recent years has been the "discovery" of foliage. For the shade gardener, interesting leaf colors and textures have always been worth cultivating. Hybridizers and nurseries have obliged with a tremendous number of new choices, from myriad new hostas in every hue from blue to gold and all sorts of variegations, as well as less familiar but equally worthy choices such as new lungwort varieties. All sorts of different ferns have been brought into cultivation and can be found at well-stocked nurseries.

Sun gardeners are also seeking out good foliage plants, mindful that continuous shows of flower color are not always easy to achieve and, indeed, may not be desirable. The eye needs a rest and other elements to admire, such as varying contrasts and compositions. Thus perennials with striped, splashed, or colorful leaves are also popular for sunny displays.

Related to this trend is the recent interest in tropical plants, such as splashy-leaved cannas or dusky-purple elephant ears. These are not cold-hardy plants for northern regions, but are hardy in warm zones and can certainly be tucked into perennial displays (in the ground or in pots) for a jolt of leafy excitement.

Mixing with Other Plants

Perennial gardening is dynamic by nature. Individual plants are constantly changing, within one season and from one year to the next. Thus the displays they contribute to are always changing. So it is no wonder that today's gardeners are open to combining their perennials with any and all plants—whatever works, whatever appeals, whatever looks great.

In particular, combining perennials and roses is a significant movement. This trend owes much to the fact that modern roses are more varied, healthier, and more floriferous than ever before. In combination with spiky flowers such as foxgloves and certain campanulas, roses are simply gorgeous and all parties benefit from the juxtaposition.

So too are the rigid rules of the past about shrubs, which formerly were consigned to hedges and foundation plantings. A row or grouping of shrubs (in and out of bloom) still makes a fine backdrop for a perennial garden, but gardeners have discovered that some shrubs are also team players that fit well among perennials. It is possible to mix a smaller shrub with a larger perennial and have them look like partners. (The current trend towards dwarf plant selections, noted earlier, also applies to ornamental shrubs and comes in handy here.)

Nor do vines have to stay in the back or to the sides. Some clematis, for example, are beautiful rambling with little or no support through a bed of perennials. Annuals can fill gaps, but may also look so nice with their perennial companions that you decide to replace them with new ones every year.

Perennial in Containers

In addition to being beautiful when planted in the garden, perennials can also make wonderful container plants. Pots situated on the deck or patio, or even window boxes, have traditionally been planted with annuals or tropicals. Now there is no reason not to include your favorite perennials in attractive containers, either alone or in combination with other plants. Recently introduced forms of some perennials, such as gaura and black-eyed susan, are shorter and more compact, making them suitable choices. Perennials in containers are also portable and can be placed out in the garden as focal points, or set in a prominent place when in full bloom and subsequently moved to a less visible location once the blooms have faded. In a large container perennials can be used as foundation plants, and their annual companions changed out during the season.

Pushing the Envelope

In the past it was assumed that the assigned hardiness zones of a plant were set in stone. Now, it has been found that many plants will grow outside this range, particularly along the edge of a zone. In fact, there are a number of plants that were assigned hardiness ranges without thorough testing. And microclimates can occur in any garden, where there is a slightly warmer or slightly cooler location. Gardeners all across the country are experimenting with plants once thought impossible to grow in their hardiness zone, which opens the door to even more exciting possibilities for the perennial garden.

SELECTING PERENNIALS

Perennials for Today's Gardens

It's a tremendously exciting and rewarding time to be a perennial gardener. Your choices are astounding—and inspiring. Nurseries and horticulturists have the world at their fingertips like never before. Outstanding new plants are being introduced at a rate unheard of twenty or even ten years ago. There are new corydalis from China, new purple coneflowers from Germany, and new dianthus from New Zealand, just to name a few. Desirable qualities from the many new-comers—such as new colors and forms of flower and leaf, more compact growth habits, better cold hardiness, and so on—are entering the gene pool, promising even more intriguing and better plants for the future.

Advances in plant breeding and production are also expanding the offerings. Genetic codes are being cracked so that hybridizers can achieve what they are aiming for. Tissue culture and improved cultural techniques are allowing nurseries to cultivate and evaluate new plants faster and more efficiently.

At the same time, the raising and shipping of perennial plants has become very sophisticated. More and better plants are being grown more economically, and the savings are being passed on to you, the consumer. Vigorous young plants with more developed, certified-

healthy root systems are being offered, thanks to improved growing and harvesting techniques. And mail-order nurseries have shipping down to a science—from the specially cushioned packaging that assures you get a totally intact, healthy plant to the well-timed arrival (they take into account your planting zone but also carefully monitor your area's weather before sending the package).

The upshot? The "perennial palette" is bigger than ever, and plants are of impressive quality and easier to grow. Perennials solve garden problems and bring beauty. Now is a

Firecracker Penstemon, *Penstemon eatonii*

A collection of perennial geraniums: *Geranium 'Johnson's Blue'*, *Geranium pilostemon*, and *Geranium endressii* 'Wargrave Pink'. New forms and colors of perennials are entering the market at an unprecedented rate. The genetic variability of such plants as the perennial geraniums has led to the introduction of numerous cultivars and hybrids.

great time to jump in and really enjoy showing them off. Take advantage of all the terrific new plants and fresh new ideas!

Evaluating Your Situation

Perennials solve various landscaping problems in a long-term way—because they are not flash-in-the-pan plants or temporary fixes. With their durability and ever-improving performances, they deliver change and long-lasting beauty.

No matter what your gardening conditions and your area's unique challenges, there are perennials that will grow well for you. A glorious perennial garden is well within reach if you match your plants to the location. This makes perennial gardening much easier, with less frustration and less work.

Before you start to select perennials, the first order of business should be assessing your yard. Take a walk around it, at different times of the day. Observe it from indoors, looking through various windows. You don't have to take notes or draw a site map or diagram if you don't want to. The goal is simply to get an accurate and realistic picture of what conditions you have for plants.

Four important factors to consider are light, soil, moisture, and temperature, since different plants need different conditions. Look at the amount of sunshine the garden receives at various times of the day. Dig into your soil to see if you have predominantly clay, sand, or loam, and check whether the soil is moist or dry. The acidity or alkalinity of your soil is another important thing to take into account.

The first step in planning a perennial garden is to evaluate your landscape situation, not only for such physical properties as light, moisture, and soil, but also for your enjoyment. How will you or visitors approach the garden and how will you view it from the house, deck, or patio? Choose a location that will be a source of pleasure and pride. Keep in mind, the more regularly you are near the garden or viewing it, the greater chance that you will be prompted to address maintenance issues, and the more beautiful the garden will be.

LOW-MAINTENANCE VS. HIGH-MAINTENANCE

Everyone has a busy life and, like any other hobby, gardening takes time. So gardening magazines and books, not to mention plant catalogs and local nurseries, have been touting ways to make it more low maintenance and less time consuming. All this without compromising our wish for a beautiful garden. There are four ways to achieve this:

- Drought-tolerant plants require less-frequent watering.
- Compact plants require less grooming and pruning, and stay within their allotted space.
- "Self-cleaning" flowers fall off the plant on their own when spent, eliminating the need to clip or pinch them off ("deadhead").
- Stockier, shorter plants or plants with stronger stems reduce (or completely eliminate) the need for staking.

Be aware of your cold hardiness zone, and remember that heat and humidity can be as important as cold in determining what plants will perform well for you. As you evaluate your landscape, be on the lookout also for possible microclimates—is there a wall that might provide a little shelter and extra warmth as it absorbs and reradiates heat, is there a small pond nearby to moderate the temperature, or is there a downspout that might add a little extra moisture to an area?

Consider also how much work you are willing to do to change your existing conditions. Would you rather amend the soil or work with what you have? Do you want to install irrigation? Would pruning a few trees let in more light? Keep in mind that when you choose plants appropriate for your particular conditions—whether shade, sun, wet soil, dry soil, and so on—creating your perennial garden will be less work, and the plants are automatically more successful.

Light Conditions

No matter what the light conditions are in various parts of your yard, you can transform almost any exposure into an attractive perennial display. Observe sun and shade patterns in your garden areas throughout the day. Which way does the garden face—north, south, east, or west? Are there trees or structures (including your house) that cast shadows? Keep in mind also how the light conditions

One way to make perennial gardening easier is to choose low-maintenance plants, such as catmint (*Nepeta* × *faassenii*). Look for varieties that are compact and sturdy, tolerant of a variety of soil and weather conditions (particularly drought), and long blooming or self-cleaning (to minimize grooming chores such as deadheading).

For a sunny location, there are a great many perennial choices, including globe thistle, daylily, coreopsis, crocosmia, yarrow, and sneezeweed. If a plant is recommended to receive "full sun," it will prosper with at least six hours of sun a day.

change throughout the year. If you are evaluating your garden at the end of winter and you have deciduous trees, remember that later in the spring and through the summer the trees will be in leaf and will create shade.

Sun Gardens

Many perennials are sun-lovers, so if your property has plenty of sunny locations, you are in luck. You can enjoy a wide range of beautiful flowering plants. See the Perennial Plant Directory at the back of this book and search for plants that note "full sun."

"Enough" sun for most perennials is defined as at least six hours of full, direct sunshine per day. This not only allows them to grow well, but to bloom well. Of course, there are exceptions to every rule and many perennials do just fine with fewer hours and others tolerate more hours. You won't really know for sure until you try a plant in your yard. Luckily, most are quite flexible and adaptable. The display will be even better if you choose drought-tolerant plants, mulch to retain soil moisture, and water during particularly dry spells.

Shade Gardens

Shade in a garden comes from many sources, natural and manmade. Plenty of plants not only thrive but flower in shade, or at least display attractive foliage to light up the dim places. Consider a shade garden an oasis, a cool place to retreat from the heat of the day.

There is no reason to be disheartened if your yard has more shade than sun, or if the best potential gardening spots on your property are in shade. The number of attractive plants that thrive in shade is amazing—and, yes, many of them flower! Some are mound-formers with flowering stalks; others are spreading groundcovers. Interestingly, those that do flower in the shade tend to have a prolonged show because the hot sun doesn't bleach out the blooms, or stress them into wilting. Turn to the Perennial Plant Directory chapter, and scan the listings for ones that grow in "partial shade" or "full shade." From this gratifyingly wide palette, you can create a perennial garden you will enjoy and cherish.

A great many shade-loving plants are adaptable and flexible. Reference books, plant labels, and plant catalogs may tout variations

If your garden area has a little too much shade to grow the sun-loving plants you desire, consider changing the environment to let in more light, by moving or removing a fence, shrub, or tree, or pruning overhanging tree branches.

such as "dappled shade," "light shade," "part-day shade," "half-day shade," "thin shade," "heavy shade," "high shade," and so forth, but in reality, many plants are not bound by these restrictive-sounding parameters. Even when conditions are not ideal, they may still perform well enough to please you. Or they may take matters into their own hands in the coming years, gradually spreading in the directions that appeal to them, either by runners or self-sowing. It's a delightful

Helleborus × *sternii* under *Pinus wallichiana*
If you garden in the shade of pine trees the needles can create a natural mulch, but they will also acidify the soil. Choose plants that are acid loving or tolerant as to soil pH.

surprise when you find a pretty shade-loving perennial has popped up and is thriving in another part of your garden.

Deep Shade

Classic deep-shade sites are those that face north or are in dense woodlands, and areas that are backed by walls, trees, or hedges. Yet it is still possible to garden in such difficult conditions. First, do what you can to improve the soil and to reduce the encroachment of other plants.

Sometimes areas are deeply shady during the main part of summer, but in spring, when overhead deciduous trees are not fully leafed out, it's possible to have a display of plants that are well adapted to such conditions. If you grow woodland wildflowers, such as alumroot, blue phlox, or foamflower, use the wild species or seek out some of the improved cultivars for more color choices or bigger or better flowers. Many of these will go dormant by summer, but you will have enjoyed a lovely springtime show.

Other plants, valued for their attractive foliage, can prosper in heavy shade in spring, summer, and fall—in mild climates, some may even be evergreen over the winter months. For variety, seek out ones with variegated or pat-

An area with deep shade, especially where the soil is dry, can be a problem site. But a number of perennials will work, including native species such as Solomon's seal (*Polygonatum biflorum*). Many woodland wildflowers are adapted to such situations.

terned foliage. Examples of deep shade plants include hostas, lily-of-the-valley, perennial forget-me-not, hellebore, lungwort, and ferns.

Soil Types

What type of soil do you have in your yard? It's important to find out before you install a garden. The information will dictate what kinds of perennials you can grow well, or lead you to a soil-improvement project. One thing you can do is simply dig down into your soil about a foot and look at what you have—clay, sand, loam, rocks, and so on. The best way to get a really thorough evaluation, especially of your pH and any nutrient deficiencies, is to have a professional soil test done. Ask for a

referral at your favorite garden center, or look up the Cooperative Extension Service in the Yellow Pages; ask them to send you a test kit.

Soil Moisture

Another vital factor to consider when choosing perennials for your garden is the amount of moisture in the soil. Too much water can be as detrimental as too little. The "available water" for a plant is really the thin film of

Improving drainage

If you want to grow a type of plant that needs really good drainage, you can tailor a small section of the garden (or even just a space a little bigger than the planting hole) to accommodate it by adding pea gravel or Perma Till or a similar material. It also helps if the location is on a slope or mounded a little higher than the surrounding area.

water that remains on soil particles after the majority of water has seeped past the root zone. If too much water remains in the soil, filling the air spaces, the soil is considered waterlogged, and can deprive roots of oxygen. When you examine your soil, check its moisture content—does it seem dry and dusty or sandy, or after you have dug a hole is there standing water in the bottom? Also, does your region receive a lot of rain, are there regular drought periods, and in what season or seasons do your rainy periods and droughts occur?

Naturally occurring soil moisture conditions may dictate which perennials you can

Plants that do well in shade often have large leaves (hosta, lungwort, bergenia) or numerous small leaves (astilbe, ferns, bleeding heart) in order to absorb as much light as possible.

Dicentra × 'Luxuriant'

Many perennials are tolerant of wet soil, including some types of iris, such as Siberian (above), Japanese, and copper irises. Bearded iris, however, needs well-drained soil and will rot if it receives too much water.

Perennials like Missouri primrose (*Oenothera missouriensis*) have thick, fleshy roots that enable them to grow in dry, gravelly locations. Such plants typically need extremely good drainage.

and cannot grow. This is not necessarily a problem that needs fixing. There are all sorts of good perennials for all sorts of conditions, and chances are you can make good matches— that is, choose appropriate plants. This may turn out to be preferable to toiling away trying to change native growing conditions.

Damp Ground

When you sink a trowel into the soil and it pulls up moist or damp—but not soggy— dirt, your soil has plenty of moisture. Ideally it is brown in color, perhaps with some red- or yellow-hued streaks. A few of the many perennials you can grow are astilbe, hosta, bee balm, and various irises.

Dry Ground

Soil that has a high sand or gravel content, has many tree roots competing for moisture, or drains water away rapidly is considered dry. It tends to be lean (low on nutrients) and can become compacted or dusty on the surface. Plants that form deep root systems or have a taproot tend to tolerate dry ground quite well, as they store water in their roots and also are

To help you choose the best perennials for your site, take soil samples for testing by your Extension Service office. This will tell you the relative acidity or alkalinity, and alert you to any nutrient deficiencies. Be sure to tell them you are planning a perennial garden.

BOGGY SOIL

Low areas in the landscape tend to hold water longer and, depending on soil quality, drain slowly, poorly, or not at all. Ordinarily a gardener gives up on such an area, leaving it to weeds or attempting to fill it in.

But a boggy area can be a great gardening opportunity. Quite a few perennial plants tolerate such conditions and, if you succeed in introducing them, your eyesore will become a showpiece.

Be aware of your cold hardiness zone. Garden centers sometimes offer plants that could prove to be short lived in your area, whether from extreme heat or cold. Snow-in-summer (*Cerastium tomentosum*) is a Zone 4 plant that will melt in hot weather.

able to reach down for deeper moisture. Examples include false indigo, spike gayfeather, coreopsis, and evening primrose.

The Effect of Temperature

Cold hardiness and heat tolerance are the two main factors when considering how temperature affects plants. The USDA Hardiness Zones map is a guideline for cold hardiness, meaning the average lowest temperature range at which a particular plant can survive. Some plants have less trouble with enduring cold weather than they do living through high heat, especially when coupled with high humidity. Hot nights are a significant part of this, since plants need a break from the energy-intensive processes that occur during daylight hours.

Very Cold Climates

Most of the United States is in Zones 5 to 8. Those living north of these zones may feel shut out of perennial gardening because of their harsh winters. Or an individual property in an otherwise temperate zone may turn out to be especially cold, because of an exposed (unprotected) location or because it's in a valley where cold air settles.

Fortunately, plenty of perennials can endure cold conditions and still return in glory every spring. Examples include bellflower, bleeding heart, lungwort, spike gayfeather, peony, and yarrow.

Very Hot Climates

There are also regions in the country, in Zones 7, 8, and 9, that are very hot in the summer, and relatively mild even in the winter. Even Zone 6 areas can be so hot that some perennials "melt." When you couple the heat with high humidity, there are perennials that will struggle; they may make a valiant effort for a year or so, but they never reach their full potential and might not flower well. But many perennials thrive in the heat, and in Zones 8 and 9 some tropical plants can be perennial. Examples of heat-loving perennials include butterfly weed, coreopsis, sedum, rose mallow, and salvia.

Some perennials, like *Verbena canadensis* 'Homestead Purple', thrive in the heat.

Blue and green are cool colors and are considered calming. Warm colors like orange and yellow are exciting and make a strong statement in the garden. One of the great joys of gardening is discovering beautiful, perhaps unplanned, combinations—often called "happy accidents."

What Perennials Have to Offer

When you are choosing perennials, it's not only worthwhile but fun to consider "the whole plant"—not just its flowers (whose show can sometimes be fleeting). A good perennial has many qualities to offer, changing its personality with the seasons—and thus its role in your garden. In spring, you may admire its new leaves. Later its flowers take the stage. The foliage or seedpods that remain behind after the big show is over may also make an important contribution to your displays. Understanding all the aspects of a perennial's appearance will allow you to make harmonious—not to mention appealing—combinations in your borders. A better sense of all stages of a perennial's development over the course of the year allows you to make the most of your garden and to be even prouder of your displays, month after month. The following aspects of what perennials can bring to your garden are offered here as "food for thought."

Color

The colors you see have a powerful capacity to evoke a rainbow of emotions. This is as true for flower colors as for, say, paints. The pleasure of seeing color is heightened for a gardener—and anyone who visits a garden—because being outdoors also stimulates our other senses.

Perennial plants have a huge and exciting range of colors to offer, as we set out to make the most of them and to combine them with one another to create wonderful garden moods.

- *Blue and green:* These are cooling, serene hues; ideal where you want a tranquil mood or a quiet corner.

- *Orange and red:* Invigorating, fiery hues like these work well where you want to make a splashy display or to entice visitors along a path or towards an entryway.

- *Pink and purple:* Neither cool nor hot, these colors have the ability to create harmony throughout the garden, to knit various other colors together.

- *Yellow:* Its cheery radiance makes small spaces seem bigger, and keeps displays looking fresh and perky.

- *White:* White flowers go with everything, and provide rest and refreshment for the eye.

Using color in the garden in these and other ways is often a matter of inspiration. You can copy or adapt ideas from other gardens or from a picture you admire in a magazine or

Color is an important element in any garden, and is usually the first thing a visitor notices. There are endless possible combinations and the choices depend on the personal taste of the gardener.

Painted Daisy (*Tanacetum × coccineum* 'Robinson's Red') and Rock Soapwort (*Saponaria ocymoides*)

book. Even a painting, wallpaper, fabric, or any manner of ordinary objects and settings may fuel your colorful garden ideas. Experiment to see what works; modify what doesn't. And keep a lookout for happy garden "accidents," where two plants meet up without your intervention and create an appealing vignette.

Flower color and, for that matter, foliage color, offers endless possibilities. Shady areas can be lit up with carefully chosen and placed perennials. Sunny areas can sparkle with excitement. And the show will evolve with every season: The very same perennial garden can be cool and charming in spring, bold and bright in summer, and overflow with rich, harmonious hues in fall. Even winter can offer interest, when jaunty caps of snow adorn perennial seedheads that you deliberately left on the plants.

Texture

Differences in flower and especially foliage texture give great character to a perennial garden. Variety is the spice—from fine, wispy plants to bold, assertive ones. You can employ texture for many purposes.

- Create a sense of depth in a small space. Various colors, shapes, and sizes mixed together fill an area with interest.

- Add privacy with multilayered perennial displays. Your living "garden wall" steals the show and blocks distractions from view. Enough plants can even mute street noise.

- Capture or extend garden interest. Foliage texture is useful to bridge the gap when the flower show is fleeting, has passed, or is not yet ready.

- Call attention to or flatter showy plants. Plants of attractive, interesting texture can direct attention to other plants or distract from them, as needed.

A Variety of Forms

Perennial plants also come in a great range of sizes and shapes. Capitalizing on these requires

Texture can provide as much interest in a garden as color. Too many plants with similar leaves and flowers can be monotonous to look at, but combining bold and fine textured perennials gives depth and dimension, even in a small space.

Lamb's Ears, Feather Grass, Mullein

When choosing perennials think of foliage as well as flowers. Many perennials, like purple-leaved alumroot, have beautiful leaves, giving texture and variety to a garden, and "breathing space" between plants in bloom.

Consider the leaves

Don't always choose perennials solely on the basis of their flowers. When not in bloom, foliage form, color, and texture are available to take the stage. Foliage can become an important garden element. Consider the purple-leaved alumroots, deservedly popular perennials. Their intriguing foliage is slightly reminiscent of the shape of maple leaves, yet they are low, mounding plants. Their unique colors bring richness and interest, especially to partially shady nooks that might otherwise have too many green leaves. And their leaf texture is fascinating, with smooth, shiny, or slightly hairy leaf surfaces that capture and play with light over the course of a day.

savvy placement. You need to know how broad or tall a plant will become, even if it's quite small when you add it to your garden. Take into account its natural growth habit. In these ways, it becomes possible to use perennials to create certain useful effects.

- *Boundaries, garden "walls," and property lines:* More traditionally defined by shrubs or trees, these important garden barriers can also be supplied by perennial plants. For creating a line or edge, mound-forming perennials are excellent. If you want a little height or screening effect, choose perennials that produce vertical flowering stalks.

- *Groundcovers:* When you don't want the "living carpet" of your garden to be lawn, or when it can't be (such as when there's insufficient sunlight), turn to perennial groundcovers. Naturally low-growing and sprawling, they will fill in where you want them to. The trick is to select one whose cultural needs match the site you have in mind, so it can thrive without much fuss.

- *Weavers:* Perennials of low or medium height and loose profile make a nice addition to any border because they weave together, or create a recurrent theme, within the display.

- *Focal points:* One spectacular perennial or a small grouping can deliver a commanding presence in a garden. Ideally, a focal-point plant is one that looks attractive viewed from various angles (ideal growing conditions will really help).

- *Small wonders:* A small garden, a small garden room or featured area, or even a tiny courtyard or patio, can be made into an impressive, in-scale perennial garden by using small-sized perennials and dwarf cultivars of perennials usually seen in larger sizes.

Perennials come in many forms, from tall and linear to low and creeping. Whatever your landscaping need, whether it's a screen planting or groundcover, there are perennials to serve the purpose.

Sea Thrift (*Armeria maritima*)

What Perennials Suit Your Taste?

This is a personal matter and perhaps you don't quite yet know the answer! In which case, you can experience the adventure of exploring perennials until your personal taste and style become clarified. Many practical factors weigh in, of course, but such an incredible range of perennials is available these days, you are sure to find what you want—and to succeed in creating the look you want—with searching and experimentation.

Or perhaps you know what you like and you want to work to achieve it in your perennial garden. The two most popular styles are big and bold, and soft and pastel.

Big and Bold

A perennial garden that makes an exciting impression is easy to come by. The plants you choose and the way you arrange them will make it happen. Some ways to do this include the following.

- Choose perennials with big blossoms.
- Choose large-size perennials with distinctive foliage.
- Select a mix of bright primary colors.
- Increase impact by grouping several individuals of the same plant, or grouping like colors.
- Repeat a color or form by interspersing several plants of the same assertive-looking perennial throughout the garden.

There are many choices of color schemes for a perennial garden. Planting combinations can be bright and bold, or soft and pastel, or can vary from one part of the garden to another. Gray or silver-leaved plants serve as connectors or bridges between plants of varying colors. Colors that are similar yet different (such as blue, lavender, and pink) can blend easily while still providing pleasing visual interest.

A bold plant can be a focal point in the garden, such as a striking variegated *Agave americana* with its sword-like leaves, set amongst a groundcover planting of delicately textured *Geranium incanum.* Other perennials that would serve the same purpose as the agave include yucca, bearded iris, and cardoon.

Soft and Pastel

Gentler hues and more airy plant forms create a romantic, old-fashioned-looking garden. To maximize this, try some of these ideas.

- Intersperse plants with rambling or weaving habits for a casual feel.

- Add white, which always seems to give pastel plants near it an extra glow.

- Include gray-foliaged plants, which flatter pastel flowers and contribute to the garden's overall softness.

- Site your pastel garden against a dark backdrop. A dark wall or hedge really shows it off, and never competes.

Shopping for Perennials

Once you have a pretty good idea which plants you want for your garden, it's a great feeling to go get them. Timing is fairly important. Ideally, you want to bring home your perennials as close as possible to planting day—not because they are especially frail (that's unlikely), but because plants in peak condition transplant into garden soil best.

If you join the throngs down at the local garden center on the first warm weekend in spring, you might not be able to get high-demand favorites. So have a few alternate selections in mind, just in case!

Perennials can be obtained as bare-root or potted plants, or grown from seed.

Monkshood

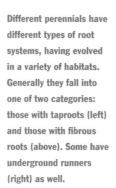

Daisy

Different perennials have different types of root systems, having evolved in a variety of habitats. Generally they fall into one of two categories: those with taproots (left) and those with fibrous roots (above). Some have underground runners (right) as well.

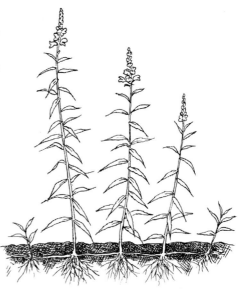

Obedient Plant

Bare-root Perennials

Bare-root perennials are generally sold by mail-order nurseries. Some perennials are more practical to sell this way, for individual reasons: For instance, baby's breath and false indigo have root systems that are sensitive to being moved in and out of the ground and various pots too many times.

What are bare-root perennials? They are dormant, usually two-year-old field-grown plants. They should have been harvested in prime condition the previous fall, and kept in climate-controlled cool storage to assure they will stay dormant—in storage, during shipping, and until you are ready to plant them. They consist of a hearty root system and some trimmed-down stems; little or no leaf growth should be evident.

Be sure to check for plant quality and health. Don't worry if the trimmed-back stems show no signs of growth or greenery as yet—they're not supposed to. However, the

stems should appear thick, not wispy, and show no signs of damage or rot. The all-important

GARDEN TIP

Mail-order nurseries are a good source

Mail-order nurseries are a great place to get good and interesting perennials. Unlike local garden retailers, who deal in large, mass-market volumes, catalog companies are able to bring you plants you won't find anywhere else.

Perennials grown in pots can be planted whenever the ground is workable in the spring, or even in the fall.

GARDEN TIP

Avoid potted plants in bloom

It's so tempting to buy a potted perennial that's already showing color, either in already-blooming flowers or bursting-open buds. But there are compelling reasons not to do this. On the ride home, or within a day or two, those flower petals tend to fall off. A new perennial's first priority when you transplant it into your garden soil is to invest in root growth. And a young plant may find getting established while maintaining flowers too exhausting. If you do bring home a young perennial with flowers or buds, you would be doing it a favor to trim these off before planting, so it can expend its energy on root growth, where it is most needed at this time. It won't be long till those you lost or took off are replaced with new ones.

roots should be crisp and light brown or white. (Black, mushy, or stringy roots are not viable on most bare-root perennials—if there are only a few, just pinch them off.)

Container-Grown Perennials

Perennials come in a variety of pot sizes, from 2 inches to 2 gallons or larger. These are sold by both mail-order nurseries and local retailers. The larger the plant the more mature it is, and the more immediate the gratification, but a smaller plant will catch up quickly if planted in an appropriate site and given good care. Consider also how big a hole you want to dig.

When checking for quality and health, examine all parts of the plant. The foliage should be in good shape, nice and green, with few or no spots, curled edges, or yellowed leaves (a few flawed leaves can be pinched of but many flawed leaves is a sign of poor health). Make sure the plant is pest-free: Look on leaf undersides and in the nodes (where the stalk meets the stem) for small bugs, sticky residue, or webs. If flower buds are evident, they should be plump and solid, not squishy, deformed, or discolored. Finally, check that

the plant is well rooted by turning it over or sideways and thumping the pot lightly. The plant and its soil mix should not tumble out, and you may also see a few roots peeking out of the drainage holes. For most species, these should be white and "crunchy."

Perennials from Seed

Some choice perennials can be grown from seed. This is an option if you want to try something rare or unique, if you want to try your hand at an engrossing and rewarding gardening project, or if you are simply frugal. Purchase perennial seed from the catalogs of mail-order seed houses and nurseries (or their websites). Or try seed exchanges, via the Internet or through a local garden club.

There are several advantages to growing perennials from seed. It's a great way to raise a lot of plants affordably. Plant diseases are never carried over in seeds, so if that's a concern for the perennial of your choice, you can skirt the issue this way. Seeds may also be the only way to obtain certain rare perennials.

To grow perennials from seed you need sterile growing mix, small pots or cell trays, and a place to keep the sowed seeds warm. You will also need to carefully monitor the progress of the seedlings so they receive the right amounts of light and water. The results can be well worth the extra effort and patience.

Understanding How Perennials Grow

When you make informed decisions about perennials, your vision for your perennial

Many perennials can take a year or more to get established and begin to reach a mature size. Some perennials, such as purple coneflower (*Echinacea pupurea*), may take a year to bloom since they first put their energy into building a root system. But this is all part of the process that ensures perennials will live for several to many years. So, what you may lose in "instant gratification" you will gain in long-term benefits.

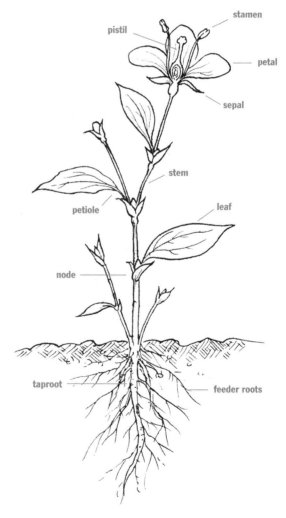

A typical perennial plant has flowers, leaves, stems, and roots, though in a variety of arrangements.

Spiderwort (*Tradescantia virginiana*)

A perennial given sufficient "elbowroom" will achieve its natural height and width, and be more beautiful and healthy.

garden will most closely match what really happens in your yard. Careful choices now will surely save you extra time and effort down the line—in moving plants around, taking them out, constantly cutting them back, or urging them on with fertilizer.

Growth Rates

Perennials are not like annuals. They are not "instant-gratification" plants and they don't always provide quick color. Instead, perennials are a long-term investment—one that pays off later. Generally speaking, they devote their first year in your garden to establishing themselves in their new home. They do this by extending their root systems into your garden soil. All this takes place out of sight. Meanwhile, "top growth" in the form of stem, leaf, bud, and blossom growth may be limited that first year and even sometimes during the second summer. Be patient! The big payoff comes in the third

and following years, when your perennials have settled in and those root systems can finally fuel vigorous top growth.

Mature Sizes

All perennials, and their various cultivars, have a known "mature size," a maximum height and width they can reach. They generally attain this only after several years of growth. Naturally, these numbers may vary according to the health of a perennial and how happy it is in its particular garden setting.

Sufficient light also affects mature size—a plant that's not getting quite enough can become leggy or sprawling, while a well-sited one will be more compact and full. Climate is also a factor—cold climates cause certain perennials to be somewhat smaller than usual.

But you should always investigate a plant's mature dimensions, or mature "footprint," so you know what to expect and can plan to accommodate it.

PLANTING AND GROWING PERENNIALS

IN THIS CHAPTER:

- ■ **When to plant perennials**
- ■ **Site preparation**
- ■ **Propagation techniques**
- ■ **Installing the plants**
- ■ **Post-planting care**

Success with Perennials

A great looking perennial garden is not difficult to attain—there are no mysterious secrets or complicated techniques. If you've chosen appropriate varieties and healthy plants, you are already on your way. The next order of business is to give them the best possible start. Plant them at the right time, give them good soil to grow in, and place them with care. It's as simple as that. They'll repay your efforts by thriving in their first year and looking fabulous for many years to come.

When to Plant Perennials

Whether you are putting in young plants or more mature ones, the planting-time principle is the same: Make it easy on them. The middle of summer is a poor time—hot days lead to thirsty, stressed plants, which is a challenge for established perennials and too trying for young ones. And obviously winter is just too chilly and short of sunlight, depending on the severity of your climate, and the soil can be frozen and unworkable. The "shoulder seasons" of spring and fall are your best bets.

Spring Planting
Spring is the traditional time to plant perennials, and with good reason. The plants you

Hebe (*Hebe* 'Variegata'), Wild Bleeding Heart (*Dicentra eximia*), Creeping Raspberry (*Rubus pentalobus*), and Creeping Soft Grass (*Holcus mollis* 'Variegatus')

buy are young and eager and spring affords them a very good start. The days are getting longer and temperatures are rising, and the soil has warmed up. Water—so critical in a young perennial's early days and weeks—is plentiful in the ground, thanks to winter run-off and spring rains. Time is also on the plants' side, as a whole summer season stretches ahead, with good, friendly growing conditions forecast for at least several months.

A wise approach to successful perennial gardening is to plant young plants in the spring at the start of the growing season, when the soil is warm and there is ample rainfall, and plenty of time for the new plants to get established before the heat and drought of summer.

If you can't plant your newly purchased plants immediately, put them in a protected location away from hot sun (morning sun is fine) and drying winds. Remember to check them daily to see if they need water—plants in containers can dry out quickly.

Hardening Off

Small seedlings and slightly larger young perennials benefit from a chance to acclimatize to life outdoors in your yard even before they go into the ground.

If you raised the perennials from seed indoors, or know for a fact that your supplier grew them in a greenhouse before you purchased them, this process is mandatory. Otherwise, the shock of being moved straight into garden soil may prove too great, and your new little perennials may struggle and die.

If perennials have been grown indoors or in a greenhouse it is advisable to slowly acclimate them to life out of doors through a transition process called "hardening off."

Called "hardening off," this process involves putting the seedlings outside in a sheltered spot. They'll need protection from direct sunlight, wind, and cold air. Good spots include a patio or porch with an eastern exposure, a bench or table under a big tree, a screened-in porch, or a cold frame, provided you prop open the top. Bring them in at night or if it's stormy. Keep them evenly watered. Wait at least five to seven days before planting them. This allows enough time for them to experience and adjust to outdoor life.

The Right Day, the Right Time

Keep plant stress to a minimum by planting on a cloudy or misty day. The moist air will help prevent drying out and any rain will even water the new arrivals for you. The watering you do will soak in without worry of evaporation—and thus you will have given the roots their best start.

Ideally, do the work in the late afternoon, so the new plants don't have to face the heat of the noon sun on their very first day in your garden. Morning is fine, too, so long as you remember to water well right after planting, and perhaps provide a little shade to protect the plants from afternoon sun.

Chinese Silver Grass, Blue Oat Grass, Sedum, Asian White Birch, and Scotch Pine

Autumn is an excellent time to plant perennials. The heat of summer has diminished, nights are cool but the soil is still warm, rain has begun to fall more regularly again, and the sunlight is less intense.

Fall Planting

Spring can be a hectic time in the garden, while fall is a time to slow down—and, for many a gardener, an opportunity to take a break, reflect on the season past, and clean up the garden. What some people don't realize is that fall is also an excellent time to plant perennials! And nature is ready to help: The soil is still warm, fall rains spare you at least some of the time and effort of watering the new plants, sunlight is less intense, vigorous summer weeds are nearly finished for the year, and spring is a wetter, muddier season than fall in some regions, so planting in fall is easier and more enjoyable.

Fall is also a fine time to move perennials around within your garden, or to divide and replant others. Because the plants are starting to go dormant, digging them up and tampering with their roots is not as stressful for them.

WHEN YOU CAN'T PLANT RIGHT AWAY

Sometimes installing or adding to your perennial garden becomes a lengthy project. A shipment may arrive midweek and you can't plant till the weekend. Or you might devote an afternoon to prowling the local garden center, but not be able to plant your purchases for several days. The key is to keep the plants alive and well, but avoid tempting them into vigorous growth just yet.

- **Bare-root plants:** These can be stored for a few days in a refrigerator, cool basement, or garage, any place where they will be cold but not freezing. This keeps them in a suspended state of animation, that is, nearly dormant. If, however, they appear to be breaking dormancy and generating a bit of greenery, go ahead and pot them. A rich mix (equal parts of compost, garden soil, and soilless potting mix) is good. Potting them will also give you the opportunity to harden them off.

- **Container plants:** New plants may arrive in small pots or cell packs. Either way, their resources are limited because they are confined to a small space—there's not a lot of soil mix around their roots, and they will need water, as small containers dry out quickly. Buy yourself some time by keeping the pots in a sheltered spot away from hot sun and drying winds. Water them daily. If you can't plant for a full week or so, use this time to harden them off.

Fall is a good time to divide and move perennials in your garden. To divide a peony, for example, first cut back stalks and dig the established plant from the garden. Remove soil from its roots with a spray of water or by loosening with your hands. Cut sections apart with a sharp knife or pruners then replant the sections at the same depth the original plant was growing.

Give your fall-planted perennials as much time as you can to start growing in place before winter comes and dormancy begins. In other words, don't wait too late. If the plants only have two or three weeks before a frost hits, they may succumb. Ideally, you want to get them in the ground a good six to eight weeks before any frost is expected.

Aftercare for Fall-planted Perennials

Less work is involved in planting perennials in the fall. Here's what to do—and what *not* to do.

- *Water them on planting day:* No matter how damp the ground is or how soon you expect rainfall, this is a good policy

A vital step in the planting process, at any time of year, is to water the newly installed plant immediately. This will settle the soil around the roots and provide moisture to stressed and damaged roots.

because it removes air pockets in the soil and provides moisture to roots stressed by the planting process.

- *Do not fertilize them:* Fertilizer stimulates the entire plant, and you do not want to cause these perennials to put on new growth right now. Fresh new young leaves and stems are vulnerable to cold damage, and cold weather is coming.

- *Mulch:* As with perennials planted in spring, an inch or two is usually sufficient. Remember not to pile mulch too close—don't let the mulch touch the plant's crown or main stems. At this point in the year, the purpose of a light mulch is to simply hold in soil warmth and moisture.

- *Later provide a thicker, protective winter mulch:* When it becomes clear that winter is arriving and all the other plants are going dormant, assume your fall-planted newcomers are, too, and protect them accordingly.

What to Expect

When you plant perennials in the fall they respond a little differently than spring-planted ones. Because of the cooler temperatures and less intense sunlight the perennials tend not to put on much top growth or to try to flower. Instead, their energy is directed into their roots. Fall-planted perennials spend their time

Tools for preparing a new garden area include shovel, garden fork, weeder, mattock, edger, loppers, rake, and hoe.

***Sedum* × 'Autumn Joy'**

Fall-planted perennials will emerge from dormancy in the spring with vigor and often show more robust growth and more prolific flowering than spring-planted counterparts (which have not yet had time to become established and store the energy necessary for blooming and stem and leaf formation).

Site Preparation

The single most important thing you will ever do for your perennials is to prepare good soil for them *before* you plant. This is the key to their success, now and in the future.

For growing perennials, your soil goals are to:

- Dig deeply enough to accommodate their root growth comfortably.

- Add some organic matter, which improves soil structure.

- Provide good drainage. The vast majority of perennials do best in well-drained soil (too much water or standing water leads to rot, and growing in overly dry soil is stressful for many plants). The way to improve drainage is to add soil amendments that help—which ones and how much, depends on what kind of soil you are starting with.

getting established in their new home, settling in and expanding their root systems. Of course, when the soil and air grow colder, fall-planted newcomers respond by going dormant. You should then mulch them for the winter, along with the rest of your garden.

When spring returns, you'll finally get to see the big payoff! Your fall-planted perennials will emerge from dormancy gradually, already acclimated to outdoor life and your garden's soil and microclimate. They'll soon surge into vigorous growth—and can be bigger and more impressive than any spring-planted perennials you may be adding.

Before starting a garden project of any size, check your soil for structure, moisture, nutrients, and pH.

■ Make nutrients available to your plants. A humus-rich, fertile soil naturally provides important nutrients. Fertilizer also helps. Just remember that a moderate soil pH is important; if your soil is too acidic or too alkaline, nutrients in the soil will be unavailable to your plants.

Soil Test First!

A soil test is a worthwhile investment in your perennial garden's future. Again, doing it now—before planting—is smart, because you'll be better able to deal with the soil-improvement recommendations. Private labs as well as the Cooperative Extension Service can perform the test for you; contact them for a kit and instructions for taking samples. The fee is usually low, no more than a few dollars.

When you send in your soil sample, remember to tell the lab that you are planning to grow perennials (their suggestions might be different if you were planning a vegetable garden instead). If you are concerned about

The roots of trees and shrubs can compete with perennials for water, nutrients, and space. A shallowly rooted groundcover such as dwarf mondo grass can provide a bit of color and texture. Or you can add a layer of soil over the roots, or place potted plants on top of the ground to create visual interest.

your soil's pH, that's an extra test and you need to request it. There are also soil test kits available at local garden centers or through mail-order garden supply companies for checking the pH yourself.

One last note: Plan ahead. Most labs take four to six weeks to analyze your soil and send you the results. Use this time to lay out the boundaries of the bed, and perhaps start loosening the soil in preparation for mixing in amendments.

COPING WITH ROOTS IN THE SHADE GARDEN

Trees and shrubs create shade and also fill up the ground in a shady area. Their roots hold them in place and nourish them. These roots, however, can become your enemy when you are trying to plant shade perennials, because they may frustrate your digging efforts. And young plants will not be able to compete with them for soil moisture and fertility.

You can chop, prune, or dig them out (thereby possibly endangering their vitality and health), or you can give your shade-loving perennials their own soil. For best results, spread at least 6 to 8 inches of soil over root-infested ground before planting perennials there. (Avoid completely covering over a tree or shrub's entire root zone, or you might smother it.) Alternatively, strategically place pots of shade-lovers throughout the area, on the surface of the ground or sunk down to their rims.

If your property is affected by stresses, you may have been discouraged in your perennial gardening efforts. But take heart—it is still possible to grow perennials and have a beautiful display.

- **Improving poorly drained soil:** You may dig in humus or sand to lighten the area and improve drainage (but not when the soil is quite wet, because you may damage soil structure). Installing drainage pipes, tiles, or gravel drainage pathways under the ground's surface are options, though these involve a lot of effort and expense. The cheapest, easiest solution is to build raised beds on top of the soggy ground, fill them with excellent soil, and create the perennial bed of your dreams.

- **Improving moisture retention:** You should add plenty of organic matter, or humus—and be prepared to keep adding more in the years to come. Mulch your perennials after planting to help hold in soil moisture. If this becomes a losing battle, installing raised beds is always a practical option.

An easy test for checking the drainage capacity of your soil is to dig a hole and fill it with water. If the water drains through fairly quickly (less than thirty minutes) the drainage is adequate. If several hours later the water still hasn't drained through, your soil has poor drainage.

Soil Structure

Not every region or even every garden is blessed with ideal growing conditions and perfect soil. While you can alter whatever soil you have to make it more hospitable to various perennials, in some instances you can get a good display without much fuss. Also, be attuned to perennials that actually prefer your particular growing conditions.

If you plan to work with the soil you've got because of financial or physical limitations, or some other reason, there are still plenty of options. Remember that soils that occur in your yard also occur in the surrounding area, and natural, uncultivated fields and woods still have plenty of plants that are growing well. Fashioning a good-looking garden is still attainable.

Soil types are measured or identified by their composition: their ratios of various-sized soil particles (sand, clay, and silt), which is called the structure of a soil. The three basic soil types are clay soil, sandy soil, and loam. In addition to soil particles, most soils also contain about one-quarter water and one-quarter air (which plant roots also need to thrive).

Clay Soil

Clay soil has notoriously poor drainage and thus is often soggy and slippery. However, it may be quite fertile. Some plants tolerate these

Prairie Coneflower, *Ratibida pinnata*
Many plants not only tolerate but thrive in clay soils. While clay is difficult for the roots of some plants to penetrate (and for the gardener to dig) and can alternate between extremes of wet and dry, it is also high in nutrients.

conditions fairly well. Abundant (at least 30 percent) tiny clay particles make a soil that is dense and poorly drained. When wet, it's sticky and slippery and water may pool on the surface. Clay soils are very slow to dry out, and slow to warm up in springtime, which delays planting. Clay contains nutrients that plants like, but unfortunately the nutrients are often "locked up" and unavailable. Plants that tolerate heavy clay soil include butterfly weed, prairie coneflower, blazing star, and sunflowers. To improve it, dig in humus.

Sandy Soil

Sand is a large soil particle, and genuinely sandy soil may contain upward of 35 percent sand or more. The result is light, porous ground. Water passes quickly through—too quickly for some plants—and carries away any soil nutrients in the process, making sandy soil notoriously infertile.

Drought-tolerant plants can grow in sand, such as false indigo, yarrow, black-eyed susan, and beard-tongue. As with clay, the addition of humus will help.

Undoing construction damage

If your home is a newer one (especially in a new tract), or if it has recently been switched from septic to town sewers, chances are that heavy equipment has compacted your soil. The ground may also contain rubble and building debris. The topsoil layer may have been stripped off and not replaced, or not adequately replaced. None of these problems is insurmountable! But soil improvement must be dealt with now, and all at once, so that you can enjoy gardening on the land for the rest of your days living there.

This is a time for professional advice. Have a landscaper look over the situation with you. In the spot where you'd like to have a perennial garden, discuss your options. It may need to be power-tilled, by you or someone else, or you may elect to install a raised bed on the spot. Perhaps all you need to do is order a nice truckload of topsoil or loam. Find out, take action, and try not to cut corners. The success of your future garden depends on good soil.

Goldenrod, *Solidago* species

Sandy soil has low nutrient levels and poor moisture retention. Yet many perennials grow well in a sandy location. These are typically plants that require extremely good drainage, and don't have high nutrient needs.

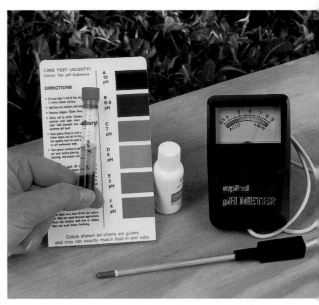

If you don't want to send a soil sample to a lab for testing, home kits for checking your soil's pH are available from your local garden center or a garden supply company.

Loamy Soil

Loam is the ideal soil for many plants, having equal percentages of sand, clay, and silt. So its soil structure is loose enough to allow good drainage, but it also holds the right amount of moisture. Typically it has organic matter included as well.

Most perennials thrive in this medium because it is balanced and well aerated. Loam soils will also retain sufficient nutrients in the root zone.

Make it a practice to add organic matter annually at least, either in the form of "top-dressing," by which you scatter and spread it on the surface of the soil or, when practical, by digging it into the ground several inches to a foot down.

Soil pH

The soil in your yard may be typical of soils native to your area, and present its own set of gardening challenges. But before you try to alter or remedy a soil you perceive as difficult, confirm your hunch with a professional soil test that includes an analysis of soil pH.

Radically changing a skewed pH requires professional advice, a willingness to continually dig in amendments, and patience. That said, nudging an "iffy" pH up or down a point or so is completely doable—again, follow the soil-test recommendations. Note that most perennials are perfectly happy growing in neutral ground, somewhere near 7.0. The addition of organic matter can help to moderate both high and low pH.

Some perennials, such as wintergreen (*Gaultheria procumbens*), need an acidic soil.

There are many soil amendments available, both organic and inorganic, including (left to right) compost, COIR (made from coconut hull fibers), vermiculite, peat, perlite, and sand.

Adding amendments to the soil increases the water-holding capacity, improves drainage and soil structure, encourages beneficial soil organisms, and moderates pH.

Acidic Soil

Soil that tests lower than 7.0 on the pH scale (between 1.0 and 6.9) is acidic. It may be acidic thanks to acidic tree leaves or needles, as well as plentiful rainfall. There are plenty of acid-loving plants. Some favorites are coral bells, certain ferns, bleeding heart, and calla lily. If you wish to make your soil more neutral, you will usually be advised to dig in ground limestone—how much depends on the results of your soil test and the area you are treating.

Alkaline Soil

Soil that tests higher than 7.0 on the pH scale (between 7.1 and 14.0) is alkaline. Drought-tolerant plants fare best. Try sea holly, sedum, ornamental salvia, and verbena. In areas with minimal rainfall, salts build up in the soil and may even appear on the ground's surface as a whitish crust, making the soil very alkaline. To make the soil less alkaline, flush the area with clean water. A soil-test professional may also suggest that you add powdered sulfur or peat moss—how much depends on the results of your soil test and the area you are treating.

Good Timing

Ideally, you should break ground for a new perennial garden in the fall. There often seems to be more time then anyway, with the flurry of summertime activities behind you, and fall is a natural time to tidy up and assess the garden. Soil in the fall is still perfectly work-able and, indeed, may be less wet than spring ground. So the project won't be as muddy. Also, you'll be adding various amendments, and it's beneficial to let them meld and settle over the winter months.

But sometimes you will do the new-bed preparation work in spring, out of necessity or impatience, which is fine. Do the work as early as is practical, and allow the improved ground at least several days or a week to settle before adding any plants. There is nothing wrong with preparing beds in the summer, but the ground is often hard and dry and difficult to work. And summer is not the best time to be planting new perennials anyway.

Recommended Organic Amendments

These are the basics of any soil-improvement project. They provide a number of important benefits to your perennial garden.

- *Increased water retention:* So you don't have to water as often, and your perennials are better able to withstand dry spells.

- *Improved drainage:* So water moves through the soil slowly enough for

Compost is an excellent soil amendment, improving both nutrient levels and soil structure. There are a variety of ways to create a compost pile: a structure of stakes and plastic netting, stacks of straw bales, a garbage can with holes punched in it for aeration, or pre-made bins available from garden centers or garden supply companies.

roots to get the moisture they need, but quickly enough to not cause rot.

- *Looser soil:* So nutrient-bearing water can enter and there are beneficial air spaces, providing oxygen to roots and giving roots room to grow.

- *A favorable environment for beneficial soil organisms:* These organisms, such as earthworms and mycorrhizal fungi, break down organic matter into a form roots can use and maintain air spaces in the soil (worms also contribute their own organic matter, called worm castings).

- *Neutral soil pH:* To create a more moderate, plant-friendly setting, where soil nutrients are available and stress is minimized.

The following materials are all good sources of organic matter. If they are fresh, they should be aged or composted for a few months to a year first. If in chunks or large pieces, chop them up so they'll mix in better and break down faster. Use whichever ones are most readily available to you, either in your own yard, or from an inexpensive supplier such as a local garden center, farm, landscaping firm, or municipal compost pile.

- *Compost:* Homemade is best, because it's usually a nice, rich blend, and you may have plenty on hand. Garden centers also sell it in bags.

- *Rotted manure:* Any vegetarian animal waste can be used (cow, horse, sheep, pig—never dog or cat!). However, it must be aged or dry. Fresh or steaming-hot manure can burn young plants.

- *Peat moss:* It must be dampened before you dig it in, or it will not hold moisture well. You can buy bags at a garden center. Never add peat moss to soil that has already tested acidic, as it is acidic itself.

- *Leaves:* Fall leaves work well and can be chopped up first so they break down faster. Use a shredder, or run over them with a lawn mower a few times. Note that oak leaves are acidic, and maple leaves may be full of seeds that germinate into small seedlings all over your perennial garden.

- *Sawdust:* Don't use sawdust from wood that was chemically treated or you may do your garden more harm than good. And fresh sawdust will rob the soil of nitrogen. Use sawdust that has had a chance to sit for several months and rot.

A wide variety of products are available for adding to your soil to improve its quality.

- *Hay or straw:* Either of these, in aged form, makes a decent soil amendment, as long as they are weed-free.
- *Grass clippings:* If you have a lawn, you have plenty! Don't use clippings, however, if you fertilize your lawn or treat it with a weedkiller. Grass clippings are best when piled up and composted for a while.
- *Other materials:* Worm castings, seaweed, alfalfa meal, apple pomace,

WHAT IS HUMUS?

Soil organisms—from microscopic ones to roving earthworms—break organic matter down into a material called humus. Humus binds nutrients that plants need to thrive. It holds these nutrients in the soil in your plants' root zones, so they can access them, thereby allowing your perennials to grow strong and healthy.

ground corncobs, peanut hulls, and mushroom compost—any of these can be beneficial. Again, let them compost or rot a bit before adding them to the garden.

Digging Deep

When preparing new ground for the first time, or rejuvenating an area to put in a new, improved garden, you need to break out the shovel or hand-held tiller. You will want to do a thorough job and dig deep for these reasons:

- *Ease:* It's so much simpler to do this work at the outset, before any plants are in place. You won't disturb, dislodge, or damage anything important.
- *Long-term benefits:* You are providing space for long-term residents, not short-term tenants.

If your soil is inhabited by earthworms it is considered good soil. Earthworms not only loosen the soil by tunneling through it, they add their own organic matter, called worm castings. They are only one of a host of organisms, both visible and microscopic, responsible for aerating and enriching the soil and breaking down organic material into a form usable by plants for growth.

How deep you dig when creating a new bed area depends partly on your soil. If your soil is loose and rich, you might not need to dig further than 6 or 8 inches. If your soil is poor you might need to dig deep to create an environment conducive to thriving root systems, and to improve drainage.

GARDEN TIP

Good fungi

While some fungi, such as powdery mildew, are considered problems in a garden, there are also beneficial fungi living in the soil. These fungi attach to the roots of plants and extend fine threads between soil particles and into organic matter, absorbing water and nutrients and bringing them back to the plant. Adding a good mycorrhizal fungus to the soil can help poor, damaged soils by improving soil structure, and aid plants by increasing nutrition, drought resistance, and protection from soil-borne diseases. There are a variety of products on the market, including Root Boost, MycoStim, Bio Grow, Plant Success Tabs, and Endorize.

How Deep Is Deep Enough?

You will hear different things about the important issue of depth. Some gardeners are fanatical, and insist on excavating to a depth of one or more feet—which is a big job! Others reassure you that 6 to 8 inches, the root depth for many perennials, is sufficient. Make your own decision based on how much energy you want to put into the project, and also how good the soil is. If the new bed will consist of a plant-friendly blend of good indigenous soil mixed with one or more organic amendments, shallow digging is probably fine.

If your native soil is poor (of poor quality, drains poorly, or has a too-high or too-low pH) and if digging down reveals a dense, inhospitable subsoil layer, the Big Dig is probably advisable. In either case, the idea is the same: to give your perennials' roots their best shot—loose, friable, fertile soil in which to grow and prosper.

Hole-by-Hole Preparation

Sometimes you cannot dig up an entire bed. Either it's already in good condition, or it's just too big, or you don't have the time or energy. Digging individual holes for individual plants is always an option. The goal is to give the roots enough room to grow. Here are the basic steps:

1. Bring the plant with you and keep it nearby so you can plant it quickly, before its roots dry out.

2. Dig a hole, ideally twice as wide and twice as deep as the present root system.

3. Using a trowel or your fingers, scratch the sides and bottom of the hole to loosen the soil, to help the roots move into your garden's native soil.

During the process of digging you might encounter obstructions. Tree roots can be cut out of the way, provided that removing them will not compromise the health of the tree.

Keep up the good work

Organic matter breaks down over time. So you'll need to keep adding it to your perennial garden, to continue giving your plants its many excellent and important benefits. Always add it to new beds or planting holes. In established beds, make it a habit to add more every few months, at season's end, and when spring returns. Many good mulches are organic and will break down and add organic matter to the soil while they protect your plants (but remember, because they break down, mulches will need to be renewed periodically).

4. Refill the hole with a mixture of the indigenous soil and organic matter.
5. Follow the planting instructions outlined later in this chapter.

Dealing with Obstructions

As you dig, you are likely to encounter some obstructions: Clods, rocks, weeds, and roots

REJUVENATING WORN-OUT SOIL

There are some telltale signs that your yard's soil is depleted or worn out. Close inspection will show that it exhibits at least one of the following woes, maybe more.

- Compressed or compacted
- Powdery or dusty
- Devoid of earthworms
- Lifeless (maybe even the weeds are not looking healthy!)
- Not even roots are able to work their way into the area.

Your first instinct might be to revive the area with a dose of balanced fertilizer. But it's far better to improve the soil structure first. Mix in plenty of organic material, such as rotted manure, compost, composted leaves, or dampened peat moss. After that, the improved soil should be ready and able to support a nice perennial garden.

are the most common. Generally speaking, you want to remove anything that will get in the way of root growth.

- *Clods:* These are nothing more than compacted clumps of soil, held together by moisture. But a clod can obstruct plant growth as surely as a rock of the same size. Break clods apart by hand or, if necessary, with the flat back of a trowel, and return the dirt to the bed.

- *Rocks:* Extract little ones and set them aside. Remove big ones by excavating around them with a shovel and prying them loose, with a crowbar if necessary. If a large rock simply won't be moved, leave it in as a garden element and plan to plant around it.

- *Weeds:* For weeding to be really effective you need to remove their entire root systems. Use a hand weeder if necessary. A tool called a "dandelion weeder" (or "asparagus fork") has a long thin handle and a forked-tongue blade that works well to extract dandelions and other tap-rooted weeds. A little three-tined hand cultivator will loosen the soil so you can tease out the root systems of others. As for weed seeds, it's a fact of life that disturbing the soil brings dormant ones to the surface, perhaps to germinate. If you can't get them now, smother them with mulch at planting time and keep a lookout for them as the season unfolds, plucking or hoeing them out while they are still small.

- *Roots:* If trees and shrubs are growing close by, it's risky to haphazardly chop

Weeds can often be a nuisance in gardens. Remove them before you plant in a new area and continue to watch for them throughout the growing season. Weed seedlings often crop up around a new planting since during the process weed seeds were brought to the soil surface. One handy weeding tool is a three-tined hand cultivator.

and maul roots in the area where you are installing your new perennial bed. You might really damage a plant you want to keep. If possible, leave the roots undisturbed and plant perennials around them. If it turns out the roots are absorbing too much water and nutrients, you may have to remove them after all, or move your perennials. If you find a network of roots in your chosen site, and no valuable plants nearby to trace them to, you can dig and pull and lop them as much as you are able. Of course, if your digging reveals a host of obstructions, you might be compelled to reconsider the entire project. Perhaps you need to place your new perennial bed in a more hospitable location, or perhaps you would be better off erecting a raised bed on the site.

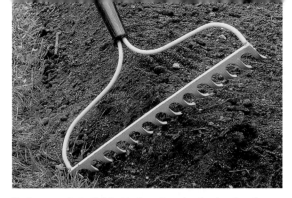

To give a new bed a finished look, and create a level surface for installing your new plants, rake over the soil surface.

Finishing Touches

No matter how intensive your digging project, before you stand back and declare the job finished, you should do two little things before calling it a day:

- *Rake over the entire bed:* It looks nice and fills you with pride, but there are also practical reasons: It smoothes over little hills and fills little valleys, and may turn up a few straggler clods or stones that you need to remove.

- *Water:* The easiest way to do this is to place a sprinkler right in the middle of the bed. Give the entire area a good soaking. This will settle the soil.

You can create more perennials to add to your garden or give away to fellow gardeners. The three main methods of propagation are seeds, cuttings, and division.

Before beginning a propagation project, clean trays and pots in a solution of one part bleach and ten parts water. This will kill any organisms (such as damping-off fungus) that might damage seedlings, newly rooted cuttings, or young divisions.

Propagating: Making More Perennials

There are several methods of propagation: division, cuttings, and seed. If you have the inclination and the time, it's fun to see if you can multiply your perennials. The following is an overview of your options. A great deal of research and experimentation has been done in this field, so if raising your own perennials using these methods really intrigues you, find a book or two with specialized, detailed information.

Dividing Established Perennials

Dividing your perennials is good for them and good for your garden. Sometimes, over the course of its life in your garden, a perennial cries out to be divided, or cut up into small pieces and replanted. For certain perennials, this is cosmetic—the crown, or innermost part of the plant, has become bare and the only thriving part is on the outer

Catmint, *Nepeta faassenii*

Dividing a perennial not only creates more plants, it can revive plants that are overgrown and declining in vigor. To divide a perennial you can either dig up the entire plant and cut sections apart, or cut the plant apart while it is still in the ground. In either case, keep the root system intact as much as possible.

Some perennials, such as daylilies, have fleshy roots, making division easy. One method of dividing a daylily is to pry it apart using two digging forks.

perimeter. For others, regular division is rejuvenating. Their roots have become crowded and the plants just aren't flowering as abundantly, all of which division relieves. You may also choose to divide a perennial just because it's getting too big for its allotted spot. Whatever your reason, the upshot is you end up with more and healthier plants.

Always divide plants during a period when they are not at their peak. A perennial that is flowering or growing strongly at the height of summer resents this disturbance. Furthermore, summer-divided and replanted perennials may struggle in hot weather. It's much easier on them in spring or fall. Work on a cool, still, cloudy day if possible. Hot sun and wind create extra stress for the plants.

- *Spring divisions:* Early spring is an excellent time to divide, move, and transplant perennials. Wait until they are up and growing, at least 2 or 3 inches high. The pieces, once replanted, should respond well to their inner urges to grow, as well as to the warming soil, spring rains, and warmer air.

- *Fall divisions:* Hold off on dividing plants in the fall until the perennials

show clear signs of slowing down. The flowering should be finished, and the foliage starting to die (cut it back and cut any stalks down before proceeding). As the ground has not yet frozen, transplanting the pieces is doable. The newly planted divisions can then be watered in and mulched for the coming winter.

Ways to Divide

Most mature perennials have clumping or dense roots. You can dig them up and divide once they're out of the ground, or you can chop them into sections right in the ground. Whatever you decide, the principle to remember is: Keep as much of the root system intact as possible. Shallow and incomplete cutting will chop off roots and result in small pieces that may be too damaged to grow into new plants. Always use sharp tools, whether a shovel or a garden fork or a sturdy knife.

Dividing a Perennial, Step by Step

Dividing many perennials is an easy project, and can be beneficial to plants that have grown in upon themselves, have died out in the middle of the clump, or have expanded out of bounds to crowd other plants in the

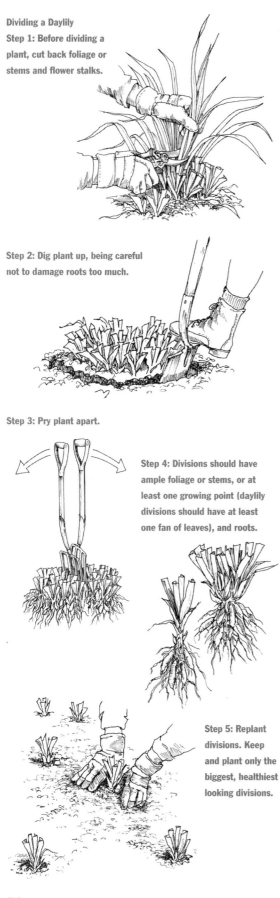

Dividing a Daylily
Step 1: Before dividing a plant, cut back foliage or stems and flower stalks.

Step 2: Dig plant up, being careful not to damage roots too much.

Step 3: Pry plant apart.

Step 4: Divisions should have ample foliage or stems, or at least one growing point (daylily divisions should have at least one fan of leaves), and roots.

Step 5: Replant divisions. Keep and plant only the biggest, healthiest looking divisions.

garden. For successful plant division, follow the steps below.

1. Define the size of the project. If foliage or flower stalks are in your way, chop them back. Use a shovel or trowel to outline the root area with short slices.

2. Dig up the plant and evaluate the extent and size of the roots. To do this, you may need to brush soil off with your hands or a spray from the hose.

3. Pry the plant apart. If it's big and dense, two garden forks inserted back-to-back in the middle and pulled outward should do the trick. If it's a smaller plant, use a trowel or knife. Very dense, entangled roots may need to be teased and pulled apart by hand after the initial cut with a sharp tool.

4. Make divisions. Each piece should have at least one growing shoot (and maybe a few leaves) plus a substantial section of roots. Discard unpromising pieces such as a spent inner crown or sections with damaged, dying, or spindly roots.

5. Replant the pieces. Treat the divisions with care, because they are now new young plants. Give them an appropriate spot in good soil, provide them enough elbowroom, and water them in well. Mulch when you are finished.

Cuttings

There are two types of cuttings, stem and root. Both methods require cutting a healthy portion from the plant and placing it in an environment conducive to forming new growth. The formation of new roots on the

When dividing bearded iris, cut back foliage before digging and soak rhizome divisions for thirty minutes in a solution of ten parts bleach and one part water. This will kill any disease organisms that might enter the cut ends and lead to rot.

cutting is the critical stage and a young plant is not ready to be put into the garden (or even into a larger container) until it has grown an ample root system. Often new shoots are also produced at the same time the new roots are growing. That is a sign the cutting is still viable, but the production of new roots is the key to a successful new plant.

Stem Cuttings

These are small divisions made of short, young shoots and no roots. They need to have a terminal bud at the top and a few side buds (tucked in above the junction of a leaf and the main stem). Each cutting should be of soft but vigorous growth, about 6 inches or less in length.

Take stem cutting in late spring or early summer, when the source plant is already growing well.

Using a sharp knife, scissors, or even pruners, carefully cut stem sections of new growth from the mother plant (do not rip or tear). Cut it off cleanly, so that at least one node will be below the soil line. Strip off lower leaves. Then stick the cutting no more than an inch deep in a flat or pot of 1:1 peat-based soil mix and sand. Keep the cuttings moist and warm (in a greenhouse, warm well-lit room, or a cold frame).

Watch for new top growth. But the real test is that when you gently tug on the cutting, roots resist and hold the cutting in the mix. Once you are sure your cuttings are well rooted and thriving, you can move them one by one to pots or, if sturdy enough, out into the garden.

Some perennials you can raise from stem cuttings are summer and creeping phloxes, bee balm, aster, turtlehead, obedient plant, and salvia.

Taking Stem Cuttings
Step 1: Cut sections of new growth 3 to 5 inches long.

Step 2: Remove lower leaves and any side shoots.

Step 3: Dip cut ends into rooting hormone and stick into sterile soilless mix. Be sure at least one node (point where leaves or side shoots emerge) is below the soil level.

When sowing large seeds or sticking root or stem cuttings, poke a hole in the soil first. This is especially helpful if you have applied rooting powder to cuttings and don't want to rub it off as you insert the cutting into the soil. A handy tool to use is a dibble, made especially for this purpose.

Root Cuttings

Healthy sections of roots are placed in a soilless mix and raised in a cold frame or propagator.

Take root cuttings in late winter or early spring, so the procedure will not traumatize the mother plant, and when the root pieces will be poised to grow.

Use a sharp knife to cut fleshy, mature root pieces about 2 to 4 inches long. Cut the top end straight (the end that was nearest the crown of the mother plant) and the bottom end slanted, so you can distinguish them. If the root pieces are thick enough, insert them into prepared pots or trays (a 1:1 mixture of peat-based soil mix and sand is fine) vertically and right side up. If they are slender, lay them horizontally. Top off with sand, and keep moist and warm.

The appearance of shoots and small leaves after several weeks shows that the pieces have rooted and begun growing. Let them grow a while longer, until you judge they are strong enough to be moved up to individual pots. Eventually, about the time warm weather returns, you should be able to move the new young plants outside into the garden. Some perennials you can raise from root cuttings are acanthus, Japanese anemone, Oriental poppies, summer phlox, sea holly, black-eyed susan, and bleeding heart.

Seed

Probably the most challenging way to create new plants is from seed. While some perennials are fairly easy to propagate this way, some require special treatments, such as stratification (a period of cold and damp) or light, and take several months or even a year to germinate and begin growth. Some seeds won't germinate until they have had a succession of warm periods and cold periods, to break down certain chemical barriers in the seeds, trigger growth, and soften hard seed coverings.

You can purchase packets of perennial seeds from a garden center or specialty catalog (the latter is a great source of unusual perennials). If you collect ripe seeds from perennials in your garden, realize that those from hybrids or cultivars may not be viable or

Seed Sowing
Step 1: Moisten potting mix.

Step 2: Fill small pots, trays, or cell-packs with moist potting mix.

Step 3: Sow seeds a few to a pot or cell. Seedlings will emerge in varying lengths of time, depending on the species.

Step 4: Water newly sowed seed and young seedlings from below.

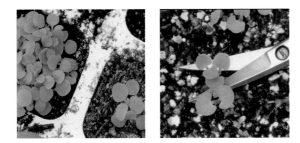

Sow seed thinly, only a few to a small pot or cell. Crowded seedlings will compete for moisture, nutrients, and light and can be difficult to separate into individual plants later. To have only one healthy seedling per pot you can either pull apart seedlings after they are sturdy enough (with at least two or three sets of true leaves), or cut away all but one developing seedling.

may not "come true" (that is, the seedlings may not resemble their parent).

For purchased seed, sow indoors in late winter or early spring. This way the young plants have a chance to get started and should be ready to go outdoors in late spring and early summer. For collected seed, you can sow it in late fall and coddle the seedlings through the winter months or set the flats outside over the winter.

Most perennial seeds germinate just fine in flats of sterile potting mix, lightly covered over with a dusting of sterile sand or vermiculite. (It should be sterile to avoid damping-off disease, which causes young seedlings to flop over at their base and die.) Tiny seeds do not need to be covered. Give the flats warmth, even moisture, and indirect light. Carefully move the seedlings to pots when they reach an inch or two high and have at least two sets of true leaves. (The first leaves to emerge are called "seed leaves" or cotyledons and their purpose is to provide the energy to get the young plant started; true leaves emerge later.)

Germination rates vary. Some perennials sprout and grow within weeks or months. Others appear to be a failed project, but germinate the following year. To find out what to expect, read the seed packet carefully or look up your perennial in a seed-starting reference book such as Nancy Bubel's *Seed-Starters Handbook* or Ann Reilly's *Success with Seeds*. Some perennials you can raise from seed are balloon flower, coral bells, Stokes' aster, and cardinal flower.

GARDEN TIP

Gathering seed

If you want to try your hand at growing plants from seeds out of your own garden, first make sure the seed is ripe since it won't continue to ripen after it has been removed from the flower head. Flower heads or seed capsules or pods should be thoroughly dry and "crackly," and the flower should obviously not still be blooming. Most seed is dark brown or gray when it is ready, but some seeds are light colored.

Installing the Plants

When the time has come to plant—the bed is finally ready to receive the perennials—it's an exciting day! Here are a few tips to help you accomplish the job quickly and efficiently. The goal is to get the plants into the ground properly, so they experience minimal stress and can begin growing and beautifying your yard.

Preparing the Plants

Although you can put plants into the garden soon after purchasing them, it will be better

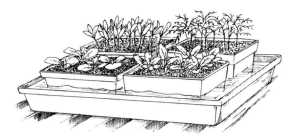

It is important to water sowed seed and new seedlings from below so the seeds are not brought to the soil surface or washed to the edge of the pot, and tender seedling stalks are not bent over by the weight of water droplets and damaged.

if you take a little time to prepare them. If there's time, or if you believe it's warranted, you should "harden them off" so they'll make a smooth transition. Beyond that, there are a few planting-day preparations you should do.

For Bare-root Perennials

Rehydrate them a few hours ahead of time. Soak their roots (not the entire plant!) in a bucket. Then bring them, bucket and all, to the planting site. If you can't do this, or don't wish to, then just keep their roots moist by draping a damp cloth over them until they go into the ground.

For Potted Plants

Water them a few hours beforehand (so they are damp but not soggy; the roots and stems should be full of water or "turgid"). Immediately before planting, pop them out of their pots one at a time. Loosen the roots a bit; if some of the potting soil comes loose, mix it into the soil from the hole. Examine the roots. If some are damaged or rotten, snip them off with clippers. Groom the top growth a bit as well, trimming it back an inch or two, so the

roots will have less to support. The plant will soon recover.

Seed-grown Plants

Even though you have kept seedling plants growing in pots until their root systems are big enough to be transplanted to the garden, they might still be small plants. Water them thoroughly thirty minutes to an hour before planting so they have a chance to drain a bit. Wait until you are in the process of planting to remove them from their pots or cell packs; if you remove them too far in advance of planting they will quickly dry out. Slightly loosen the roots very gently since they're still young and fragile—you don't want to damage

Soak the roots of bare-root perennials to rehydrate them before planting them in the ground. And be sure to water thoroughly after planting.

A cold frame can be used to hold over plants prior to planting.

Before planting a potted perennial, tease the roots apart a little.

For seed-grown plants, handle them very carefully when putting them in the ground and water immediately. The root systems are not as big as a plant that has been growing in a pot for many months.

the few roots you have on a small plant. Carefully place the plant in the hole and press loosed soil around its roots. Water immediately since planting is stressful and young plants don't have the moisture reserves of a larger plant.

GARDEN TIP

Helping rootbound plants

Sometimes when you extract a young perennial from its pot, you discover it has become rootbound. Roots are so dense and crammed in that they may be circling around and back on themselves. Tease them loose as best you can, so they can start to grow downward and outward in the garden. In more extreme cases, you can take a very sharp knife and carefully score the dense rootball two to four times at evenly spaced intervals, cutting in about a half-inch deep. This slices open some of the roots, which induces them to produce tiny new "feeder roots" once in the ground.

Proper Planting, Step by Step

1. Dig an ample hole: ideally, twice as wide as the root system. It should also be several inches deeper than the farthest reach of the current roots, so new roots can expand into welcoming ground.

2. Place loose soil in the bottom for the roots to grow into. Pure fertilizer is not recommended, as it can burn the roots, but organic additions are acceptable.

3. Loosen and tease apart the perennial's roots, so they will be ready to grow into their new home.

4. Set the plant in the hole at the proper planting depth. For most plants the crown should be at soil level, but there are exceptions such as bearded iris and peonies, which prefer shallow planting.

5. Holding the plant upright and in place with one hand, thoroughly backfill soil into the hole with the other. Press firmly so the plant is well anchored.

6. Use soil (not mulch) to build up a shallow basin—1 or 2 inches tall is usually sufficient—around the base of the plant to help hold water.

7. Add support if needed. If the perennial is likely to be sprawling or floppy, or to grow tall, now is the time to install a stake next to it or a cage right over it.

8. Give every plant a good soaking. Watch the water soak in, and repeat.

Proper planting will ensure that your perennial will quickly settle in and grow successfully. Dig a hole that is neither too deep nor too shallow, allowing the plant to be at the same depth it was in the container. Remove the plant from its pot just prior to placing it in the hole, loosening the roots carefully. Fill in firmly around the roots with soil then water and add a layer of mulch.

Proper Spacing

When you plant small plants, it's tempting to place them close together. You will soon rue this decision. Judge how far apart to place young perennials by finding out what their mature width is expected to be. Allow for that "footprint," or more. If you are planting several of the same plant use the mature width as a guide. For example, if you are planting three of the same type of plant, and each one will ultimately be 1 foot wide, space them 1 foot apart from each other.

To free a plant from its pot, remove any roots growing out of the drainage holes, squeeze or press the sides of the pot or tap it from the bottom, and carefully pull or shake the plant out. If your potted perennial seems tight in its container and won't easily come out, cut off the pot with scissors or pruners so you don't damage the plant trying to pull it free.

Post-planting Care

On planting day it's important to take a few moments right after planting to finish up. You are not really through for the day until you take care of these final touches.

- Lay down a light mulch around each plant (an inch or two is usually sufficient). This shelters the plant from soil temperature fluctuations and premature drying out. It also helps smother weeds. Run the mulch right up to the stems or crown, but not touching, which can encourage rot.

- Insert a label in the ground near the plant, so you can remember its name. Plastic labels can be purchased at garden centers, but Popsicle sticks and tongue depressors can also be used.

GARDEN TIP

Walk the plank!

A newly prepared perennial bed tends to be soft and fluffy in texture. So get a board or plank to use on planting day, and walk or kneel on it as you work. True, it presses down on the garden soil, but it disperses your weight, which minimizes the compaction.

Some plants need to be planted shallowly. When planting bearded iris, be sure the rhizome is at the surface, and is not under the soil. Also, do not cover the rhizome with mulch.

After planting put down a light mulch.

Label new perennials so you will remember what you have planted.

Provide shade for newly planted perennials.

When planting a bare-root perennial, build up a mound of soil in the bottom of the hole, hold the plant upright with one hand, and scoop soil around the roots with the other hand. Plant it so that the crown is just below the surface of the soil.

■ Provide a little shelter from hot sun, even if you've just planted sun-lovers. Their first few days will be easier. Use lightweight lawn chairs, plywood tents, screens, or whatever you have on hand.

In the ensuing days, even perennials touted as "low maintenance" need tender loving care for at least their first few weeks, if not their entire first season. Visit them often and do whatever needs to be done.

Water frequently, unless the weather is rainy. Once or twice a week is a good rule of thumb. Watch for weeds and remove them promptly if they appear. Young perennials simply can't compete with aggressive invaders. Renew the mulch layer if it breaks down or gets washed away. Keep a lookout for pests and diseases and intervene quickly if they appear. If your plants are sited appropriately, in well-prepared ground, chances are there will be no such problems. But you don't want to be caught napping!

MAINTAINING PERENNIALS

IN THIS CHAPTER:

- **What to expect from your perennials**
- **Watering, fertilizing, and mulching**
- **Weeding and grooming**
- **Winter protection**
- **Pests and diseases**

What to Expect from Your Perennials

Proper care of your perennials is sure to bring out their best. But bear in mind that every garden is a community of living things. This community changes over time, as the plants adjust to their setting and to one another. You the gardener will grow in knowledge and experience as you get to know your perennials as individuals and as members of a larger group. The best-laid plans may be changed by nature (as when a storm drops a tree branch on a flower bed or a prolonged drought brings stress). Or your perennial garden may change according to the level of care you are willing and able to provide.

But there are some general "perennial *plant* truths" you can count on:

- A plant's first year is formative. That is, a newly introduced perennial will spend its first season in your garden getting established. Root growth is the highest priority—and this, of course, is occurring out of sight underground. So enjoy your new perennial's first year, but realize that the best is yet to come.

- There is no such thing as no-maintenance plants. Especially newly planted ones. In order for them to thrive, you must nurture young perennials. Some established ones might continue to require

your attention—trimming back and shaping, frequent deadheading, for instance—to look their best. Certain perennials are definitely worth a little extra effort.

- You will discover more about each perennial's personality, sometimes in the first year and certainly in ensuing years. Assertive plants will grow lustily and spread out, increasing their bulk and sometimes their numbers. Less outgoing plants may need a helping hand from you to stand out.

Red Hot Poker (*Kniphofia uvaria*) and
Lily of the Nile (*Agapanthus africanus*)

There are also some "perennial *garden* truths" to be aware of as you enter this grand adventure:

- A perennial garden is a work in progress. You are never truly "finished." This isn't just because the creative process evolves and you get new inspiration or enthusiasm. This "medium" of living plants has countless variables. Plants have life cycles and life spans; they react and adapt to their immediate environment and your local climate. And perennials might behave a little differently from one year to the next.

- Plants seem to have a mind of their own. Sometimes they frustrate us and sometimes surprise and delight us. As an experienced botanical garden professional once remarked, "They often take the brush right out of our hands and paint their own next scene."

- Garden maintenance is work. But it can be minimized for efficiency, and it is not drudgery. It is an absorbing, results-oriented effort that yields visible, gratifying, and often thrilling results.

Watering

Let's say you're gardening in a "typical" season, meaning that the garden has plenty of natural moisture early on from melting snow, run-off, or springtime rains. Summer becomes hotter and drier, then autumn brings cooler days and, eventually, drenching rains. In this scenario watering a perennial garden is mainly a summer job.

But there are atypical years and perennials that benefit from extra moisture (certain irises, for example), and those that struggle with too much water (such as lavender, which can rot in damp ground). The key, then, is never to assume anything. Check your plants regularly. Or, more properly, check their soil.

Soil that is wet holds it shape when squeezed (left) and may drip water, soil that is dry feels sandy or dusty and won't hold together when handled (middle), and soil that has the right amount of moisture feels damp but crumbly.

How Much Water Is Enough?

Unlike annuals, most perennials tend to be naturally deep-rooted plants. Of course, downward and outward growth takes time—sometimes years. Deep watering encourages the roots to grow deep and long, whereas light watering keeps root growth shallow. The roots go where the water is!

Generally speaking, well-soaked soil down to at least 6 or 8 inches satisfies the water needs of most perennials. This is accomplished by occasional deep soakings, not by intermittent sprinklings.

Get your perennial garden on a watering schedule. A good, deep soaking once every week or two is a good place to start. But of course this schedule can be modified for many reasons:

- After a good, soaking rain, skip a watering.

- For young plants, regular water is more important.

- Plants growing in a raised bed or quick-draining soil dry out more quickly than a traditional garden bed and require more frequent irrigating.

- During a spell of dry weather, you must water more frequently.

- Plants in trouble—wilting, dropping their leaves, or other signs of obvious distress—need extra moisture immediately.

In time, as the garden matures and the plants grow deeper roots and become established, once-a-month watering may suffice if there has been plenty of rain; once every two weeks when it's been dry, depending

There are a number of tools to help you keep your garden well watered. A rain gauge measures rainfall amounts. A soaker hose is an efficient way of irrigating a garden bed, delivering water close to the root zones of the plants.

on your climate and soil, and the types of plants you're growing. If you live in a part of the country that is naturally dry, consider growing drought-tolerant plants adapted to your region.

After you've finished watering a plant or an area, and no water remains puddled on the surface, check to see if the watering was adequate. If the soil is loose, simply poke down with your finger. Better still, slice into the ground nearby with a trowel (but avoid cutting into a root system) and have a look. If the ground is damp to a depth of 6 or 8 inches, chances are good that your watering was sufficient. If only the surface is moistened, water more.

Certain perennials are always going to need more irrigation than others. Be ready to provide supplemental water to the following:

- Traditionally thirsty species.

- Thirstier species that are growing among drought-tolerant companions.

- Young plants with new, confined, developing root systems.
- Plants that share their space with a resource-grabbing tree or large shrub.

Watering the Entire Bed

Irrigating a large flower bed can be time consuming, so it's wise to put some sort of watering system in place. Drip-irrigation lines are highly efficient, delivering water exactly where it is needed through small emitters along their length. However, it's best to install them before planting, since digging and burying in place is required.

Low-tech methods include snaking a soaker hose throughout a bed or setting up a sprinkler. Either of these can be moved midway through the watering process, if necessary, to get full coverage of the bed.

Standing over a large flower garden with a hose or watering can is the least efficient way to water. It's time consuming and requires patience and endurance. You may get bored and move on before your perennials have been adequately soaked. Better to use one of the systems recommended above.

Sometimes an individual plant might need a little extra water, requiring you to spot water with a hose or watering can.

Spot Watering

Sometimes plants need to be watered individually. It's important to deliver the water directly to the root system, generally right at the base of the plant and perhaps an inch or two out from the farthest reach of the foliage. Be neat. There's no point in wasting water on bare ground or possibly encouraging weed seeds to germinate.

If you can deliver the water personally, use a hose or watering can. If you use a hose, a soaker attachment delivers the water more gently. Alternatively, bring a water-filled plastic bottle or jug, or even a long-necked wine bottle, to the spot; hold your thumb or hand over the opening, deftly turn it over and plunge it into the soil near the plant. Soil will now plug its opening while allowing water to seep out. In this way, water is delivered slowly, and you don't have to stand there. Come back later and remove the bottle, or refill it for another dose, as necessary. (Granted, this is not a very attractive method, but it's temporary and gets the job done quite well.)

Make a basin

Mound up soil or mulch in a low berm (1 or 2 inches high) around a perennial, preferably at planting time. This prevents wasteful run-off, holding water in and forcing it down into the root system below.

Watering Options for Perennials

Watering Can

Advantages: You can visit each plant individually, taking a closer look at it as the water sprays down. Delivers water evenly and moderately.

Disadvantages: Not practical if you have lots of perennials to water. You may have to make several trips per plant to refilling; a big planting can be a laborious watering job.

Bottle or Jug

Advantages: Delivers water exactly where you want it, right into the thirsty plant's root zone, at a slow rate.

Disadvantages: Looks unattractive. Requires that you install and monitor it.

GARDEN TIP

Get a watering wand

A watering wand screws on to the end of your hose, not only extending your reach but also delivering water to your plants in a soft, diffuse shower. Some come with a valve near the top end so you can shut off the water temporarily while you transfer the aim elsewhere. Watering wands are inexpensive, usually no more than $20. Cheaper ones tend to leak and work poorly after just one season, so spend a little more and get a good one.

Hose

Advantages: Delivers water directly to the basin and a perennial's root system.

Disadvantages: You have to move it from plant to plant. If you "babysit" the hose, you could get impatient and not water adequately.

Caption

Sprinkler

Advantages: Ease! Also delivers water slowly and steadily. Can water a larger area.

Disadvantages: Wet leaves of some perennials can develop unsightly water spots, or even moisture-related disease problems. To minimize these possibilities, water in early morning so drops that fall on the foliage can evaporate. Evening watering can lead to disease problems, and watering in the middle of a hot day just wastes water to evaporation.

Conserve water!

To water in an efficient and conservative way, here are some tried-and-true techniques:

- Water in the early morning or late afternoon, when there is much less evaporation.
- If puddles form or run-off occurs, turn the water off for a while; resume after the excess has soaked in.
- Create a basin around individual plants by mounding up an inch or two of soil; this traps the water in place so it soaks in right where you want it, instead of running off.
- Mulch your perennials to hold in soil moisture.

Bubbler

Advantages: Ease! Also, practical—delivers water at a slow gurgle.

Disadvantages: It's possible to overwater. To prevent this, add a timer to the system.

Soaker Hose

Advantages: The ideal way to water many perennials or a large flower bed. Delivers water slowly, directly to the root areas. Can be put on a timer.

Disadvantages: If you leave it in place, it's not a very attractive sight in the garden (unless you can find a way to hide it from view, like covering it with mulch). But pulling it out of the garden—and laying it back down again each time you want to water—may be a lot of work. Once the perennials fill in, you won't really notice a soaker hose.

In-ground Systems

Advantages: Ease! Also, efficient—they provide water directly to the root area, at a measured rate, so there's little waste or run-off. Thus, these systems are an excellent choice

Fertilizing your perennials can give you healthier, more productive plants, and correct nutrient deficiency problems in the soil. Timing and application rates are very important, so follow label directions carefully.

for areas with regular droughts or water restrictions. Also a time-saver, if you have lots of perennials needing water. It can even water when you are away if you add a timer.

Disadvantages: Depending on the type you choose, and the extent of the system you want, it can be costly. Also, it's easier to install *before* you plant anything, so if your garden is established, installation might require more care to avoid damaging plants.

Fertilizing Your Perennials

Before you feed your perennials, consider this: Is it necessary? If the bed you are growing them in contains plenty of organic matter, fertilizer may not be needed. If the soil is not very fertile or has poor texture, it's wiser to spend some effort improving it rather than relying on constant fertilizing to take up the slack.

Some gardeners never fertilize, feeling that their plants are growing in sufficiently decent soil and that extra pampering is simply extra work. These gardeners probably won't grow plants needing regular fertilizing or eventually remove plants that don't live up to their expectations. It's a "survival-of-the-fittest" approach, and it certainly has its merits. Luckily, a great many common perennials handle this system just fine since they don't require fertilizer to thrive.

CRITICAL NITROGEN

Nitrogen is undoubtedly the most important nutrient your growing perennial plants require—it is constantly in demand. Decomposing organic matter continually releases nitrogen, which is why it's so important that perennial garden soil have plenty of organic matter. The forms of nitrogen found in common fertilizers and organic matter need to be broken down by bacteria to make the nitrogen available to plants. Which is why nitrogen isn't accessible when the soil is cold (and bacteria aren't active), noticeable particularly in early spring when new growth might be yellow from nitrogen deficiency.

Nitrogen is soluble in water, making it reach plant roots quickly. But this solubility also means it is readily leached from the soil, which is why some gardeners apply it more often than they apply other fertilizers. Yet the old adage of "too much of a good thing isn't good" holds true—too much nitrogen fertilizer can delay flowering (since it favors the growth of leaves and stems); create weak, succulent green growth; and burn the roots of new plants and seedlings.

Labels on fertilizer packages should indicate the amounts of nitrogen, phosphorus, and potassium, typically as a ratio such as 5-10-5.

In any event, never broadcast fertilizers, lime, or other amendments haphazardly. You may be wasting your time and money, and damaging the environment. It's much wiser to find out what, if anything, is needed, and how much.

Test Your Soil

To determine whether fertilizing is even necessary, have your garden soil tested. This is a simple matter of digging up soil samples from various parts of your yard where you wish to grow perennials, mixing them together, and sending a portion (dry) to a professional lab.

Be sure to note that you plan to grow perennials (as opposed to vegetables) so the lab technicians can make appropriate recommendations about how to improve your soil if necessary. If fertilizer or a particular nutrient is deemed necessary, the lab will also supply you with an application rate. For instance, "add one or two pounds of nitrogen per 1,000 square feet per year" is typical advice.

How Fertilizing Works

Fertilizer is plant food. It nourishes your perennials, helping them make new growth. It's important to understand that fertilizer does not cause cell growth. Rather, its nutrients support cell growth by providing energy.

Many fertilizers supply three basic nutrients to plants—nitrogen (N), phosphorus (P), and potassium (K). Labels on bags and containers of fertilizer always express their presence in this order, as a ratio. For example, a 5-10-5 fertilizer contains 5 percent nitrogen, 10

SLOW FOOD VERSUS FAST FOOD

"Slow" plant food is slow-release fertilizer. These products break down over time, gradually dissolving and gradually releasing their nutrients to your plants. One good dose of slow-release fertilizer at the beginning of the growing season can keep plants going for months. One good dose, indeed, may be all that's needed each spring.

Chemical slow-release fertilizers are granular products, pellets, or sticks, which have been treated to release nutrients slowly. Most organic fertilizers—including composted manures—also release their nutrients slowly.

A "fast" fertilizer is one that is not specifically labeled as slow. These unleash their nutrients (when watered into the soil) at once, so the plants can use all they have to offer sooner rather than later. Some gardeners prefer to use these products, applying perhaps less at a time but more frequently—for more precision control over the feeding of their plants. Most powdered, granulated, and liquid chemical fertilizers are quick release.

percent phosphorus, and 5 percent potash (the form of potassium used by plants). Each element does different things when added to your garden soil.

- *Nitrogen (N)*: Enhances the growth of leaves and stems.
- *Phosphorus (P)*: Aids the production of flowers, fruits, seeds, and roots.
- *Potassium (K)*: Increases a plant's resistance to disease and generally promotes vigor.

Certain fertilizers also offer other elements that may turn out to be beneficial for certain soils and certain plants. Some of these "secondary elements" are calcium, magnesium, and sulfur. "Trace elements" may also be furnished, including boron, chlorine, iron, zinc, copper, manganese, and molybdenum. Luckily, many soil amendments, including compost and seaweed, supply these anyway. And pH-adjusting additives such as lime and elemental sulfur also provide some calcium, magnesium, and sulfur. Actually, few good garden soils lack these nutrients, and few perennial plants insist upon them.

Basically, an application of fertilizer "jump-starts" your plants, urging them into active growth and providing extra energy. Remember, however, that it only works and delivers these benefits if you apply it properly.

When Your Perennials Need Fertilizer

When the soil has a nutrient deficiency, an application of fertilizer can help improve a perennial's appearance and performance. If a plant or plants develops a problem, take a sample of the affected plant in for examination

Applications of fertilizer can promote the production of flowers; stem, root, and leaf growth; overall plant vigor; and disease resistance.

by a garden center employee or an Extension specialist before assuming it is a nutrient problem.

Also, a too-high or too-low soil pH could be the reason that your perennials are not taking up important nutrients. The nutrients may actually be present but "locked up" and unavailable to the plants growing there. Most perennials do best in a slightly acidic to neutral soil, between 5.5 and 6.5. So before you fertilize, test the soil pH. Be sure to note when you send your soil sample to the lab that you are wishing to grow perennials so the technicians there can send you appropriate soil-improvement recommendations.

- *Too acidic:* If a pH test reveals that your soil is pH 5.0 or lower, you can bring it back into a more neutral, plant-nutrient-friendly zone by adding something alkaline. Popular sources include powdered lime and wood ashes. Apply these according to the rates recommended by the lab. Sprinkle them on the bed and water in.
- *Too alkaline:* Many perennials tolerate moderately alkaline soil, but when the

Apply granular fertilizer to the soil and work it in, either by turning the soil or scratching it in around individual plants.

pH strays into the 8.0 range or higher, you may have to improve the soil. (Note that very alkaline soils also tend to be dry soils, which may also account for plants failing to thrive there.) To make such soil more neutral or acidic, you can dig in some dampened peat moss or a compost of oak leaves and pine needles. The soil testing lab will have specific recommendations.

Nutrient Deficiencies

Nutrient deficiencies can be major or minor. Problems due to a lack of minor nutrients are less common generally. Below are a few of the more serious, major nutrient deficiencies.

Plant Symptom: Leaves are not thriving— they're small, pale to yellow, sometimes with bluish-purple undersides. They may turn completely yellow and fall off.
Nutrient Deficiency: Nitrogen

Plant Symptom: Leaves are small, but not yellow. Leaf undersides exhibit areas of reddish-purple that eventually spreads to entire leaf.
Nutrient Deficiency: Phosphorus

Plant Symptom: Stunted plant growth, with slender, fibrous, hard stems.
Nutrient Deficiency: Phosphorus
Plant Symptom: Stunted plant growth;

spindly, slender stems that die off one by one.
Nutrient Deficiency: Nitrogen

Plant Symptom: Leaves normal size, but older leaves have browned edges and may cup downward. Leaves may develop blackened dead spots or turn yellow or ashen. The trouble starts at the bottom of the plant and works its way upward.
Nutrient Deficiency: Potassium

Don't overdo!

If you are too zealous, you can do your perennials more harm than good. Always follow label instructions for application rates and dilution information, and if you have any doubts, use less fertilizer rather than more.

Signs that you've overfed your plants include:

- **Fewer or no flowers:** The fertilizer has inspired foliage at their expense.
- **Burnt edges on leaves:** This is especially true for foliar feeding.
- **Tender growth:** Your plants have absorbed too much nitrogen.
- **Shriveled, dried-up leaves:** Excessive fertilizer has drawn water from the roots, injuring them and consequently the leaves they support.

COMMON FERTILIZERS

Before applying any fertilizer, read the label directions and follow suggested application rates and safety precautions. Remember, the first number refers to nitrogen, the second number to phosphorus, and the third number to potassium. Fertilizers can be applied in several ways—as a foliar spray, as a topdressing, or mixed into the soil at planting time. Depending on the type, dry forms can be broadcast over an entire new bed or mixed into individual planting holes—use caution with the latter so you don't burn roots. Always mix fertilizer with soil from the hole (don't just throw the fertilizer in the bottom of the hole and place the roots of the plant directly on top of it) and water thoroughly after planting. Slow-release, organic fertilizers are generally so safe that it would be difficult to over-apply them and damage plants. Chemical fertilizers need more careful measurement. A sampling of fertilizers is listed below by their formulations, whether they are chemical or organic, and if they are quick release or slow release.

5-10-10	23-15-18	6-8-2	6-2-0
chemical	chemical	bat guano	milorganite
granular	powder	organic	organic
quick release	quick release	composted	composted, in bags
widely available	widely available	slow release	slow release
		order from a	widely available
10-10-10	4-3-2	specialty house;	
chemical	chicken or cricket	sometimes at farm-	9-1-0
granular	manure	supply stores	blood meal
quick release	organic		organic
widely available	composted	6-2-2	granular
	slow release	cottonseed meal	slow release
14-14-14	need to obtain from	organic	widely available;
chemical	a farm	powder	stinky
granular		slow release	
slow release	5-3-2	widely available	4-12-0
widely available	fish emulsion		bone meal
	organic		organic
20-20-20	liquid, concentrated		granular
chemical	slow release		slow release
powder	widely available;		widely available
quick release	stinky		
widely available			

Plant Symptom: Plant growth is stunted. Stems are thin and become hard and woody. If you dig up a plant you discover that the roots are brown or poorly developed.
Nutrient Deficiency: Potassium

When and How to Fertilize

The optimal time to fertilize perennials is at the start of the season, in springtime—about a week or two before planting time. This way, you'll apply fertilizer when the plants are poised to make rapid growth and the benefits of the fertilizer will be maximized. Never just

The amount of fertilizer you use depends on the size of your bed, the types of plants you are growing, and the makeup of your soil.

Phosphorus

Phosphorus is one of the "big three" nutrients, aiding in root development and bloom production. It is available to plants as phosphate, which bonds to soil and is nearly insoluble, dissolving so slowly that only a little at a time is accessible to plants. Three common types of fertilizers containing phosphorus are rock phosphate, super phosphate, and bone meal. These supplements are more effective if mixed into the soil at planting time, so the slowly dissolving phosphorus is closer to the root zone. Overuse of quick-release fertilizers with high phosphorus, particularly for turf, has led to water pollution in many areas. If applying water-soluble fertilizers in granular form, sweep any excess from sidewalks or driveways into the beds so run-off water doesn't carry it into the water supply.

dump plant food directly onto a plant's root zone or directly into a planting hole, as this can burn a plant. Instead, follow these general directions:

- *For a new bed:* Scatter dry or granular fertilizer over the surface, then dig it in to a depth of several inches (so it gets into the root zone, the area where the roots of your perennial plants will be growing). Or mix with soil in planting hole.

- *For an established bed:* Distribute dry or granular fertilizer around the emerging plants, and scratch it in carefully with a rake or clawed hand tool, to a depth of at least an inch or two. Be careful not to or dislodge roots or rootballs as you work.

Then water well: Plants can absorb the fertilizer's nutrients only in liquid form. Some perennial gardeners continue to fertilize plants throughout the growing season, every month or so, up until mid- or late summer (stopping then so that the plants will have a chance to slow down as cooler weather approaches). In areas that are irrigated often or in regions with high rainfall, some nutrients can be leached from the soil (especially nitrogen), which can require more frequent fertilizing.

How Much Fertilizer?

The amount of fertilizer you should use varies widely, from as little as 1 pound per 100 square feet to 10 pounds per 100 square feet of garden. Of course, it can vary depending on what kind you are using and whether it is slow release or fast, organic or chemical. Highly concentrated fertilizers need to be applied more sparingly. The amount you use also depends on how much ground or how many plants you are treating. With fertilizing, more is *not* better. Moderation is the key. Two weeks to one month is enough time to judge whether you have fertilized plants properly.

Organic Versus Chemical Fertilizers

Generally speaking, organic fertilizers are best for perennial gardens. Not only are they good for your plants, they are gentle on the soil.

Foliar feeding of perennials delivers plant food quickly.

Mulching is one of the best maintenance practices for your garden. For a new bed, apply mulch to the top, rake smooth, and plant through the mulch. Or install plants first and apply mulch carefully around them.

They are "slow food" and release their beneficial nutrients over time, providing long-term effects and saving you work. Examples include homemade or store-bought bagged compost or humus, composted animal manure, fish emulsion, cottonseed meal, milorganite, blood meal, and bone meal.

Chemical fertilizers are available in granules, powders, and concentrated liquids. They need either to be diluted according to label directions or watered in so they will be activated and so they don't come into direct contact with roots and injure (burn) them.

Granted, chemical fertilizers are a cheap and easy way to deliver soil nutrients, but you can't count on them to maintain soil fertility. The truth is, organic content of any soil is constantly being washed away and lost—especially cultivated soil. If you depend exclusively on chemical fertilizer, you will end up using ever-increasing amounts. A chemical, quick-release fertilizer is often used at planting time to jump-start plants, and to fill in between the time of planting and the time when slow-release, organic fertilizers become available.

Foliar Feeding

Foliar feeding is simply spraying or misting fertilizer (diluted with water, of course!) onto your plants. It's a quick and easy way to give your perennials a periodic boost during the summer months. It can be especially beneficial for those plants that have a longer bloom period.

Either dilute a commercial chemical fertilizer according to the label directions, or brew some "manure tea" (soak a small sack of manure or even compost in a bucket of water overnight or longer). Add this mixture to a hose-end sprayer, set the nozzle to "fine" and spray away! Be sure to get the undersides of the leaves, too, for they will also absorb the nutrients. Work on a cloudy day, or in the morning or late afternoon, to minimize evaporation and maximize absorption, and to avoid burning the foliage if you're using a chemical fertilizer.

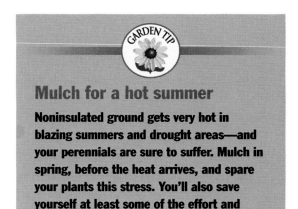

GARDEN TIP

Mulch for a hot summer

Noninsulated ground gets very hot in blazing summers and drought areas—and your perennials are sure to suffer. Mulch in spring, before the heat arrives, and spare your plants this stress. You'll also save yourself at least some of the effort and expenditure of supplemental watering.

Mulching Perennials

Laying down mulch in your perennial garden is not a "must," but few things you can do for your plants will be as good for them. It's not much effort, and the results are well worth it. Among the benefits:

- Your perennial garden looks neater and more attractive.

- Weeds are inhibited, meaning less competition for your plants, less work for you! If a few weeds do show up, they are easier to pull.

- Soil moisture is held in, so you don't have to water as often.

There are several materials that can be used as mulch, such as straw, grass clippings, pine needles, and leaves.

Bark mulch, either shredded or chips, gradually decays, adding nutrients to the soil.

- Soil temperature fluctuations are moderated, which allows especially young plants to get established faster and allows older, established plants to prosper with less stress.

- Soil renewal is encouraged, because mulches break down and enter the soil over time.

- Prevents a crust from forming on the soil surface, allowing better water penetration.

Best Perennial Garden Mulches

Use whatever looks best to you. And use whatever you can get easily and in quantity, for mulching a perennial garden properly can take plenty of material. Here are some favorite choices:

Shredded Bark or Bark Chips

Advantages: Looks neat and attractive, stays in place. Slow to decay. Free, if you chip your own (let it age a bit first—fresh wood chips rob the soil of nitrogen). Easily available at any garden center.

Disadvantages: If from pine trees, it's fairly acidic, which can make the soil pH too low.

Grass Clippings

Advantages: Cheap. Readily available. Easy to apply.

Disadvantages: Decays quickly and must be replenished often. If you have used weedkillers (herbicides) or nitrogen-heavy fertilizers on your lawn, their residues might harm your perennials. If your grass went to seed before you cut it, grass seed can germinate in your garden, which will require weeding later. Less attractive than other mulches, and can become compacted or slimy.

Compost

Advantages: Adds nutrients to the soil while it breaks down. Free and plentiful if you already have a compost bin or pile.

Disadvantages: Fresh compost may burn foliage due to high content of salts or minerals.

Rotting Leaves

Advantages: Smothers weeds very well. Helps hold in soil moisture well.

Disadvantages: Not especially attractive. If there are seeds (from maples, ashes, and acorns from oaks), they can germinate and become a weed problem.

Gravel mulch can keep away slugs and add warmth to the garden bed as it reflects heat.

Hay and Straw

Advantages: Cheap. Easy to apply.

Disadvantages: May contain weed seeds! Can harbor rodents, especially over the winter months. Doesn't look natural.

Mushroom Compost

Advantages: Organically rich—provides very good nutrition for the perennials as it breaks down.

Disadvantages: Hard to find. Must be well composted, not fresh. May be high in salts.

Cocoa Hulls

Advantages: Looks terrific!

Disadvantages: Can blow away in a stiff breeze. The chocolaty smell, usually appealing, can compete unfavorably with fragrant perennial flowers.

Pine Straw

Advantages: Loose and fluffy, allowing good air circulation around plants. Once the bales of pine straw (really pine needles) are placed near the garden, it's lightweight and easy to spread. Looks nice.

Disadvantages: Can acidify soil as it breaks down. Might not look natural if pine trees are not common in your area. Breaks down fairly quickly and needs to be reapplied.

Sawdust

Advantages: Long lasting. Looks neat.

Disadvantages: Needs extra nitrogen to break down properly (which you will have to add). If it's too deep, it makes a dense, impenetrable layer.

Gravel or Stone

Advantages: Nice neat look. Easy to apply. No need to replenish over the course of a season. In cool climates, reflects welcome warmth and light onto the perennials. Controls slugs and snails. Good for plants susceptible to crown rot.

Disadvantages: No benefits to the soil. Doesn't look natural in some regions. Can make the garden too hot.

Plastic (landscape fabric, garden plastic, black plastic)

Advantages: Keeps weeds out. Holds in moisture and warmth. Can be left in place for years.

Disadvantages: Can be difficult to put in place (before or after planting—tricky at either time). Inhibits access of water and fertilizer. Hampers soil renewal projects, normal perennial spread, and garden redesign. Unattractive.

Good Timing

Because one of its most valuable benefits is keeping weeds under control in the garden, the best time to put mulch down is before the weeds even appear. Mulch your perennial garden—or renew last season's mulch—in mid-spring. Another good reason to mulch in early spring is that because your perennials

When spreading soil, mulch, or amendments around plants, be careful not to pile it up on stems or cover crowns.

are just starting to emerge and are not very big yet, it's much easier to work around them, and you can see where they are so you don't mulch over them.

The Right Way

While it makes sense to just toss mulch by the shovelful onto shrub beds or tree areas, you can't do this in your perennial garden. You must deliver it more carefully and have good aim. Take your time. If your garden is full of plants, wade into the garden, use a bucket, and scoop out what you need with a trowel. An inch or two deep is sufficient for most settings and for most perennials.

Ideally, you want to spread the mulch over each plant's root zone, but not right up against

Keep mulch handy!

If you are mulching a large perennial bed, it will save you a lot of back-and-forth if the material can be piled up nearby. If you order a bulky truckload from a local garden center, or just bring home a few bags, do yourself—especially your back and knees—a favor and create a convenient staging area as close as possible to where the mulch will be used.

There are a wide variety of weeding tools available. Choose one that fits your hand and suits your needs.

its crown or stems (which can encourage pests or rot). Some gardeners make sure of this by creating a small, round, shallow trough for each plant. While the plant is still young, this "bowl" will be visible, but before long, foliage and flowers will hide it from view.

Don't forget to cover open areas of your perennial bed with a layer of mulch as well. This way, any perennial weeds should be smothered before they can gain a foothold, and any weed seeds present in the soil will have trouble germinating in the total darkness. Eventually, as the summer goes by, your burgeoning perennials should cover the open areas.

To remove weeds from the perimeter of a bed, cut a deep edge and dig out the weeds to the inside of the line. Make a trench or install edging to keep weeds from growing back into the bed from the lawn.

A scuffle hoe cuts off the tops of weed seedlings, and can also pull up patches of shallow-rooted weeds, roots and all.

Weeding

You've planted a splendid perennial garden, full of promise. You've laid down your spring mulch thoroughly and carefully. In a perfect world, your perennials would thrive and the weeds would stay on their side of the fence.

But the reality of gardening is that weeds are aggressive little plants, and they will do their best to grow in the excellent ground you've prepared and take advantage of any opening. Weeds aren't just unattractive marauders. They also steal resources from the plants you want to grow, and may harbor insect pests or diseases.

And so, the battle begins. Striking early—in springtime—will give you and your garden the edge, and save you time and tedious weeding later in the season. "An ounce of prevention is worth a pound of cure," as the old saying goes.

Maintenance Weeding Basics

Weeds pop up in a garden at any time in the season. They may have lain dormant until a scuff of your boot, a swipe of a garden tool, or a less-than-thorough new planting project occurred—and enough light and air were supplied to allow them to swing into action. Or a bird or other animal may have introduced them to the bed. Or when you added a new plant to the garden weeds or weed seeds were hiding in the potting mix. Weeds are nothing if not resilient, resourceful, and opportunistic.

If you look closely in spring, just as your perennials are reappearing, you may spot weeds close to their crowns. These must go!

And sooner rather than later, because the weed roots can intertwine with the perennial plant until it is impossible to pull up one without pulling up the other. Also, a close-neighbor weed steals water and soil nutrients from the desirable plant and may even cause it to grow in a lopsided or distorted way. Get it out of there while they're both still young! (If by accident, you pull up both, quickly replant the "keeper"—if it's young and the season is spring, it should make a full recovery.)

- *Weed early in the season:* It's easier to pluck weeds out when they are smaller. Also, late spring and early summer soil tends to be moister, and weed roots are easier to extract from damp ground.

- *Pull up weeds anytime you see them:* Don't toss them aside randomly. Make a little pile or throw them in a bucket—and get them far away from the garden as soon as you can.

- *When in doubt, hold off:* If you are not sure if an emerging plant is a weed or just a volunteer seedling from a desirable perennial, keep an eye on it. By the time it flowers, you should be able to identify it. But be realistic. If it keeps

GARDEN TIP

Keep other invaders out, too

The springtime trenching technique can be put into practice if any other aggressive or nurtured plant abuts your perennial bed. Classic "encroachers" include pachysandra, vinca, and ice plant.

growing and it still doesn't look like a familiar or desirable plant, don't wait—get rid of it.

■ *Get the roots:* Many weeds are like the Hydra in the Greek legend—cut off the head and a dozen more grow back. So try to be thorough. A good, sharp, piercing weeding tool is a great weapon because it can reach down deeper than your probing fingers.

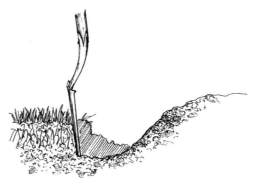

To establish a boundary between the lawn and a garden bed, cut along an edge, dig a trench, remove the sod, shape the trench, and either leave the trench open or install edging as a physical barrier.

- *Don't let them go to seed:* If weeds are already producing flowers, you are nearing the danger zone. Many weeds produce and disperse incredible amounts of seeds (dandelions are a classic example). If you are too busy to pull the weeds out, at least rip off the flowers as you pass through the garden (and throw them away, in case any have viable seeds) and return later to finish the job.

- *Patrol the vicinity:* Your perennial garden, on any given day, may indeed be weed free. But if weeds are growing a few feet away or around a corner, your achievement may be only temporary. Get rid of weeds growing nearby, too.

- *Avoid weed-killer herbicides:* These herbicides may be warranted in weed-infested areas, or be worth using on a lawn you're trying to improve, but they are not recommended for use in or near perennial gardens. The risk of harming or killing the good plants is too great.

An edging of bricks laid flat can provide a mowing strip.

Keep Lawn Grass at Bay

Unlike other plants that are unwelcome in your perennial beds, lawn grass is in your yard on purpose. You cut it, fertilize it, and aerate it. And because you take such good care of it, it tends to grow lushly. If it abuts your garden, lawn grass will do its best to invade. But the good news is it's possible to keep its questing roots away. Here's what to do:

1. Decide where the boundary is, where the lawn should stop and the garden should begin. Using a sharp edging tool (a half-moon edger or a shovel), cut a continuous line to define the edge.

2. Now make a trench. Move out into the lawn a few inches and cut a line parallel to the border you just established. Depending on the type of lawn grass you grow and the tool you are using, this trench may be up to three or more inches deep.

3. Extract the sod within the trench.

4. Shape the trench. The lawn side should go straight down, so the grass roots will be persuaded to follow that course rather than to try to cross the trench. The garden side, on the other hand, should be sloping.

5. Leave the trench open or fill it, but not with soil or any possible growing medium. Leaving it open works because roots simply can't grow across open air. Some gardeners like to pour in pebbles or gravel, lay bricks, or insert plastic or aluminum edging. Examine and renew the trench every spring.

You can deadhead by pinching off bloom stalks between your thumb and forefinger, or by using clippers.

Grooming

One of the great joys of perennial gardening is caring for the plants as they grow, and helping them to look their best. After the physical effort of digging and planting, this sort of work doesn't seem like work at all— indeed, it's more like pleasurable fussing and primping. It's an excuse to enjoy and admire your plants at close range, and to fine-tune the display.

Deadheading

This is just a fancy gardening term for removing faded, spent flowers. Sometimes you can just pinch them off, while others are better snipped or clipped off. You should deadhead your perennials every time you pass by—get in the habit. That way, it will never become a chore and your garden will always look great.

Deadheading doesn't just keep your plants looking neat, or return the viewer's focus to the developing or freshly blooming flowers. It also keeps your perennials blooming longer! It is a plant's natural life cycle to go from bud to bloom to seed. If you interfere before the flower fades and seeds start to develop and ripen, you arrest this natural process. Seed production is very exhausting for a plant and uses a lot of its resources. When you deadhead, the plant continues to flower in an effort to produce seeds.

Some perennials, like chrysanthemums, benefit from disbudding. In this case, you may remove the central flower bud (usually the largest and the first to open if you leave it on the plant), which will encourage the remaining flowers to be larger.

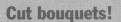

Cut bouquets!

Growing flowering perennials gives you the thrill of harvesting your own homegrown bouquets. However, you may hesitate even as you head out to the garden, snips in hand, with the intention of filling a vase. You may fear that the garden will lose color. Not to worry. Cutting blooming flowers for arrangements is essentially a form of deadheading. Many perennials will respond to the absence of flowers by generating more.

Deadheading encourages a perennial to continue producing blooms by not allowing flowers to go to seed.

Staking helps tall plants stand upright. Use a sturdy stake, and soft twine so the stem is not damaged.

Staking

Some perennials can't really stand up on their own. Their flowers may be heavy, or their stems not strong enough to support the show. Overly rich garden soil and not enough sunlight can also cause plants to be floppy. Whatever the reason, you may be tempted to offer a little support.

If you do feel support is needed, consider your options and pick the most appropriate or easiest one for the plant in question. And act earlier rather than later. The longer you wait, the larger and floppier a plant grows and the more difficult it becomes to work with. For instance, peonies are best staked when their foliage is just emerging in early spring. That way the stems can grow up and through and around the support. Early-season staking also means you run less risk of harming the root system.

Hardy chrysanthemums benefit from pinching during the summer to make them bushier and produce more blooms, and from disbudding later in the season to produce more large flowers. Disbudding means removing the largest, central flower bud.

SHOULD YOU STAKE?

Lending support to a plant that seems to need it is a matter of choice. If you really don't want to spend the time and effort, perhaps you should forgo growing that particular plant.

- **Advantages:** Stakes hold up floppy plants and allow a better display of their flowers, which would otherwise be hidden or facing inward or downward.

- **Disadvantages:** Support devices are often visible, even as the plant grows, and some gardeners feel they look intrusive and unattractive in the garden.

Wooden, Bamboo, and Plastic Stakes

Plunge any one of these into the soil adjacent to a perennial you know will grow tall and wispy—a delphinium, for instance. It's best to do this early in the season when the roots are just emerging from dormancy; the plant will recover from any damage you might cause. The cheapest and most low-tech option is worth trying, and it can look natural and charming. You can erect a tent or dome shape of twigs over a young perennial. Just be sure to pick sturdy stems and to insert them far enough into the ground so that they do not wobble.

Bear in mind the ultimate size of the plant's base or rosette and don't put the stake too close. Several inches away is fine. Then, as the plant grows, anchor its main stem to the stick at intervals. If you are concerned about harming the stem, use soft rags or yarn tied

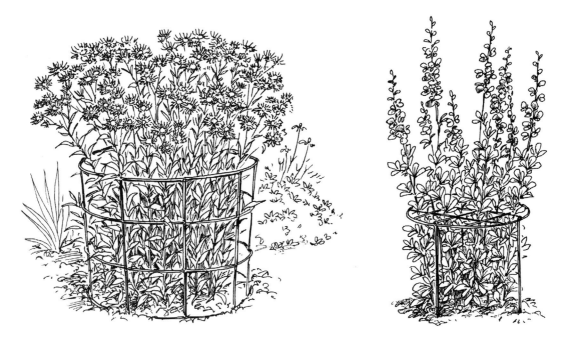

A multi-stemmed plant can be supported with either a cage (left) or a hoop and staking kit (right).

To install a hoop and staking kit, first place the gridded section over the plant just as it is coming out of the ground in spring, then as the plant grows taller lift the grid and attach the stakes.

first to the stake, and then looped gently around the stem. This allows for movement in a breeze as well.

The thickness of the stake needed can be a matter of trial and error. A stout one may seem excessive while the plant is young, but could end up leaning or even toppling under the weight by late summer. For extra stability plunge a stake into the ground as deeply as you can. The type of stake you use, and even the color, is a matter of taste. Be prepared to replace wooden ones every year; they tend to weather a lot and rot, at least the portion that is underground. Bamboo stakes also decay over time.

Cages

Wire cylinders are made expressly for perennial plant support and are available every spring from garden centers, as well as mail-order catalogs. They share the same basic goal: to hold up most of the plant. As it grows, the foliage will fill and even poke out of the sides (eventually hiding it from view). At mature size, the plant will spill out over the top (also hiding the top edges from view). With its lower and main bulk so thoroughly supported, the plant will be able to show off its foliage and flowers without any flopping.

Hoops and Staking Kits

There are also hoops of various sizes, typically with a ring of wire attached to stakes. Staking kits are simple contraptions that look like a lawn furniture table, with three or four legs for support. Atop the legs is a round, mesh "tabletop" that the foliage and stems can grow up through and eventually hide from view. Hollow sockets at the tops of the "legs" allow legs of another kit to be stacked on top, so even taller floppy perennials can be accommodated. Staking kits and hoops are available from garden centers and garden-supply catalogs.

Cutting Back

There are only two times in the gardening year that you should be cutting back your perennials—spring and fall. Both are, strictly speaking, optional, but make a difference in plant health and the garden's attractiveness.

Spring Cleanup

As winter recedes and warmer weather returns, you are eager to get outside. The garden is reawakening. A survey of your perennial beds may show a bit of a mess: dead or winter-damaged foliage, brown crowns, old leaves and other debris lodged in tangled stems, and so forth. A little tidying up is in order.

Perennials (like New England aster, above) can be cut back in the fall after they've finished flowering and are starting to go dormant, or in early spring. Ornamental grasses (top) should be cut back in late winter.

During spring cleanup, be careful not to damage emerging stems and buds, such as those of peonies.

Bring along your clippers, but wield them with care. When you look closely, you are likely to see some signs of life way down inside the rosettes of many perennials. Leave anything green, of course. Clip off anything brown (old stems, twigs). Remove all leaves and old flowers or seedpods, and take the debris to the compost pile. Cut back stems, but not too low—you should be able to see a few live, swelling buds on each stem.

The Fall Routine

Drastic cutting is allowed in fall. It's actually fun and satisfying—you are tangibly putting the garden to bed for the winter.

Cutting down dead and dying flower stalks is the first order of business. You should also shorten or chop back bushy perennials to within a few inches. This creates a "stubble" look, which helps hold your winter mulch in place. But first run a rake through the garden and get out any debris you missed.

You may decide to spare perennials that offer winter interest. Several tall ornamental grasses hold up in cold weather and look beautiful in the snow. *Sedum* x 'Autumn Joy' and purple coneflower seedheads can hold a jaunty cap of snow that is a charming sight on winter days.

Frost on hollyhocks.

Winter Protection

Perennials follow an annual cycle. Most emerge each spring, grow and bloom through the summer, start to slow down in fall, and go dormant over the winter. (There are exceptions, of course, such as spring-blooming wildflowers, which are often dormant in the summer and begin to emerge in late winter.) As they do this year after year, perennials tend to grow deeper roots and form an ever-larger, more robust plant or colony of plants. Remember to give new, young perennials a little extra protection though.

And so, after all this energy has been expended, winter becomes a time of rest. Your perennials need to head into the winter months in good shape. Many times they appreciate a helping hand from you—a little grooming, a little protection—to bring them through the winter and to delight you once more the following year.

Hardiness Zones Demystified

When it comes to perennials, you see cold hardiness zones referred to frequently. The zones, taken from the U.S. Department of Agriculture Plant Hardiness Zone Map, are referred to in plant catalogs, on garden center tags, in reference books, in gardening magazines, at garden club meetings, and in conversations between avid gardeners. It's important to understand that hardiness zones are guidelines, not immutable rules. Winters vary. Conditions at higher elevations are different from those at lower levels. Over time your own garden will show you what you can and cannot grow.

In addition to cold hardiness, heat tolerance is also important, particularly in certain regions. The concept of heat zones is a relatively new idea, developed by the American Horticulture Society, but there is increasing interest in this concept and you will likely see more about it as time goes on. The U.S. has been divided into twelve zones based on the average number of days in the year when the temperature is over 86 degrees F, the temperature at which a plant can suffer damage from heat. For more information on the AHS Plant Heat-Zone Map, visit the website of the American Horticulture Society at www.ahs.org/publications/heatzonemap.htm.

The USDA Map

The U.S. Department of Agriculture has divided North America into ten zones. The coldest zone is Zone 1 and the hottest is Zone 10. Most of us garden in less extreme conditions. Zones 5 to 8 cover most of the United States. As the climate changes, the boundary lines may shift. And even within your own yard, there may be warm areas and cold pockets ("microclimates"). The zones are based on the average lowest wintertime temperatures. A plant described as hardy to a particular zone means the plant can survive winter there.

But you can push the limits of some

If you live in a colder zone and want to grow plants not hardy in your area, you can remove them from the garden and keep them over the winter. For cannas, cut back stalks, dig up the plants, and pot them up for storage in a place where they won't freeze, such as a garage or basement.

To keep dahlias over the winter, dig the bulbs from the garden, clean off the soil, cut away any rotten or damaged parts, and bury them in peat moss. Store where it stays cool but does not freeze.

plants. If you live in Zone 5 you can probably grow a Zone 6 plant (especially if it's planted in a warm part of the yard and mulched for winter). A Zone 8 or 9 plant in Zone 5 will need to be dug up and stored over the winter, or just used as an annual. Microclimates can even be created for plants that might be "iffy" with hardscape features like a protective fence or wall, or heat-absorbing gravel mulch.

Beyond the USDA Zone Map

Like most rule systems, there are exceptions to the USDA Zone Map. Or it might be more accurate to say that the USDA information is not the whole story. A low-growing Zone 6 plant may survive in Zone 4 with adequate protection. A plant rated hardy to Zone 4, however, might perish in Zone 6 because of more active freezing and thawing cycles over the winter months. A perennial that does well in the humid Gulf Coast Zone 8 may fail in the dry heat of a Southern California Zone 8 garden. In the South the minimum winter temperature is not as important as the maximum temperature and the humidity levels.

Basic Winter Preparation Chores

This routine, of course, can be tailored to your own garden and the amount of time and energy you have to devote to it. But here are the basic steps for getting your perennials ready for winter, so that they'll have an excellent chance of returning in good shape next spring.

- *Late summer:* Reduce watering a bit and cease fertilizing, so the plants can slow down. Pinch off fading foliage. Pull weeds before they go to seed.

In very cold regions, some plants warrant special protective measures.

- *Fall:* Cut faded perennials down to a few inches. Clear out all debris and compost it. Give the bed one last good soaking so the roots are well hydrated before the ground freezes. After first frost, lift and store tender bulbs and tubers such as tuberous begonia, gladiola, and dahlia.

- *Late fall:* Lay mulch over the entire perennial garden, tucking it between the plants' crowns. The depth will depend on how severe your winters are and how much snow you receive. Mulching 2 to 4 inches deep is the minimum for protecting most common perennials from winter temperature fluctuations in most parts of the country. A mulch of 6 to 8 inches, or even more, may be warranted in harsh climates. Marginally hardy plants should get special treatment—either dig them up to spend the winter indoors or in a cold frame, or cover them well with extra mulch.

- *Over the winter:* If you are strolling outside and observe that the fall-applied mulch has become patchy or if snow cover is poor, throw on more mulch. Or move snow from parts of the yard where it's too high and toss shovelfuls over your perennial garden. And if you notice that, by unlucky chance, a plant has been disturbed by frost heaving (meaning it has been lifted out of the ground by repeated ice formation in the soil and thawing), firm it back into the ground immediately.

GARDEN TIP

Branches over the bed?

Where available and warranted, evergreen boughs can be laid over a perennial bed after other winter preparation steps have been completed. These catch and hold snow, adding an extra layer of protection. It's worth doing, especially, if your perennial garden is in an exposed location and wind blows the snow into drifts instead of letting it settle into a blanketing layer.

GOOD WINTER MULCHES

You can use whatever is plentiful, cheap, or close at hand for this job. Some of these will settle and break down over the course of the winter months, but that's okay. This process adds texture and organic matter to your perennial bed soil.

Winter mulches perform two important functions for your perennial garden: They help keep an even soil temperature, and they help prevent the plants from being heaved out of the ground during freeze-thaw cycles.

Salt hay and straw are excellent winter mulches. Even if they contain weeds, winter's cold temperatures won't allow these to germinate or grow. Fall leaves, which may be plentiful in your yard or neighborhood, are another option, especially if you can shred them first.

Choose the right size of container for your perennial, or divide it into smaller pots.

Nest a plastic pot inside a clay pot for a perennial needing moist soil.

For winter protection or to control an aggressive plant, sink the perennial, pot and all, in the ground.

Surround potted plants with straw, leaves, or pine needles to protect roots from the cold.

Caring for Perennials in Pots

Most perennials can, at least in theory, thrive in a pot. Ones that form deep taproots may struggle, however, unless you are able to provide enough room (false blue indigo, for instance). Here are some ways to help the plants thrive.

- Provide a big enough pot.
- Make sure there's a drainage hole in the bottom.
- Site the pot before filling it with potting mix, if you can. This helps you try out different locations to find one that best suits the pot and its plant. Also, a filled pot can be heavy, making moving it *after* filling and planting a struggle.
- Use an appropriate pot. If moisture-retention is important to your perennial, use plastic or, if you prefer the look of a clay pot, simply nest a slightly smaller plastic pot inside. (Clay pots wick moisture away from root systems.) Of course, if you are growing something drought-tolerant, go ahead and put it in a clay pot.
- Provide a good growing medium. Use a fertile potting mix, perhaps mixed with a little good soil from the garden.

If you like to garden in containers you can still grow perennials, as long as you follow a few basic maintenance practices.

- Visit often for maintenance. Water often because potted plants tend to dry out quickly. Fertilize for a better show. Groom fading flowers, leaves, and stems.

- Turn the pot occasionally. Even shade-loving perennials lean towards a source of sunlight after a while. If you turn the pot a quarter-turn every few days or so, growth will be more even.

- Provide winter protection. A root system in an aboveground pot is vulnerable to cold. Either plunge the entire thing, pot and plant, into the ground for the winter and cover with a mulch, or hold the perennial in semi-dormancy in a cool (non-freezing) protected location for the winter (water only a little bit and don't fertilize until spring returns).

Pests in the Perennial Garden

Perennials are basically trouble-free. This is even truer when you have chosen locations and soil that are appropriate for them. Problems are possible but not inevitable. Occasionally, however, a plant signals its distress—and you must first identify the source and then decide what to do.

The good news is most plant maladies are caused by poor culture, not by a pest or disease. This can be remedied not by garden chemicals but by changing something about the plant's environment—where the plant is growing, what kind of soil the plant is growing in, or how much or how little water and fertilizer you are providing.

Growing a variety of plants can make for a healthier garden.

Prevention

Gardening will be easier and less time consuming if you avert potential problems. Here are some classic preventative measures that will make a huge difference in keeping your perennial garden healthy and thriving.

- *Grow the right plant in the right place:* Plants are weakened by the stress of trying to adapt to too much sun, too little sun, poor soil, or inadequate space.

- *Be tidy:* Dead or dying leaves and stems or too many weeds add up to a debris-filled garden. Diseases can gain a foothold or pests can move into the shelter you've inadvertently provided, and foray out to attack your plants.

- *Grow a variety of plants:* Bugs have favorite foods and plant diseases have favorite targets. Plant diversity can thwart them or prevent the spread of a problem.

- *Don't crowd your plants:* Plants that are growing too close together get less air circulation, or you are less likely to notice when they are drying out or being attacked by a fungus or pest.

Diagnosis: Cultural Problems

When a perennial appears to be in distress, your very first question should be: What is causing its failing health? It's well worth checking, or double-checking, reference books and catalogs to find out if you are growing it in the right place. Or perhaps some cultural condition is not right and can be corrected. If one of the following problems is troubling a perennial in your garden, it could be quite

Goatsbeard, *Aruncus dioicus*
Many plant problems are actually related to culture, rather than pests. Wise plant choices, proper siting, and good maintenance practices can avert many health issues.

easy to fix or you might need to move the plant to a more suitable location.

- *Too much water:* Leaf stems (petioles) turn downward and leaf edges curl, indicating that the soil is so saturated that oxygen is not reaching the roots. The roots are probably damaged.

- *Not enough water:* The plants wilt. Leaves develop browned margins.

- *Too much fertilizer:* Lots of lush, floppy growth and few or no flowers.

- *Not enough fertilizer or infertile soil:* Stunted, weak growth.

- *Too much sun:* Bleached-out or yellowed leaves. Wilting.

- *Not enough sun:* Spindly, leggy growth as plants lean toward a source of light.

- *Cold damage:* Plant is heaved out of the ground, roots and all. In the spring growth is slower than normal and foliage is thin and yellowing. Plant dies back from its tips.

- *Heat damage:* Wilting. Death from the stem up.

- *Poor soil:* Stunted growth, poor flowering, smaller or fewer leaves.

- *Salt damage:* "Burned" leaf margins and tips. Small or malformed leaves. Salt deposits on leaf surfaces. Growth slows and halts.

- *Overly rich soil:* Excessive, floppy leaf and stem growth.

Diagnosis: Pests

Pests in the perennial garden are possible but not certain, so don't be paranoid or discouraged. Suspect a pest if you actually see one. If you've seen rabbits in the yard or you garden in deer country and your perennials are being nibbled, you can safely assume they are the culprits. Or you may find weevils lurking at ground level or aphids crowding the leaves of your perennials.

Even as you seek information, consider your tolerance level. Is the damage so debilitating or life-threatening that you are prepared to declare war on the pests and perhaps even spray garden chemicals or set out poisons? Cosmetic damage where only a few leaves, buds, or flowers are marred may not be so bad. Your perennials may be able to survive it and you, too, may be able to live with it.

Getting Expert Help

If you are not sure what is troubling your perennials, or if you spot a bug that you suspect may be a nibbling pest, but you are not sure, investigate. There are numerous reference books on the topic. But an experienced gardener, a local garden center staffer or landscaper, or a Cooperative Extension Service biologist can give you a faster and perhaps more accurate identification. Ideally you should provide that expert with two pieces of evidence: a plant or plant portion that has experienced the damage and one or more actual bugs. If that's not practical, try taking a few good photos. The person who helps you identify the culprit should also be able to advise you on treatment options.

GARDEN TIP

Insects that change

Identifying insects can sometimes be complicated by the fact that many look different at different stages in their life cycles. You may dismiss tiny, harmless-looking pupae that you notice while out digging in the soil, but live to regret your indifference or ignorance when they emerge later as mature insects to attack your prized perennials. Or an insect may look menacing and turn out to be a friend, not a foe. For example, an immature ladybug is about half the size of the adult and looks completely different.

Common Perennial Insect Pests

The following are by no means all the pests that can mar or kill your plants, but they are the culprits most often seen. Realize that the majority of insect pests do most of their damage when they are still young and hungry and growing rapidly. At this stage you may be able to pick and kill them or blast them away with the hose. Full-grown adult pests, however, may move or fly faster or have a waxy shell that resists insecticidal sprays. So it is often wise to take a little time to get to know your pest and its life cycle before deciding how and when to act. Please note: Low-toxicity, least harmful tactics are listed first. Try these before escalating to more toxic alternatives.

Aphids

Description: Tiny, soft-bodied, green, orange, yellow, red, or black.

Damage: Suck plant juices, especially on young tip growth.

What you can do: Spray them off with the hose repeatedly over several days until they are eradicated. Or treat entire plant (including top and bottom of leaves and stems) with insecticidal soap or an insecticide.

Larvae or Grubs

Description: Small, curled, white or gray wormlike larval stage of several types of insects.

Damage: From early fall to spring (depending on how cold your winters are) they dine on plant foliage and roots. They tend to favor older, lower leaves. Notched leaf margins are a

Japanese beetles are a common garden insect pest in some regions, favoring plants in the rose and mallow families. They can also be damaging in their larval or grub stage, feeding on plant roots.

telltale sign that they are at work in your garden.

What you can do: Place small wads of newspaper at the base of the affected plants in the morning and gather these up each evening; destroy both the paper and the snoozing bugs it has trapped. Uproot the affected plant and pick them out of the roots and destroy them. If the soil seems infested, move that plant to a far corner of your garden in the hopes of avoiding their recurrence. Treat the soil with beneficial nematodes, available from local garden centers or by mail; introduce them in early fall, when the eggs are hatching. Treat the soil at the base of the affected plants, at two-week intervals, all summer, with an insecticide labeled especially for combating the specific pests.

Four-lined Plant Bugs

Description: A small reddish beetle when young, it matures to exhibit four parallel lines on its one-quarter-inch body.

Bees are beneficial insects in a garden, pollinating flowers so they will form seed.

Damage: Sucks plant juices, especially on the tops of leaves, particularly on younger leaves. They hide underneath. Leaves may become pockmarked.

What you can do: If their numbers are small and they aren't quite at the flying stage, you can pluck them off and squish them. Otherwise, you can resort to spraying with homemade or store-bought insecticidal soap.

Consider the Risks

Use insecticide sprays and poison baits only as a last resort. Some are very general and may kill many more creatures than the intended targets. You don't want to kill beneficials while aiming for pests and inadvertently upset the balance of nature in the process. You can cause *more* pests to appear the following year, if you've killed off their natural predators!

If you are convinced you need to use such a remedy, read the label very carefully, not only to make sure you are spraying for the right pest, but also for application and dilution instructions. The label will also inform you of what other creatures may be

THE GOOD GUYS: BENEFICIAL INSECTS

Another strong argument for accurate insect identification is that while you may have spotted an insect or insect colony among your perennials, it might be one that either does no harm or eats harmful bugs, including some of those described above. Other insects are very likely pollinators. These "good guys" are the insects you want to leave alone, at every stage of their development, to prosper and do their work in your garden.

- **Bees:** Pollinators.
- **Butterflies and moths:** Pollinators.
- **Ladybugs:** Eat soft-bodied pest insects, including aphids, mealybugs, scale.
- **Lacewings:** Eat soft-bodied pest insects, especially aphids.
- **Spiders:** Catch and eat all sorts of insects in their webs.
- **Ground beetles:** Eat other insects and sometimes prey on snails.
- **Praying mantis:** Eat a variety of insects.
- **Syrphid flies:** Their larvae eat aphids (and the larvae of ants, termites, and bees).

The praying mantis is an insectivore, eating other insects in the garden, both good and bad. Their egg cases look like tan-colored cotton candy wrapped around plant stems. Learn to recognize the different stages of beneficial insects so you can encourage them in your garden.

affected; some chemicals are toxic to fish or bumblebees, and some could harm children or pets. Some may harm your skin or eyes, so you must wear protective gear when spraying. The magnitude of the threat the target pest poses to your perennials needs to be carefully weighed against these important risks.

Other Pests and What to Do

A menagerie of other pests can trouble your perennial garden and cause minor or major damage; the following are the most common. Again, if you know exactly what the culprit is you can take steps to fight back and protect your plants. Please note: Low-impact, least harmful tactics are listed first. Try these before escalating to more toxic alternatives.

Of significant concern in recent years is the proliferation of deer. Because native habitat is shrinking and predators are fewer,

deer have not only multiplied in many areas but are brazenly wandering into yards and gardens in search of food. However, as this problem has increased, so has research into its solution, both by scientists and homeowners.

Slugs and Snails

Description: An inch or longer, depending on the species, these soft-bodied pests are slimy and neutral in color. The head has antennae and their tail ends are tapered. Snails have protective shells that they can retreat into.

Slug damage on hosta leaves.

Ladybugs and ladybug larvae can consume scores of aphids in a season.

Damage: They are especially active in spring (when conditions are moist and foliage is young and succulent), but can eat your plants year-round in mild climates. They do most of their destructive leaf-eating at night.

What you can do: Try to make your garden a drier place—make sure air circulates and soil drains well (and that water from heavy rains can drain off). If possible, encourage their predators, which include birds, turtles, and snakes. Handpick and destroy them (you'll collect the most if you go out at night with a flashlight when they are active). In the daytime find them under stones and boards. Making the soil surface damaging to their tender skin has worked for some gardeners; try fresh wood chips, gravel mulch, or diatomaceous earth. Copper strips placed strategically around the garden or around favorite plants has also discouraged them; apparently, their slime interacts with the copper and they get a minor electric shock. The time-honored method of setting out pie pans of beer each night works fairly well, too,

but emptying the tins of drowned slugs in the morning is unappetizing work! A safe, natural product called Sluggo is also a remedy. It's an iron phosphate material that, once eaten, causes the slugs and snails to stop eating. As a last resort, try poison baits, which are sold at garden centers, usually in pellet form.

Rabbits

Description: Wild rabbits are brown or gray and are generally smaller and leaner than the pet-store kinds.

Damage: They adore tender young seedlings. Although they favor the vegetable garden, rabbits are happy to raid a perennial bed as well and can nibble a plant right down to ground level if they find it tasty or they are hungry enough.

What you can do: You can sprinkle various bad-tasting or bad-smelling substances around the vulnerable plants, including blood meal, bone meal, wood ashes, hot pepper flakes, or rock phosphate. You may have to reapply these after a rain. You can cage vulnerable plants in "rabbit fencing" (lightweight wire mesh of 1 inch openings or smaller). If the problem is severe, you may have to enclose the entire perennial bed in wire mesh; sink the lower edge down about a foot into the ground all around, if possible, so the rabbits can't crawl under it. As a last resort try a catch-and-release trap.

Moles and Gophers

Description: Moles are fairly small and gray; gophers are larger and brown.

Damage: They tunnel under your garden and

Mole

lawn, creating holes and dirt piles and damaging plants from below. Moles don't eat plants they eat destructive grubs, but they also like to eat beneficial earthworms. Gophers eat plant roots and a sign of a gopher-damaged plant is one that looked fine the day before but is now completely wilted.

What you can do: Flood their tunnels with the hose. Surround your perennial bed with wire mesh sunk as deep as two feet into the ground. Trap them. Poison them (with bait sold for this purpose or naturally poisonous seeds such as castor beans).

Mice, Shrews, Chipmunks, and Voles

Description: The types most often seen in garden settings are small, brown rodents with long, hairless tails; shrews have distinctive pointy noses and voles have shorter tails than mice.

Damage: Plants are not their only source of food, though they will nibble on roots, young leaves, and seeds. They do like to eat the succulent bulbs of favorite spring bloomers, especially tulips (they shun daffodils, which are toxic to them).

What you can do: Keep sheltering mulch to a minimum. Erect wire cages around plants you

Deer are less inclined to eat certain plants, including yarrow and wormwood.

think they are damaging (plant your tulip bulbs in underground wire cages). Flood their tunnels, assuming you can find their entrances. Set baited traps in early spring when they are very hungry and their numbers are still low. Get a cat!

Deer

Description: Any species of deer found in North America can become a garden pest. Most often you will see mothers (does) and their babies (fawns), in pairs or groups.

Damage: Deer raid gardens for food year-

To ward off deer, a deer fence is the most reliable approach. Other tactics include burlap screens around susceptible plants during peak times and repellents such as predator urine suspended nearby. Plants can also be sprayed with a chemical deterrent or hot-pepper solution that makes the plants taste bad.

DEER-RESISTANT PERENNIALS

One of the simplest ways to combat nibbling deer is to grow plants they don't like. A lot of grassroots and professional research has been done on this subject, and you can experiment and find what succeeds for you. Below is but a sampling of recommended plants.

Ask for these and others at your local garden center. If you shop for your garden by mail, either from the Internet or from a catalog, you will notice garden suppliers increasingly are flagging deer-resistant perennials for you. Jackson & Perkins has pioneered an entire listing headed "Deeresistible™" perennials, which takes out the guesswork—and also reminds you that these plants, although shunned by deer, still look beautiful in your garden! Please note: As a general rule, deer most often avoid plants with a strong scent or a bad taste.

- Anemone
- Astilbe
- Bee balm
- Blanket flower
- Bleeding heart
- Boltonia
- Candytuft
- Catmint
- Cinquefoil
- Columbine
- Evening primrose
- False indigo
- Forget-me-not
- Foxglove
- Globe thistle
- Hellebore
- Joe-Pye weed
- Lavender
- Lily-of-the-valley
- Lungwort
- Lupine
- Monkshood
- Poppy
- Purple coneflower
- Russian sage
- Salvia
- Sea holly
- Seaside daisy
- Turtlehead
- Verbena
- Veronica
- Wormwood
- Yarrow

round, but especially in summer when native vegetation is dry and the garden is lush and edible. They will also visit the garden in winter and early spring when woodland or meadow food is in short supply.

What you can do: The only sure way to keep deer out is a special "deer barrier fence," which is too high to jump over, has a skirt deer can't crawl under, and may include electrical wires. There are different designs and you can review your options with a good local landscaper, or get plans from a nearby Cooperative Extension Service office. If that's not affordable or practical, there are other tactics, including everything from hot-pepper spray for plants to suspending repellents from shrubs and trees around your yard, such as bags of human hair (from the barber shop), predator urine, or bars of Irish Spring soap. If deer are a chronic problem for you, you should certainly landscape defensively by using plants deer don't like to eat. Although a hungry deer will eat almost any plant in your yard, they do tend to shun certain ones.

Diagnosis: Plant Disease

As noted previously, a happy perennial is a healthy perennial. If you have chosen wisely and planted in an appropriate setting, it's unlikely your plants will get sick. However, it can happen—and if it does, you can successfully combat disease.

Disease Prevention

Avoid disfiguring or fatal plant diseases before they have a chance to move into your perennial garden. Here are some tried-and-true prevention tactics.

One way to prevent or lessen disease problems in the garden is to plant resistant varieties. *Phlox paniculata* 'David' is less prone to powdery mildew, a common problem on summer phlox.

- *Match plants to their site:* Find out if they prefer it wet or dry, sunny or partly shady, and accommodate these requirements from the very start.

- *Choose resistant varieties:* If you love phlox and bee balm but fear powdery mildew, be wise and practical: Seek out the newer resistant varieties.

- *Be tidy in the garden:* Diseases fester and breed in plant debris. Take it out or rake it out, but don't leave spent foliage or dead plants lying around in the garden.

Thinning out stems or leaves improves air circulation around plants, diminishing disease problems.

- *Groom your plants and dispose of affected plant parts:* Sometimes a few leaves will show signs of disease (mildew, browning, yellowing). Remove them from the plant and dispose of them.

- *Water carefully:* Fungus and rot can get started if your usual watering method inadvertently soaks foliage or saturates unopened buds. And diseases can travel from one plant to another in water droplets. So make sure the water is delivered as close to the surface of the soil as possible, where it can soak in promptly. Water in the morning so the hotter sun later in the day can evaporate lingering water drops.

- *Improve air circulation:* Still air traps and nurtures diseases. Create more space and let air in and around your plants by not planting them too close together, or by thinning their foliage or stems from time to time.

Common Diseases of Perennials

Most perennial plant diseases have a fungal origin, though some are bacterial. These thrive in damp conditions where air circulation is poor. Here are the ones you would be most likely to encounter. Please note that low-impact, least harmful tactics are listed first; try these initially. Generally speaking, unless a disease is very obvious or quite advanced, a quick, responsive cleanup may be all that's needed.

Crown Rot

Description: This disease can come on suddenly. Shoots turn yellow and dry up. Close inspection of the plant's crown and surrounding soil reveals a webbing of white fungal strands.

Damage: This rot appears when weather gets hot and very humid. It can kill a plant and

GARDEN TIP

Bag it!

When you survey your perennial beds looking to see that everything is healthy and thriving, bring along a plastic bag and a pair of clippers. Put diseased or questionable leaves, branches, buds, or flowers into the bag as you go. This way you won't accidentally drop anything back into the garden and you'll confine the disease. When you're done, don't forget to dispose of the contents properly. (Tossing diseased plant parts on a compost pile is unwise unless the pile gets hot enough to kill fungus spores or bacteria.)

spread to others. It can also contaminate your garden soil.

What you can do: Promptly get rid of all affected plants, roots and all. Treat the soil with a fungicide labeled for this disease. If you then replant in the same area and the problem recurs, you may have to get rid of the soil and haul in new, healthy dirt.

Gray Mold, Botrytis Blight

Description: Plants develop distorted flowers and leaves, become blackened, and a grayish-brown mold appears. Buds fail to open.

Damage: This disease mars plant appearance and thwarts bud development. It disables the plant and, left unchecked, eventually kills it.

What you can do: Remove and destroy affected parts immediately, and clean up around the base of the plant. Improve air circulation around the plant and, if possible, soil drainage. Use a fungicide labeled for the specific plant and this disease, and follow application instructions to the letter (usually spraying is done in early spring).

Leaf Spot Fungus

Description: Foliage slowly develops round, yellow or yellowish-green spots. These may darken over time.

Damage: It looks unhealthy, and can spread to other leaves and nearby plants.

What you can do: Immediately remove and destroy affected leaves. If you've caught the problem early enough, that may be all you need to do to control or eradicate the problem. Also, keep plant foliage dry when you are watering.

Powdery mildew on bee balm.

Powdery Mildew

Description: Grayish-white leaf spots and patches, which can eventually coat an entire leaf.

Damage: It may look bad, but is rarely fatal. It's a sure sign of damp, humid weather.

What you can do: Pick off and get rid of affected leaves. Keep the rest from getting wet when you water the plant, and water in the morning. Do whatever you can to improve air circulation around the plant. You can spray with a sulfur- or copper-based fungicide.

Rot

Description: Plant parts or entire plants turn brown and rotten. There may also be a foul smell and oozing sap.

Some plant problems can be unattractive, but might not kill the plant or prevent it from flowering. Only you can decide what is acceptable and what is obtrusive enough to warrant treatment.

Rot on a dahlia rootstock.

Do a good fall cleanup, so the spores can't overwinter in plant debris. You can spray with a fungicide labeled for rust on perennials.

Wilt

Description: Affected plants falter and wilt.

Damage: This is actually a broad catchall term for a variety of diseases, both fungal and bacterial, that cause perennials to wilt. Unchecked, the plants will die. Gopher damage to roots can also cause wilting.

What you can do: Act quickly at the first sign of a problem, removing entire affected plants. Don't respond by watering more! Instead try to increase air circulation and improve drainage.

Damage: Bacteria have gained a foothold in the plant starting from the roots or rootstock. Unchecked, it is fatal.

What you can do: Remove and discard all rotten plant parts as soon as you observe them. For irises, you may have to dig up or further expose the tubers to cut out the rotten parts. It's also a good idea to expose the healthy part to bright, hot sun for a few days before replanting.

Rust

Description: Small rust-colored or brown spots or spores appear on leaves and sometimes stems; tiny, jellylike "horns" (rust-colored or yellowish) may also appear.

Damage: A bad case completely disfigures a plant's foliage but is unlikely to kill it.

What you can do: Pick off and destroy affected leaves. Check carefully and remove even those that are barely affected, as it will surely spread.

Prevent contagion

If you are patrolling the garden and clipping out plants and plant parts that may have fungal disease, don't become part of the problem and spread it. Swab the cutting edge of your tools with rubbing alcohol from time to time. Wear gloves or wash your hands before and after dealing with a diseased plant.

If you have qualms about using a chemical spray to treat a disease or pest, consider safer remedies, such as this combination for use against powdery mildew.

Spraying Advice

Spraying diseased perennial plants is usually drastic action, to be undertaken only if the problem has escalated and spread and you cannot seem to control it by other methods. You should first clean up the garden—there is no point in spraying leaves or buds that are already on their way out. In some cases you need to drench the soil where the disease has originated and is proliferating, not spray the plants themselves.

Make sure you have identified the disease correctly. As with plant pests, you can consult good reference books or show affected plant samples (or a good photograph) to an expert, if you are uncertain about the diagnosis.

A well-stocked local garden center will have a range of fungicides and sprays. Examine the labels very carefully and choose appropriately. When you apply any garden chemical, do so on a windless day and be sure to wear protective clothing, gloves, and eye gear. Follow the label directions regarding timing of application; some chemicals are only effective in early spring or late fall. And follow the label directions regarding dosage and dilution to the letter—more is not better. If it rains shortly afterwards, however, you may have to reapply.

Finally, if spraying a plant, be thorough. Wet even the undersides of the leaves and pay careful attention to the lower leaves, which are the most vulnerable (because they are closer to the soil and farther from beneficial light and air).

DESIGNING WITH PERENNIALS

IN THIS CHAPTER:
- Home landscape help
- Garden styles and theme gardens
- Mixing perennials
- A few simple design principles
- Creating visual interest
- Perennials with other plants

Home Landscape Help

So diverse and versatile are perennials, that when a gardener has a special goal or landscaping need, chances are good that a plant (or plants) can come to the rescue. Again, the solutions provided are bound to be long-lasting, because perennials stay and prosper, looking better and more impressive with each passing year.

The joy of growing perennials is doubled when you can arrange the plants in pleasing ways, so that they look great and thrive. First, it's time to do some planning—a process that is fun, intriguing, and ultimately very satisfying.

Realize also that creating your garden is an ongoing project, and you can revise your plans as the years go by. In time you may decide to increase or add garden areas as you find the time, energy, and inspiration.

To get started you need to do some clear-eyed assessing:
- What kind of garden will look nice with your house?
- Who will use or visit your garden, and how will it be viewed?
- How much time do you have to devote to garden maintenance?
- What assets do you want to enhance and what liabilities do you want to minimize?

Let's tackle these issues one at a time. First realize that there are no right or wrong answers. Think things over. The choices are yours.

There are nearly infinite ways of arranging and combining perennials to create a garden that suits your house, your needs, and your taste.

111

Your garden should complement the style and size of your house.

Luckily, unlike some home-improvement projects, gardening is quite flexible and forgiving. If you put in something then change your mind later or get fresh ideas, the landscaping *can* be changed. This is a living canvas for the artist in you.

Suiting Your House

Ideally, you want a garden that flatters your house: one that looks like it belongs, that seems "right." This important issue leads to several questions:

What style is your house? If your house is formal, a formal garden is appropriate. If you have a ranch house or a bungalow, a looser, more casual garden seems better. If you have a cottage, an English-style garden would work, whether traditionally formal or overflowing with plants. If you have a big old Victorian, a larger, more sprawling garden, perhaps with some larger or taller plants, will look good. If

you live on a street where all the houses have similar architecture, consider if you want your garden to stand out or fit in.

What color or material is your house? Harmonizing garden flowers and foliage with the color of your house and its trim is fun (if you want to paint it new colors or change the color of the siding, the entire project becomes more ambitious, but also more exciting). Plain, unpainted wood can be a handsome backdrop for a great range of perennials. Brick is less flexible—in particular, red and other hot colors don't seem to stand out well against a brick background, although contrasting colors will. As for stone or stucco, certain bright colors seem to warm up the look of these houses.

What about scale? If your house is large or rambling, little "vignette" gardens or rock gardens may seem lost or too small. If your house has two or more stories, a garden needs some mass and height to make an impression. If your house is small, perhaps you don't want to hide it from view with too much garden. If your house is large and the yard is small, consider ways for the plants to embrace and flatter it (keeping the design full but simple, with repeating plants, seems to work). On the other hand, if your house is small and your yard is large, you may want to add garden areas that gradually connect the house to its surroundings.

How much lawn do you want? Lawns require a lot of work to look good, including frequent mowing and watering, plus seasonal fertilizing. But your family may want a lawn, or your neighborhood may require it. Even so, you may be ready to replace some or all of your lawn area with perennial gardens. To spare your back and to see how smaller-lawn landscaping works for you, it's wise not to remove all of the lawn at once. Instead, steal a little more of the lawn for perennial gardening each year.

What are the hardscape features? Most yards come with some built-in structure or structures that you must work your perennial gardens around. It may be a building such as a garage, carport, or shed. (Don't forget to accommodate the garbage can area and compost pile.) Then there are fences and walls, gates and arches, hedges or boundary plantings that may be too big to chop down or remove, windbreaks, the occasional large tree, or a grove or orchard area. Sometimes perennials can hide or disguise these elements. Sometimes they can share the stage.

Visitors to Your Garden

It's important to consider the regular visitors or users of your garden when you are still in the planning stages.

- *Children:* They run or ride their bikes around the yard. Their balls and Frisbees inevitably land among the flowers. They need their own space, too—a play structure, a sandbox, a spot for a tetherball or basketball hoop, a place to park bicycles. Watch where children go and allow them practical boundaries. Otherwise you'll be forever lamenting damaged plants and scolding the kids for causing the damage.

- *Adults:* Will you be entertaining in your yard? Perennial gardens can impress and delight visitors; strategically placed and

designed perennial gardens can also bring a sense of enclosure or privacy or enhance a great view. Decide where you want to put a patio, deck, or terrace and how big it will be. Plan where outdoor furniture will go, including tables and chairs, garden benches, and even a hammock. Think about where the grill will go, and perhaps a chimnea. Work your perennial garden plans around these elements, so that your plants are safely out of the way of traffic but can still be admired.

- *Pets:* Cats are pretty accommodating and really only need to be discouraged from treating fresh new garden soil like a

Consider how much lawn you want or need. While a lawn can be high maintenance, it can also frame your garden, and provide a place for recreation. Instead of removing a lawn area all at once, turn portions of it into garden over time until you've achieved the right balance.

A garden can be a wonderful habitat for wildlife. To encourage birds to visit your garden, provide food (including plants that make berries and seed loved by various bird species), water, and opportunities for shelter, such as birdhouses.

wonderful new litter box. Dogs either need a run area or have to be walked elsewhere so they won't damage your plantings.

- *Wildlife:* If you garden in deer country and want to succeed with perennials, you have options. Ultimately your best defense is a deer fence. For smaller creatures, from rabbits to groundhogs, fencing or other deterrents may be necessary. Birds and butterflies may be very welcome and you can encourage them by growing certain perennials.

How Much Time Do You Have?

This is a tough question! We'd all like to believe that we have ample time and energy to realize the garden of our dreams. The key here may not be to scale back your ideas, but to shift your attitude. Caring for a perennial garden shouldn't be a chore. It should be an adventure. Ideally, the journey becomes as fulfilling as the destination.

That said, be realistic about the effort and time involved:

- Installing and planting the garden requires a significant initial time investment.

- The work is cyclical, which keeps it interesting and dynamic. Spring is generally a time of planting, feeding, and mulching; summer involves mostly grooming and weeding; fall is cleanup time and time to prepare the perennials for winter.

- You need to visit your plants often so you'll notice what they need. (As side

benefits, you'll also get to know them better and enjoy them more.) Decide whether you can get out there daily or just on weekends.

Experienced perennial gardeners have devised many timesaving tricks. These help you have more garden beauty for less effort.

- *Use smart siting*: If you position plants where they prefer to grow, they will require less effort to maintain and to look good. They'll do the work for you!

- *Grow low-maintenance plants*: Easier (less fussy, healthier) perennials will require less care.

- *Mulch*: This nourishes the soil, keeps weeds down, and holds in soil moisture.

- *Spend less time watering*: You might install a drip system (better to do this at the outset than when the garden is already in place). Or simply put a soaker hose or sprinkler on a timer.

Ultimately, it's tricky to plan or schedule exactly how much time you will devote. You need to jump in and learn about yourself as a gardener, as well as about the plants you've chosen. Realize also that a perennial garden is less and less work as the years go by. The plants become established and prosper with less coddling from you. Also, you become more experienced and efficient at meeting their needs and helping them look their best.

How Do You View the Garden?

As a practical consideration, this question is more important than most of us realize. It has to do with how we live with our garden. Once you identify your viewing relationship, you can better plan to maximize your visual enjoyment.

Structural "tricks" can help you. Lower-growing, sprawling plants increase the sense of a horizontal plane, while taller and fuller plants create boundaries and backdrops. Stepping up gradually from one to the other fills a garden. Techniques using color make the most of various viewing opportunities. Remember that darker colors recede and brighter ones advance.

A variety of garden elements can also help you make the impression you want. A fence stops the eye and establishes a backdrop, as does a dark hedge or windbreak planting of columnar trees. A trellis or pergola creates vertical interest or defines a "garden room." A fountain, pool, or piece of statuary can also create a focal point around which you build a garden picture.

Of course, you may view your garden in more than one of the following ways. It helps to be cognizant of what your viewing angles will be *before* you plant, so you can plan ahead and really enjoy your garden.

From the House

Depending on whether it's a bedroom or kitchen window, a living room bay window, or a sliding glass door opening onto the back patio, views from the house can be small and tight or more expansive. But a frame always circumscribes them. Therefore it makes sense to create a pleasant scene within the frame. It may only be part of the entire perennial garden, but make whatever you most often see from indoors a priority. It may be a view

A fence or fence section can be a backdrop for a garden bed, or screen a view, both from the house and from the road, providing an attractive focal point and establishing a boundary for the garden.

of your favorite plants or favorite colors, or plants that present an ever-changing scene from one season to the next, so the view is not static or predictable.

From the Driveway or Road

Whether it is you and your family viewing the garden or people walking or driving by, the way your garden looks from the driveway or road is important and should be a design

A garden can create a transition from the house into the larger landscape, and provide privacy for a deck or porch.

priority. You may want to hide your home and the rest of your yard from view, for privacy's sake or to diminish road noise. Or you may want to draw in visitors or passersby with an inviting design.

From a Porch or Deck

One of the great joys of outdoor living is admiring a nice garden. Plants can embrace or enclose a porch or deck. They can create a sense of transition from house to a "hardscape," such as a patio or gazebo, to living plants. Space and view permitting, a perennial garden can also entice people to enjoy or enter a greater expanse.

What Are Your Assets and Liabilities?

Any landscape will have good and bad aspects. Site assets include a lovely view, large existing trees, satisfactory landscaping or permanent hardscape features already in place, or a water feature. Site liabilities include an unattractive view, poor drainage, or an overgrown tangle of weedy shrubs and vines. The goal is to plan garden areas that make the most of the good things and minimize the impact of the bad things.

Take stock of what is and what is not under your control or changeable (you can alter things on your own property but not on your neighbor's side of the fence), and what you can afford to do. You can plan a garden to frame a nice view of the mountains or a nearby pond, but you would undoubtedly want to block a view of a dumpster or a highway. Look at the big picture and decide what will stay and what needs to change before making any detailed landscape plans.

Garden styles can be formal or informal. Formal gardens typically are symmetrical, have a limited number of types of plants (though there can be variety within a type, such as in this multi-colored collection of bearded irises), have firm edges and boundaries, and use either straight lines or simple curves.

Garden Styles

Various garden styles have gone in and out of popularity, and show up in different locations and with different sorts of homes. You may already have a sense of what you like. If you're not sure or you're seeking inspiration, look at several other gardens. Look around your own neighborhood or visit a local botanic garden, which may have a variety of displays intended to show options that succeed locally. Thumb through gardening magazines or spend a few hours browsing the gardening section at a bookstore.

Formal or Informal?

One quick way to decide what sort of garden you want is to choose between formal and informal. The very shape of your garden can establish this: Straight lines and geometric shapes are formal, and free-form lines and curves are usually informal. Within these boundaries, select plants that suit the style:

- *Formal:* Compact, uniform-looking plants that naturally grow neatly or

are maintained (clipped) to look tidy. Keeping it simple and uncrowded is very effective—mass a few of the same plants or choose simple forms. A garden also looks more formal when it is appropriately in scale with the house and yard.

- *Informal:* Rambling, lush-looking plants give a perennial garden a look of spontaneity and bounty. Let them spill out over the edges or extend the boundaries by climbing a wall or fence, as with a vine. Avoid patterns and symmetry. Instead, tuck in random numbers of plants and the occasional surprise (one splashy plant or even a whimsical detail such as a sundial or birdhouse on a pole).

A perennial garden's context can also further the mood you are trying to establish. Clipped, velvety lawns or neatly trimmed boundary hedges frame and enhance formal beds. On the other hand, a less highly maintained lawn, in a yard already populated by lushly growing shrubs or trees, welcomes more informal beds.

To create an attractive edge to your border or bed, define the shape, dig down along the line, remove any sod or weeds, turn and amend the soil, and make a trench or install edging material or both.

Finally, the lay of the land can help. Flat yards, especially those with broad expanses of lawn, are naturally more formal. A yard with its own quirky hills, dales, curves, and corners calls out for informal perennial displays. There are exceptions, of course, and with enough effort you can mold your landscape the way you want it. But it's less work and more satisfying to work with what you've got.

Theme Gardens

For a satisfying garden show with your perennials, you may settle on a theme garden. Stick to the theme, making sure every plant you choose contributes to it.

Cottage Gardens

Americans covet this English garden style. A cottage garden can be made in almost any climate or soil—and a cottage is not required. The formula, translated to our shores, is loose and freewheeling. A cottage garden is now understood to be a smallish garden that is not "designed." Plants are well tended but allowed to express their natural exuberance.

A cottage garden is in a way "organized chaos." Within its boundaries plants are allowed to display their natural tendencies, intertwining and overlapping. But what might appear as wildness is actually the result of careful planning.

HOW TO DEFINE A BORDER

If you plan a formal border, the straight lines that define its boundaries are fairly easy to establish. You can lay boards, pipes, or anything straight, or you can erect a wooden stake at each corner and connect them with string to give you a pattern for cutting a straight bed edge. If you plan an informal border, one easy way to define it is to use the garden hose. Trail it along the ground and create curves where you think you want them.

Either way, before you put shovel to soil and commit yourself to the outline, it's a good idea to stand back. Leave the markings in place and go into the house and look out at the area, or walk down the drive or sidewalk and approach it. Wait a day and observe the area at different times of day. This "trial run" will help you get a clearer idea of whether it's the right design for you and your yard. Like a road planner, you might want to make your border shorter or narrower now, but allow for future expansion.

When your border's outlines are set, it's wise to make a small trench all the way around to ward off the encroachment of lawn grass, and perhaps install edging.

Such a garden doesn't just happen, however. The most enchanting ones involve thoughtful choices by the gardener. Cheerful color achieved through a rich mixture of different types of flowers and a healthy dose of foliage is one of the hallmarks. Scent, too, is an important component of these spaces and many cottage gardens are heavily fragrant.

Certain design elements or accents contribute to the overall feel and success of a cottage garden. You may, for instance, wish to mimic its British origins by making the embracing boundaries predominantly plants (vines or roses on trellises or hedges used as "living fences"). If your yard seems too big for the intimacy you want to evoke, create several smaller garden "rooms."

Attracting Butterflies and Birds
Enticing beautiful winged creatures to become a part of your garden requires that you do a little homework. You need to find out what they eat, so you can grow those plants. It also helps to know what the butterflies or birds consider to be suitable shelter, so they will be persuaded to stay around.

You also need to commit yourself to organic gardening, and thus tolerate a less-than-picture-perfect display (nibbled leaves,

To attract butterflies to your garden you need to provide food for both the winged adults and their caterpillars. Butterflies favor flowers with multiple small flowers in a cluster (such as phlox, sedum, blazing star, and pincushion flower), and flowers that offer "landing pads" (such as those in the aster family), allowing them to perch and reach numerous nectar sources.

While hummingbirds will visit a variety of blooms seeking nectar, they particularly like brightly colored, tubular flowers.

especially). Butterflies and birds are vulnerable to garden chemicals and using these to control pests and diseases or to kill weeds can place the winged beauties at risk.

Luckily, many lovely perennials attract and nurture butterflies. Don't forget to take the caterpillar stage into account; certain caterpillars really prefer to eat certain plants. And once they emerge from their cocoons, the butterflies may remain in your garden or revisit it often if the color and scent of your flowers appeal to them and the nectar is plentiful.

As for birds, perennials with edible seeds (purple coneflower, for example) will entice

migrating songbirds. But that's in the fall, and you may wish to have the birds around at other times. A birdbath set out in the open is a big draw. So, too, are birdhouses and birdfeeders appropriate to the species you wish to attract. A flower-filled perennial garden also attracts birds indirectly: Your flowers have insects around them, as pollinators or pests, and birds will come to eat these bugs.

A Cutting Garden

If you like to pick homegrown bouquets, both to beautify your own home as well as to generously give away armloads of flowers to garden visitors, you can plan for it. First and foremost, it's a good idea to devote an entire area just to this purpose, so you won't be depleting your perennial displays every time you pick.

Some gardeners actually don't bother to design a cutting garden to look especially nice—though it often does anyway—and instead install plants in rows. This configuration makes for easier, faster harvesting.

For best results, choose heavy bloomers, ones that produce lots of blooms per plant and that respond to cutting by producing still more. Other important criteria include long, strong cutting stems (so dwarf plants and groundcovers are "out"), the ability to hold petals for a while without wilting or "shattering," and, of course, good color.

GARDEN TIP

Butterfly favorites

- Black-eyed susan
- Blazing star
- Butterfly weed
- Coreopsis
- Joe-Pye weed
- Pincushion flower
- Purple coneflower
- Sedum
- Summer phlox

Bird favorites for seed

- Aster
- Black-eyed susan
- Goldenrod
- Purple coneflower
- Sunflowers

Hummingbird favorites

- Autumn sage
- Beard-tongue
- Bee balm
- Cardinal flower
- Columbine
- Delphinium
- Foxglove

Try a mix

Many perennials, including some exciting new introductions, come in mixes or blends. While such plants might be tricky to work into a carefully planned perennial border, they are ideal for a cutting garden. They bloom simultaneously and are all more-or-less the same height, so every patch becomes an instant, multicolored bouquet! Look for mixes of mulleins, lilies, lupines, and delphiniums.

When cutting flowers of perennials for bouquets, cut to just above newly formed or forming flower buds, or nodes, so the plants will continue to bloom, and so your garden won't be left with unattractive bare stalks.

Many annuals fit the bill—cosmos, cleome, zinnias, snapdragons, and so on—but so do many perennials. The big advantage with a cutting garden composed of perennials is that you don't have to replant it every year.

Fragrant Perennial Gardens

Colorful perennials always delight the eye, but if they are also wafting sweet scents, our sense of smell awakens and our pleasure doubles. This is as true outside in the garden as it is in bouquets you harvest and bring indoors.

Many perennials make beautiful, long-lasting bouquets. They can be included in the perennial border, or a separate cutting-garden area can be created.

Cutting garden candidates

- Baby's breath
- Black-eyed susan
- Coreopsis
- Delphinium
- Foxglove
- Globe thistle
- Indian blanket
- Lady's mantle
- Lavender
- Lily
- Shasta daisy

Fragrance is available in a wide range of plant types, from perennial groundcovers and low-growers to taller, bushier plants. Many of them are long-bloomers, too, which makes the season of enjoyment last longer. So an attractive fragrant perennial garden full of variety and different heights is completely attainable.

Scented herbs extend the range of possibilities—indeed, certain ones with especially showy flowers have become so popular with perennial gardeners that they are "crossover

Take advantage of fragrant perennials, including herbs like oregano, by positioning a bench or hammock nearby.

GARDEN TIP

Fragrant favorites

- Bee balm
- Catmint
- Lavender
- Oregano
- Oriental lilies
- Peony
- Phlox
- Pinks
- Russian sage
- Red valerian

perennials." Some of these are lavender, bee balm, and catmint. The fragrance may reside in the flowers, the leaves, or both.

Shade Gardens

Some homeowners don't even attempt to make a garden if they have a lot of shade, resigning themselves to a dull area in dim light, perhaps under the shade of tall trees or in the shadow of a wall or fence that cannot be removed. But the amazing array of perennials that prefer to grow in the shade should change your mind.

A well-designed, well-planted shade garden is lovely to behold. It's great fun to mix textures, from bold hosta leaves to feathery ferns. A shade garden also gains a lot of beauty from a range of leaf colors: lustrous forest green, sage green, lime green, silver, and burgundy.

Nor do you have to be deprived of color in shade. Two-toned leaves that are rimmed; dappled; or spotted in green and white, silver,

or gold always add excitement, whether in their own groupings or juxtaposed with other plants. And plenty of perennials for shade produce colorful flowers; even if these have a short period of glory, their unexpected hues add interest to the view. White is always refreshing, but warm colors, such as yellows, reds, and oranges, work beautifully too. Gardeners in Asia create drama in their shade displays by inserting just one or two flowering plants in a sea of tranquil green.

Evening Gardens

This type of garden awakens the imagination and revives busy working people, because it is at its best at the end of the day when they arrive home. Its beauty and serenity offer a chance for rest, reflection, and rejuvenation.

Because evening light is dim, the emphasis is on white perennials, whose flowers and foliage stand out luminously in the deepening

A shade garden can display an attractive combination of foliage textures and colors even when it is not in full bloom.

Hosta, Maindenhair Fern, and Solomon's Seal

A meadow garden of wildflowers is the most informal type of garden design, but it can be the most attractive to wildlife.

GARDEN TIP

Shady characters

- Astilbe
- Bleeding heart
- Ferns
- Foxglove
- Hellebore
- Hosta
- Japanese anemone
- Lily-of-the-valley
- Lungwort
- Omphalodes
- Toad lily
- Yellow wax bells

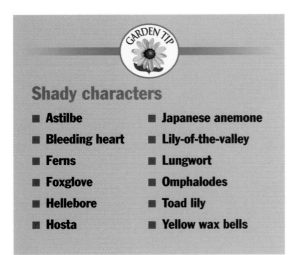

shadows. Luckily, several plants have white flowers—moths and other insects of the night pollinate many of them because the light-colored blooms are visible in the dark. Sweet, heady fragrances are a further enticement for these pollinators as well as a glorious bonus for the gardener. Add the enchantment of a little candlelight, lantern light or—best of all—moonlight, and the whole garden is aglow.

If evening enjoyment is your priority, it might not matter so much how the garden appears by day. But many white-flowering perennials do quite nicely in sun or shade settings. In sunny spots, they may need some shelter (from a deciduous tree or building overhang) from blazing midday heat, which can cause them to fade prematurely. Shade gardens adorned with white bloomers, or even just variegated shade plants such as hostas, will do double duty for you, sparkling in the day and then lighting up the evening.

Many worthwhile perennials come in different colors, but you can seek out the white cultivars. Perennials that carry their blooms visibly high, such as white Japanese anemone, or in spires, such as foxglove, are especially effective. Since you will be enjoying an evening garden during warm weather, choose plants whose bloom times are late spring or summer.

GARDEN TIP

Evening stars

- Astilbe
- Delphinium
- Foxglove
- Hellebore
- Hosta
- Japanese anemone
- Oriental lily
- Shasta daisy
- Summer phlox

Oriental Lily, *Lilium* 'Casablanca'

An evening garden emphasizes white or light-colored flowers, which often exude sweet fragrances to attract moths active at night.

The best wildflower gardens provide interest and color while still looking natural.

Wildflower Gardens

Gardens given over to the exuberance of perennial wildflowers are usually low maintenance, and they are usually informal. But some care is still required in plant selection and design. The most successful wildflower gardens look natural even as they overflow with color and charm.

Perennial wildflowers can be less work than their more domesticated cousins because they have their origins in the wild. There they evolved habits of toughness, such as drought tolerance and resistance to pests. So you don't have to fuss over them as much. Once established in your garden, they can manage well on their own. If anything, your maintenance efforts might be directed towards reining

them in, for some reproduce easily (again, a survival mechanism). This is great if you are aiming for an easy swath of color. Otherwise, simply head off unwanted seedlings by deadheading right after bloom and tugging out "volunteer" plants that pop up.

With wildflowers you should expect natural variability. For instance, flower color within a grouping or even on a single plant can vary. Within a species, bloom time or plant height can differ. Rather than fight these tendencies, embrace them! Plant plenty, and let your garden surprise and delight you at every turn and from one year to the next.

Not just any wildflower is a good choice for a garden. Rest assured that nurseries and wildflower enthusiasts have done a lot of

Some familiar garden plants are in fact native perennials, including black-eyed susan, goldenrod, and phlox.

Winning wildflowers

- **Beard-tongue**
- **Blazing star**
- **Bluestar**
- **Boltonia**
- **Butterfly weed**
- **Columbine**
- **Coreopsis**
- **False indigo**
- **Gaura**
- **Indian blanket**
- **Lupine**
- **New England aster**
- **Purple coneflower**

observing and winnowing in an effort to offer us those that have natural toughness but also good and useful qualities, such as a splashier flower show, a more uniform appearance, and a more predictable performance. Selections or cultivars of wildflowers are thus sometimes superior to the species.

Mixing Perennials

A perennial garden is, by definition, a mixture of various plants. Artfully combining them can be a source of great enjoyment. Because the same perennial can grow differently in different gardens, nobody can truly predict exactly what a combination will look like in your garden. And only you know what you prefer.

Sweeps of Color

Creating sweeps of color takes careful planning. Start by making lists of the colors you want and the plants you would like to provide these colors. Make a diagram or a drawing, or lay out the idea in color swatches—whatever works to help you visualize the garden. Finally, fine-tune. For best results, you want plants in each color in bloom at different times, so the show lasts even as it changes.

"Sweep" implies "bountiful," and the best way to achieve this effect is to grow perennials that are considered easy. Once you've identified a perennial as easy, leave it room to roam, or buy a lot of it. On planting day you may be able to tinker further. Assuming you are

Japanese Anemone, Goldenrod, and Russian Sage

For a colorful perennial garden, carefully choose and site your plants to provide maximum impact.

To enjoy your garden longer, choose perennials that flower or have colorful foliage at different times of the growing season, including fall.

Monkshood, Golden Aster, and Dog Fennel

loosely defined plan, and watch what happens. In ensuing seasons, you can decide to move plants around, take them out, or replace them with new choices.

Alternatively, you can take a more scientific or precise approach and research individual plants. Make a drawing on paper, a site map, or even a chart—again, whatever method makes it easy for you to imagine what the garden will look like. Just remember that results may vary according to the quality of the plants you purchase and the particular conditions in your own yard.

Try to aim for a range of bloom times: late spring to early summer, midsummer, and late season. Those perennials that bridge seasons or remain in bloom for a long time may turn out to be your favorites because they keep the show going. And the most exciting perennial borders feature a sequence of blooms, one plant passing the stage to another, to make a season-long parade of color and texture.

The Island Bed

Pioneered in the glorious gardens of England, the "island bed" concept translates well to the United States. It's a large perennial bed, self-contained or sited out in the open, like an island. It is intended to be viewed from all sides, which will prompt you to plant the taller perennials in the middle and the shorter ones to the outside. (You can build soil up towards the middle to further elevate the taller plants, but do not have to.) Large island or small, the look can be quite spectacular.

However, an island bed needs a reason to be. Don't just randomly construct one in the middle of a flat lawn, or it may look contrived,

installing young potted perennials, it helps to set the various pots on top of the ground throughout the garden in the areas you've envisioned for them. Then you can shift individuals around as needed.

Because perennials don't start producing their most prolific color until their second or third seasons, you may enhance your planting the first season or two by including a few annuals in the right hues.

The Perennial Border

A classic perennial border is full of variety and always has something in bloom. There are two ways to approach these goals.

For an open-ended, seat-of-your-pants approach, experiment with the planting. The first season, space and your budget permitting, install all sorts of plants, in all sorts of forms and colors. Place them according to a out of scale, or "floating," so to speak. Instead, take your cues from the layout of your property. The most appealing island beds take the place of a hedge or fence, along a naturally occurring slope or terrain change, or in an area where a division seems necessary—such as separating a yard from the street or the front yard from the back. Island beds also work fine in open areas, provided their shape is informal and other perennial gardens are not far away, so that they are part of a larger garden scheme.

The Mixed Border

More than just a perennial border, the mixed border welcomes a broad range of plants, including shrubs, bulbs, and even small ornamental trees. The great variety of plant habits, forms, and sizes creates exciting visual interest.

A mixed border, once put in place, can be a rather lawless garden. That is, plants are allowed—within reason—to be themselves. Vines can roam through the shrubs, and perennials and annuals may spread or self-sow with abandon. Here is a good place to break traditional garden rules—perhaps you'd like to insert a tropical plant, which you can tuck into place in a pot (and store in the house when cold weather comes).

One nice side benefit of a mixed border is that it tends to be naturally healthy. There's so much diversity that no one pest or disease can gain a foothold, and individual plants are able to hold forth proudly. To make a mixed border, it's best to start first with the larger plants and install the smaller ones last. Additions and

A mixed border can include perennials, shrubs, grasses, vines, bulbs, annuals, and even small ornamental trees.

evictions, in the coming years, can be dealt with case by case.

A Few Simple Design Principles

It's a thrill—and not really mysterious or difficult—to design your own garden. If you get more involved as the years go by, or have ambitious plans you don't feel confident to implement, you can always go further by reading books entirely devoted to garden design, taking a class or two, or hiring a professional landscape designer, either for a site

Planting perennials in odd numbers of three, five, or seven creates balance.

assessment or the entire installation. But the following are some basics that will help you succeed on your own.

The Principles of Grouping

Experience has shown that these four simple principles lead to attractive displays. Rules can certainly be broken, but if you start here, you will be better able to present your plants at their best.

"Stairstepping" your perennial planting, tall to short, gives the garden dimension.

- *Three to five plants:* More than one individual of a plant tends to stand out better. Also, an odd number of plants allows for a fuller, more geometric, or three-dimensional look.

- *Tall in the back, medium in the middle, short in the front:* There are practical reasons for this. The short plants will be more visible, of course, and perhaps even disguise the "bare knees" of those plants that tower above and behind them. And by "stepping up" as you move farther back in a perennial border, your garden gains dimension.

- *Gauging spacing:* When you accommodate a perennial plant's mature "footprint," it is happier and healthier and thus more attractive. Tighter spacing has its merits, though, if you want a more lush garden sooner, or want your plants to blend together or drape over one another. No matter how close you place different plants, growing them together can either emphasize their similarities (in flower or foliage color, flower shape or texture, or plant habit), or highlight intriguing contrasts because of their differences.

- *Repetition for unity:* The same or similar plants are grouped and placed at

Repetition of a color, texture, or form gives unity to the garden and leads the viewer's eye.

intervals in a perennial garden. The result is a rhythm that makes the garden look unified instead of random. It has a theme.

Designing by Bloom Season

When you are just starting out, keep your goals modest. If your garden is not large, you may find that a handful of plants in bloom at any given time is indeed enough of a show. For a larger garden, aim first for a spectacular late spring or a flower-filled midsummer and choose perennials accordingly, so you can build up your knowledge and your confidence.

It takes time and experience to achieve what the masters do: a full season of flowers from earliest spring to fall's first frost. It also takes a lot of plants, and firsthand knowledge of how they look at different times in your garden. Consider it an ongoing project, later adding plants for each part of the growing year.

Working with Color

Maybe it's a matter of taste—what you like, what you think works, what stimulates you or soothes you—but garden designers, taking their cue from artists in other mediums (particularly painters), have codified what we see and how we respond to it. They say there are reasons why certain colors elicit certain responses, why we like what we like, why we think certain plants look good together. But what you do with color principles as you consider the perennial "palette"—whether you take them to heart, tinker with them, or deliberately defy them—is up to you.

Plant perennials that flower at different times so that something is always in bloom. Here the white candytuft has nearly finished blooming, the delphinium and coral bells are at their peak, and the Japanese anemone on the right has not yet begun to flower.

Dahlia and Crocosmia

Hot colors seem to come toward the viewer while cool colors seem to recede.

Cool Colors Recede, Hot Colors Advance

Cool colors include blue, purple, white, pink, and the green of foliage. Hot colors are the opposite, and include fiery red and orange as well as bold, luminous yellow.

In paintings, as in gardens, the cooler, calmer colors seem to retreat to the darker corners or the back—even if they don't in reality. Thus cool-colored perennials, especially when grouped together, seem to retreat or be farther away. This is useful if your garden is small and you want to give it depth.

Warm colors, on the other hand, seem to dominate, to clamor for attention and admiration. They can fool the eye into thinking that the bright, cheery flowers are closer than they actually are. Try warm colors where you want to involve garden visitors, to create a sense of excitement. They can also distract or divert the eye from less-attractive sights such as a neighbor's fence or a storage area.

Neutral Colors

Gray and silver-hued foliage, such as in the favorite perennials artemisia and lamb's ears, are considered neutral. Even plain, not-very-glossy foliage plants such as various ferns, groundcovers, and certain hostas, can adopt a neutral personality in the garden.

The great virtue of neutral plants is that they succeed well with either hot or cool colors.

Paired with hot-hued flowers or foliage, they help "punch up" the excitement. Alongside cooler, softer-colored perennials, neutral plants contribute to a feeling of harmony.

Yet colorists have observed that gray or silver is not as passive as we may at first think. It turns out that it appears yellowed when placed near violet; near orange, it gains a bluish cast; and near red, there seems to be a hint of contrasting green.

In any event, neutral colors are valuable in perennial displays simply because they give the eye a rest. They keep colors from clashing. They keep the show from being overwhelming or too riotous or busy. Thus it's always a good idea to include them.

A blend of similar colors creates harmony. Neutral colors such as gray or silver enhance brighter colors of plants nearby.

Downy Phlox (*Phlox pilosa*), Salvia (*Salvia pratensis*), Wormwood (*Artemisia* × 'Huntington')

Color Harmonies

Colors that are near one another in the rainbow (or, for that matter, on the painter's "color wheel") never fail to bond in a perennial garden. Thus orange and red are natural partners, as are purple and pink. Primary colors, that is blue, yellow, and red, always look superb together, too. Pastel-themed gardens are pleasing to the eye because the softer hues are not only in the same neighborhood on the color wheel, but also share the same low intensity. Using

Yarrow (*Achillea* × 'Coronation Gold') and Daylily (*Hemerocallis* 'Silent Entry')
The yellow eye of the daylily flowers repeats the color of the yarrow, though the two plants have strongly contrasting forms.

complementary colors, such as orange and blue, purple and yellow, red and green, makes exciting combinations, each enhancing the other.

It's also rewarding to use bicolor plants to make harmonious pictures. Indian blanket flowers are red-centered yellow daisies; a good companion would be a solid-color yellow bloomer of equal intensity (such as certain coreopsis cultivars or even a yellow Asiatic lily). In a shady nook, lily-of-the-valley's dainty white bells charm in the company of a hosta with white-splashed leaves.

Contrast for Drama

It doesn't take much to generate a color splash in a perennial bed if you know how to work with color contrasts. Even one plant can change or intensify a spot. Green and white almost disappear in the landscape until you tuck in a bright red flower; suddenly, the scene is crisper and bolder. Something fiery orange emboldens a gathering of blue flowers. Hot pink combined with dark purple is exciting. Difficult-to-harmonize magenta becomes a garden asset when grown alongside silver or even lime-green foliage.

Working with Size

How big is the plant going to become? If you have a good idea, you can place the plant where it will not only thrive, but also look great for years to come. Mature plant sizes are generally listed in catalogs and on plant tags; this information is also provided for the plants in the Perennial Plant Directory later in this book. Consider not only the height but the width of the plant.

Height

For the sake of convenience, perennials are often grouped into three main categories:

short, medium, and tall. These categories are used to correspond to the traditional planting scheme: Short plants go in the front of the border, medium ones go in the middle, and tall ones go in the back.

A plant can defy its prescribed size, in which case you can treat it differently, either by moving it to another spot or trimming or pruning it back into bounds. If you find these rules too rigid and want a more informal, relaxed, diverse look, mix up your perennials as you wish. But not by too much—while it might be interesting to place a tall, "see-through" plant such as meadow rue near the front of the border, there's no sense in completely blocking a short plant from view.

Shape and Form

Perennials are also described according to their habit or shape: spiky, mounding, vase-shaped, and sprawling are the most common categories.

Billowing mounds of perennials like pink perennial geranium can soften the edge of a walkway and give continuity to a border by their repetition and by weaving in and among other plants.

A sea of any one type of plant has its merits. Lots of low, sprawling plants can weave into one another over time and create a carpet of color. A border full of plants with mounding habits has a nice uniform look. And a gathering of spiky plants, provided their flowers look good together, is a lively, appealing sight.

On the other hand, mixing these plant types together simply for the sake of mixing can create a mishmash. For this reason, you'll see the pros apply certain strategies:

- *Use repetition:* A plant of distinctive form—a spiky Siberian iris, for instance—can be tucked into a border at intervals.

- *Use echoes:* Instead of using foxgloves over and over again, put some verbascums in the next spot (both make tall flower spires).

- *Create accents:* Tuck a mounding plant among spiky ones, or a spiky one among mounding ones. Its presence will be a pleasant surprise, and the entire display will become more intriguing.

- *Alter the plants:* For example, you may feel your Russian sage plant is too rangy

Yarrow, Wood Betony, Sedum, Iris, Lavender, and Santolina

In this mixed planting, the colors of yellow and purple are repeated using a variety of plants. The upright leaves of the bearded iris in the center serve as an accent plant, contrasting with the delicate textures of the surrounding plants.

GARDEN TIP

Airy plants

Some perennials are tall but not very substantial. Their flowers rise above their foliage and wave in the breeze. Among these "airy" plants are Japanese anemone, meadow rue, and gaura. If you place them towards the back of a perennial display, they get lost or upstaged by bigger plants. So "break the rule" and move your airy plants into the center. Medium-height neighboring plants should still be visible.

and getting too big. Cut it back early in the season, even if the stems are already on their way. The plant will recover and return looking more compact.

Working with Textures

Some plants have a big, bold personality—such as hosta and Joe-Pye weed. Others are more delicate and ferny—such as astilbes and columbines. And others are somewhere in between, with a texture best described as medium—purple coneflower, for instance, and summer phlox. Because designing a handsome, dynamic perennial display is so much more than combining flower colors,

these wide-ranging textures should be taken into account. After all, unless a perennial is especially long blooming, plant form and foliage take the stage for much of the growing season.

- *Variety is the spice:* When you put together your perennial displays, try to mix up different textures. Too much sameness creates a "blob" or "mat"

This combination of upright, willowy, white false indigo and bold, sculptural prickly pear cactus shows the range of textures available in perennials.

133

GREAT DUETS: PERENNIALS WITH PERENNIALS

Here are some tried-and-true pairings that look great in any perennial display. The two plants in each grouping have similar cultural needs (that is, they enjoy similar light exposure and thrive in similar soil) and, side by side, their colors and forms put on a great show.

- Red astilbe and variegated hosta
- Black-eyed susan and ornamental grass
- Purple nepeta and gray-leaved artemisia
- Yellow daylily and red summer phlox
- Yellow coreopsis and blue campanula
- White delphinium and blue, pink, or magenta cranesbill geranium
- Hosta and purple-leaved alumroot
- Shasta daisy and white lily
- Blue summer phlox and purple globe thistle

where individual plants and their details are lost or hard to distinguish.

- *Create depth or the illusion of depth:* Layer upon layer of different textures gives a character to a display. Mixing textures can also give extra dimension. In a small garden, a multilayered scene emphasizes the plants and not the background—you can almost forget the encroaching fence, house, or driveway in an interesting little nook. You will notice that bold textures tend to appear closer, while fine textures recede. So when you place a bold-leaved plant in the foreground—a bergenia or hosta, for instance—and finer-textured ones behind it, such as ferns or bleeding heart, you'll create an illusion of depth.

- *Color can unite:* So that a display of many different textures doesn't look "too busy," try working in color harmonies at the same time. Two totally different leaf forms might be of the same or similar hue, whether chartreuse or pewter.

Creating Visual Interest

Some tricks of the garden design trade help make perennial displays more successful, interesting, and unique.

Combine perennials that not only look good together, but which have the same cultural needs.

Jupiter's Beard, Mullein, and Perennial Geranium

A decorative urn can serve as a focal point in the garden.

Strong, interesting contrasts can be achieved using flowers or foliage, in sun or shade. Here the silvery leaves of a lungwort shine at the feet of a purple smoke tree.

Leading the Eye

To coax viewers along a path or through a perennial border, you need to keep their interest moving. Garden designers do this in various ways:

- Repeat plant forms or flower colors, but vary the types of plants, to create curiosity or anticipation.

- Create a sequence. Move the color scheme along the color spectrum as the border unfolds.

- Create an outline or path that causes the end of the garden to be just out of view.

- Design so that brighter or bolder-textured plants are in the distance, tempting the viewer onward to get a closer look.

Focal Points

A focal point is a feature in the garden (it can be a plant or a garden ornament or structure) that draws your eye or is a destination, one that you want a visitor to arrive at or be drawn towards—and to pause at, enjoying the

picture you have created. Here are some ideas:

- Any dramatic plant in an attractive container, large enough to command attention, and with the plant and container in scale with one another.

- Any surprising plant—a tropical plant or houseplant (which can be moved indoors for protection if cold weather threatens).

- A significant grouping of one kind of plant, particularly those with flower spires.

- A small ornamental tree, an attractive stand-alone shrub, or a rosebush.

Contrast and Complement

Avoid sameness! Without variety in the garden, the eye finds little of interest, no place to pause and rest and savor, and thus moves on. To stimulate your own eye as well as garden visitors, inject lively colors here and there. Make bold or surprising color combinations.

Maltese Cross (*Lychnis chalcedonica*) and Catmint (*Nepeta* × *faassenii* 'Souvenir d'André Chaudron*)

Bold combinations, and the use of less-common perennials, can make a garden much more interesting.

If you have plants with variegated leaves, grow complementary-hued flowers nearby to repeat and emphasize the hue. Mix up textures. Always be on the lookout to create appealing "pictures" in your perennial displays.

Perennials with Other Plants

Perennials need not stand alone and, indeed, today's gardeners are using all sorts of imaginative plant partners to create more interest and beauty. You can work with what you've got, or tuck in additional plants. Whatever you do, remember to attend to the following basic rules for successful partnerships.

- *Choose plants with similar cultural needs:* Grow sun-lovers with sun-lovers, moist-soil lovers with moist-soil lovers, and so on.

- *Don't crowd:* Plants in too-close proximity may not grow well. Their roots compete for the same resources of soil moisture and nutrients. Their growth could become inhibited or distorted, or plant diseases that thrive in areas of poor air circulation could move in. Always allow elbowroom. If the perennial or its partner takes an opportunity to fill in a space, the result will look more natural.

- *Choose plants with similar maintenance needs:* If the perennial is drought tolerant, but its partner needs plenty of supplemental water, one of them is not going to look its best. If a perennial needs frequent deadheading to look nice and continue blooming, but its neighbor doesn't, you may be trampling in too often and causing a disturbance (inadvertently snapping off stems or compacting the soil, for instance).

The emerging foliage of the hosta, lungwort, hellebore, and lady's mantle will soon grow tall enough to hide the fading leaves of the tulips.

- *Keep everything in scale:* A large or imposing partner can overwhelm, upstage, or even hide from view an adjacent perennial. Sometimes the solution is simple: Plant several perennials per one partner plant.

Perennials with Roses

The wide range of rose colors combine beautifully with many perennials. The fact that many roses keep blooming over a long period also makes them a great asset in a perennial border, where their color can establish, repeat, or enhance the color theme. A rosebush overflowing with pretty pink blossoms, for instance, can anchor a pastel flower border. A fiery

Perennials make perfect companions for roses.

orange rose can deliver a jolt of excitement as well as continuity to a hot-colored perennial bed whose plants are cycling in and out of bloom over the course of a season.

The variety of rose forms also offers many exciting possibilities. A climber can ramble and drape over a perennial bed. A compact floribunda can fill a mid-border gap with dependable color, while a few miniature roses can do the same towards the front. Taller hybrid teas, individually or grown as a hedge, make a wonderful border backdrop—both their glossy green foliage and their elegant blooms are welcome.

Perennials with Shrubs

A perennial border that includes shrubs gains definition and heft. It gains structure. The shrubs are a relatively consistent size and form (once mature and, perhaps, with some mainte- nance pruning). Choose shrubs that are in scale with your perennials—or, if they are large, use them as a backdrop.

But shrubs can be so much more. Over the course of a season, their foliage, texture, flowers, and fruits can contribute color, texture, and

GARDEN TIP

Spring bulb cover-ups

After their days and weeks of glory, bulb flowers finally fade. Eventually all that's left is their leaves. While it's tempting to chop away all that unsightly foliage, it's foolish— those leaves are busy sending energy for next year's flowers down into the bulb, tuber, or corm. The show next spring will be greatly compromised if you tidy up too soon.

Perennials to the rescue! Several develop sufficient foliage (and sometimes even provide the additional distraction of their own late-spring flower show) to cover and disguise those unsightly fading bulb leaves from view. Examples include bleeding heart, hosta, lady's mantle, and daylily.

Perennials can make lovely combinations with shrubs, particularly when they bloom at the same time. Powder-blue forget-me-nots enhance this planting of rhododendrons.

interest to your perennial displays. Many cultivars come with colorful or variegated foliage, which also can be worked into the overall design.

Perennials with Annuals

Annuals are a good addition to the perennial garden. They offer quick and dependable color, filling temporary gaps. This is especially important in the first year or two of a perennial display, when the perennial flowers and foliage have not yet reached their full potential. Or the perennials may still be too small—there's nothing wrong with tucking in a few tall cosmos or cleomes towards the back of a border while you wait for the perennials there to fill outward and upward.

In later years, you may still find you like annuals in your displays. The gaps they fill may be color gaps—before the blue bellflowers bloom by the yellow coreopsis, you can slip

in a little early blue with some petunias or lobelias. Marigolds, and even colorful-leaved coleus plants, can ribbon through a hot-colored border to sustain the show while the perennials cycle in and out of bloom.

Perennials with Vines

Whether they climb using clinging tendrils (such as sweet peas) or tiny "holdfast" suction cups (such as crossvine), vines appreciate support. Not all perennials are up to the job, so you need to use plants that are strong, sturdy, and substantial. So it's better to wait until your perennials have matured before introducing a vining partner, and then keep

Filling space

Gaps or bare spots in your perennial garden may look awkward to your eye, even as you await the day when they are covered by the plants when they mature. At minimum, you should blanket these areas with mulch so weeds aren't tempted to move in. For temporary color, tuck in some flowering annuals—right into the ground or, if you want a flexible, versatile display, in pots that you can shift around or remove as you wish.

Japanese Anemone (*Anemone hupehensis*) and Morning Glory (*Ipomoea purpurea*)

Vines can be used in a border either on a trellis or other support, or allowed to twine amongst the perennials.

an eye on the situation so that the perennials are not pulled down or overrun.

The best approach might be to give the vines the support of a structure and let them do what they do best—provide vertical interest. A trellis at the back of a border, or a pillar or rustic twig teepee in the middle, works wonderfully. In these situations, the perennials can fill it near the base, perhaps hiding from view the vine's "bare knees," and direct attention from the ground to higher levels.

Perennials in Containers

The big advantage of displaying perennials in pots is that the show is portable. When a plant is looking great, you can tuck it into a spot where it will be shown off well, then move it

to a less visible place when it begins to flag or goes out of bloom. And by growing perennials in pots, you can try out various plant or color combinations before committing yourself and planting them in a permanent place in the garden.

The pot itself can become an appealing part of the display. Painted pots add extra color, either contrasting or complementary. A beautiful or ornate pot can be a garden focal point. Alternatively, you can hide a plain pot from view—and thus hide the fact that the perennial is potted—by installing it in the ground and covering over the rim with soil or mulch. This is worth doing if a plant is an enthusiastic grower and you want to keep it in bounds.

Seasonal interest and color can be provided by tucking in annuals among your perennials, or using potted perennials placed in the garden or on the deck or patio. Annuals and potted plants can also be used to fill empty spaces in the garden as the perennials continue to grow toward their mature size.

PERENNIAL PLANT DIRECTORY

100 Outstanding Perennials

The perennials we enjoy in our gardens today have their origins in wild places—woods, meadows, streamsides, mountains, bogs, deserts, and so forth. And many perennial plant species make excellent additions to the garden just as they are. Some species have also had improvements and alterations in plant form, flower color and size, and bloom period. These are the "garden varieties" or "cultivars" of the wildlings. And the wishes and needs of gardeners continue to be fulfilled and updated, not only by plant explorers but also by hybridizers and sharp-eyed gardeners, ever on the lookout for worthwhile variations. Nowadays there are unprecedented choices in perennials—it's never been a more exciting time to be a gardener.

To assure your success, we have chosen from among the thousands and thousands of excellent perennials a "Top 100" that meet the following important criteria:

- **Resilience:** The vagaries of any season's weather, not to mention your yard's particular soil and microclimate conditions, can put garden plants under some stress. A perennial that can tolerate a variety of challenges, still look good and produce gorgeous blooms, and return faithfully year after year, despite harsh winters or summers, is a worthwhile perennial indeed.

- **Availability:** These are not rare plants. Find them at your local garden center, or buy them through a mail-order or Internet catalog.

- **Proven performer:** Other perennial gardeners have grown these plants and found them to be tough, adaptable, and dependable. Experts have rated them highly or they have won awards, or both.

Achillea millefolium
Yarrow
SIZE (height × width): 2 to 3 feet × 2 to 3 feet
BLOOM DESCRIPTION: big flat-topped clusters of small blooms
BLOOM PERIOD: all summer
EXPOSURE: full sun
HARDY IN ZONES: 3 to 8
SPECIAL NOTES: deer resistant

Ideal in locations with plenty of sun and average soil, yarrow brings lots of color all summer long. Once established, the plants are drought tolerant and self-sufficient. They look great in sweeps, clumps, or interspersed throughout a perennial border where you want dependable color.

Yarrow's flat-topped blooms, usually up to 5 inches across, are actually tight clusters of myriad tiny flowers. Usually yellow, yarrow also comes in white, red, rose, pink, and salmon hues, or mixes of these. They always look terrific in the garden and also make good cut flowers, fresh or dried. The ferny foliage at the base of the plants even makes an attractive, gray-green, off-season groundcover.

GOOD CHOICES: peppery-red 'Paprika';
 A. × 'Coronation Gold'

Aconitum napellus
Monkshood
SIZE (height × width): 3 feet × 2 feet
BLOOM DESCRIPTION: tall spires of violet
BLOOM PERIOD: mid- to late summer
EXPOSURE: full sun to partial shade
HARDY IN ZONES: 4 to 8
SPECIAL NOTES: deer resistant

When it blooms in the latter part of the season, monkshood is a welcome sight. Gorgeous spires of helmet-shaped flowers adorn tall, graceful stems. Usually violet-blue, they can also be found in deep blue, white, and pink. The plant is clothed in divided, dark-green leaves that remain handsome all season and alternate up the stem to just short of the sensational flowers.

Monkshood blends very well with other perennials, thanks to its airy profile and medium height. Their most important requirement is rich, moist soil.

Deer and rodents shun this perennial, no doubt because its roots and leaves are poisonous. The poison can also harm pets and children, so be sure to place this plant out of their reach.

GOOD CHOICES: white 'Album'; pink 'Carneum'

Ajuga reptans
Bugleweed, Ajuga, Carpet Bugle

SIZE (height × width): 4 to 8 inches × spreading
BLOOM DESCRIPTION: small spikes
BLOOM PERIOD: late spring to early summer
EXPOSURE: full sun to full shade
HARDY IN ZONES: 4 to 8
SPECIAL NOTES: fast growing

A valuable, versatile groundcover, bugleweed delivers not only good coverage over large areas, but also color. The small spikes of flowers, usually in hues of blue, purple, or even pink, make a perky show late every spring. But it's primarily grown for its wonderfully attractive, often colorful foliage, which carries on the show for the rest of the season. The leaves of 'Burgundy Glow' are splashed with pink and cream, and 'Chocolate Chip' is chocolate-hued. 'Bronze Beauty' is bronze-purple.

Bugleweed can be grown where grass doesn't thrive, or fill in an area you don't want to fuss over. It's tough and resilient, forming weed-excluding mats over time.

GOOD CHOICES: 'Bronze Beauty'; 'Burgundy Glow';
  'Chocolate Chip'

Alcea rosea
Hollyhock

SIZE (height × width): 5 to 8 feet × 2 to 3 feet
BLOOM DESCRIPTION: tall spires with showy flowers
BLOOM PERIOD: summer into autumn
EXPOSURE: full sun
HARDY IN ZONES: 3 to 9
SPECIAL NOTES: gets quite tall

A cottage-garden classic, hollyhock is wonderfully easy to grow. Stately, unbranched bloom stalks rise up and are decorated with the prettiest, most cheerful of flowers. They come in a wide range of colors, from yellow and white and pink to lavender and bright red; there's even a nearly black (dark maroon) one called 'Nigra' that is a dramatic sight against a white wall or fence. Because of their height and carefree nature, hollyhocks are great swaying along a fence; they may also be sited at the back of a perennial border or in an entryway.

Sometimes hollyhock leaves develop a disfiguring rust disease; affected leaves should be removed and destroyed to keep the display attractive. Hollyhocks are typically biennial, but they self-sow, so capitalize on this tendency by siting them where you want them to multiply.

GOOD CHOICE: try a mix and enjoy a rainbow of hues

Alchemilla mollis
Lady's Mantle

SIZE (height × width): 1 to 2 feet × 1 to 2 feet
BLOOM DESCRIPTION: frothy chartreuse flowers
BLOOM PERIOD: late spring to early summer
EXPOSURE: full sun to partial shade
HARDY IN ZONES: 4 to 7
SPECIAL NOTES: water beads up on the leaves like quicksilver

This lovely, lush plant is a wonderful supporting player in any perennial garden. Its handsome, felted, scalloped leaves spill outward in mounds, an appealing shade of apple-green that seems to flatter any colorful flowers nearby. When it rains or early morning dew gathers on the leaves, the water beads up like quicksilver and sparkles—an enchanting sight. And the frothy chartreuse flowers are pretty and unobtrusive; they make a nice addition to late-spring bouquets.

Lady's mantle is easygoing, adapting well to sun or shade. It may also be grown in a pot and looks especially splendid in a decorative urn or terra-cotta container. If the weather gets dry, be sure to supply supplemental water so the leaves remain pretty.

GOOD CHOICES: dwarf forms *A. alpina* and *A.* 'Pumila'

Amsonia tabernaemontana
Bluestar

SIZE (height × width): 2 to 3 feet × 2 to 3 feet
BLOOM DESCRIPTION: loose clusters
BLOOM PERIOD: spring to early summer
EXPOSURE: full sun to partial shade
HARDY IN ZONES: 3 to 9
SPECIAL NOTES: attractive fall foliage

True-blue flowers are hard to come by, in the wild and in garden settings. But here is the genuine article. Bluestar not only offers the soft, versatile color, but a plant form that fits into many settings. Individual blossoms are starlike and small, no more than a half-inch across, but carried in clusters at the tops of the stems. The willowy, narrow foliage is also attractive; in fact, the plant overall makes a very appealing addition to a garden. Bluestar looks equally at home among late-blooming tulips of most any hue, alongside bright orange or red azaleas, or with early-summer perennials, bright or pastel. It can hold its own in a formal setting or bring its charms to more casual planting plans.

The plant itself is quite tough. It thrives in moderately fertile soil in full sun, but tolerates poorer soils and less sun. Pests and diseases never trouble it.

Autumn brings a surprising and welcome bonus. Though the flowers are long gone, the foliage turns a vivid shade of gold that looks splendid in the company of fall bloomers such as asters and mums.

GOOD CHOICES: *A. hubrechtii* (Arkansas bluestar); *A. illustris*

Anemone × *hybrida*
Japanese Anemone
SIZE (height × width): 3 to 5 feet × 2 feet
BLOOM DESCRIPTION: single, semidouble, or double flowers
BLOOM PERIOD: late summer to fall
EXPOSURE: full sun to partial shade
HARDY IN ZONES: 5 to 8
SPECIAL NOTES: deer resistant

Few late-season bloomers are as showy and as dependable as Japanese anemones. You can count on them to generate lots of late color, in shades of pink, rose, and white. They superficially resemble daisies and appear in profusion atop strong stalks. It gets one of its less common names, windflower, from the fact that these sway charmingly in any breeze. The plant below this show is a large, substantial mound of dark green, compound foliage.

For best results, grow Japanese anemones with ample space and against a dark backdrop like a hedge or wall where the lovely flowers will show up well. Moist, organically rich soil is key, especially when the plants are located in sunny spots.

GOOD CHOICES: white 'Honorine Jobert'; two-tone pink 'September Charm'

Aquilegia hybrids
Columbine
SIZE (height × width): 2 to 3 feet × 1 to 2 feet
BLOOM DESCRIPTION: 1- to 2-inch blossoms, sometimes larger
BLOOM PERIOD: late spring to early summer
EXPOSURE: full sun to partial shade
HARDY IN ZONES: 3 to 9
SPECIAL NOTES: deer- and rodent-resistant

For carefree, cheerful late spring color, columbines are without peer. Their flowers are produced in great numbers and wave jauntily in every breeze, bringing charm to flower borders. Their flower form is unusual and very appealing: Five sepals are centered by a boss of little yellow stamens and backed by five true petals that are usually spurred. Bicolor types have sepals and petals of contrasting shades, such as blue and white or yellow and red.

Columbines are simple to grow in full sun to part shade and average soil. Deer avoid them and rodents don't nibble them. Tiny insects called leaf miners may make tracings in the leaves, but don't harm the plant overall; simply cut off the affected foliage and fresh new growth will soon appear. Columbines reseed freely and are a great choice for any garden in need of trouble-free, exuberant color.

GOOD CHOICES: McKana Giants Mix; yellow *A. longissima* 'Maxistar'; white 'Snow Queen'; double, wine-colored *A. vulgaris* 'Nora Barlow'

Armeria maritima
Thrift, Sea Thrift

SIZE (height × width): 6 to 12 inches × 12 to 18 inches
BLOOM DESCRIPTION: small ball-shaped flower heads
BLOOM PERIOD: late spring to early summer
EXPOSURE: full sun
HARDY IN ZONES: 4 to 8
SPECIAL NOTES: excellent drainage is essential

This perky little plant is a great way to bring color into your late spring garden just as the flowering bulbs are starting to fade away. Forming a low-growing, grassy-leaved mound, the plant generates a vivacious flower show. Each blossom, a ball of tiny flowers, tops a short, bare stalk. Usually pink, it also comes in red and white.

Because of its definable, mounding form, thrift is a great choice for edging a walkway or fronting a border. It's also ideal for a rock garden. As the name *maritima* suggests, it's a good choice for a seaside garden or any setting with sandy, well-drained soil. Once established, thrift is resilient and drought tolerant.

GOOD CHOICES: vivid red 'Ruby Glow'; rose-red 'Nifty Thrifty' (which also has white-variegated foliage)

Artemisia cultivars and hybrids
Mugwort, Wormwood

SIZE (height × width): 1 to 3 feet × 1 to 2 feet
BLOOM DESCRIPTION: tiny, insignificant white or yellow flowers
BLOOM PERIOD: spring or summer (not grown for its flowers)
EXPOSURE: full sun
HARDY IN ZONES: 4 to 8
SPECIAL NOTES: deer resistant

Justly popular for their appealing foliage, the many species and cultivars of *Artemisia* make a wonderful contribution to any perennial display. Usually gray or silvery in hue, the leaves keep their cool in the heat of summer; the plants are drought tolerant and tend to look great with very little intervention from the gardener. The soft, neutral hue looks lovely among pastel flowers, makes bright flowers seem more vibrant, and flatters dark green foliage.

Horticulturists have singled out especially handsome forms for garden use. Among these is the widely grown and admired *A. schmidtiana* 'Silver Mound', whose thin, silky leaves make a compact clump (though it sometimes melts where summers are hot and humid). Although they can have the potential to run rampant, taller *A. ludoviciana* cultivars, including 'Silver King', 'Silver Queen', and 'Valerie Finnis', are good choices for mid border. For a taller form, useful as a "filler" plant, try 'Powis Castle' or 'Huntington'.

GOOD CHOICES: *A. ludoviciana* cultivars; *A. schmidtiana* 'Silver Mound'; *A. arborescens* 'Powis Castle'; *A.* × 'Huntington'

Aruncus dioicus
Goatsbeard

SIZE (height × width): 4 to 7 feet × 3 to 4 feet
BLOOM DESCRIPTION: feathery wands of creamy white
BLOOM PERIOD: early summer
EXPOSURE: full sun to partial shade
HARDY IN ZONES: 3 to 7
SPECIAL NOTES: thrives in moist soil

A subtle charmer, great feathery wands of creamy white wave above this big, shrubby plant in spring. Goatsbeard prefers a shaded or woodland garden, but it's also possible to grow it in sunnier areas provided the plant gets ample moisture.

After the flowers fade, you'll still appreciate the plant. Its delicate, textured leaves clothe the plant and are untroubled by any nibbling pests. In the fall, the leaves turn appealing shades of yellow, gold, and red. If *A. dioicus* is too big for your garden, seek out the dwarf types, including *A. sinensis* 'Child of Two Worlds' and, from Korea, *A. aethusifolius*.

GOOD CHOICES: native *A. dioicus*; *A. aethusifolius*; dwarf *A. sinensis* 'Child of Two Worlds'

Aster novae-belgii
Michaelmas Daisy, Aster

SIZE (height × width): 1 to 6 feet × 2 to 4 feet
BLOOM DESCRIPTION: small to medium, fluffy daisies
BLOOM PERIOD: late summer into fall
EXPOSURE: full to partial sun
HARDY IN ZONES: 4 to 8
SPECIAL NOTES: lovely, late-season bouquets

For exuberant, late-season color, asters are indispensable. They are also very easy and fun to grow. They adapt well to many settings and aren't terribly fussy about soil. Some gardeners like to make them the star of a late summer or fall border. For more blooms and a bushier plant, you may pinch back in midsummer.

The garden cultivars have the same natural toughness and cold-hardiness as their wild predecessors. But their flowers are larger, more plentiful, and come in more colors. There are plenty to choose from, from big, billowing ones such as sweet pink 'Patricia Ballard' to tidy, compact, rich-hued 'Purple Dome'.

GOOD CHOICES: 'Patricia Ballard'; 'Red Star'; *A. novae-angliae* 'September Ruby'; 'Purple Dome'

Astilbe × *arendsii*
Astilbe

SIZE (height × width): 1 to 4 feet × 1 to 2 feet
BLOOM DESCRIPTION: colorful, feathery spires
BLOOM PERIOD: varies, early to late summer
EXPOSURE: partial shade
HARDY IN ZONES: 4 to 8
SPECIAL NOTES: deer resistant; best in moist ground

Magnificent feathery plumes wave atop a clump-forming plant—astilbe is a real winner. Planted *en masse*, the effect is impressive, but even a single plant or a small grouping placed here and there throughout a border is very appealing. Astilbes are shade garden classics, but may also be grown in more sun in cooler regions if their roots get the moisture they crave. Try them under a stand of trees or decorating the edges of a garden pond. Even out of bloom, astilbes are attractive, with healthy, dark green, fernlike foliage.

Astilbes come in a range of quality colors, from red and purple to pink and white. Dwarf varieties are popular as edging plants and with those gardeners who have smaller gardens.

GOOD CHOICES: white 'Diamond'; bold red 'Fanal'; raspberry red *A. chinensis* 'Visions'; light pink *A. simplicifolia* 'Sprite' (1994 Perennial Plant Association Perennial Plant of the Year)

Astrantia major
Masterwort

SIZE (height × width): 2 to 3 feet × 1 to 2 feet
BLOOM DESCRIPTION: small clusters of pincushion-like blooms
BLOOM PERIOD: late spring to early summer
EXPOSURE: partial shade
HARDY IN ZONES: 4 to 7
SPECIAL NOTES: moist, well-drained soil is ideal

Unusual and beautiful flowers are the hallmark of this rising star in the perennial world. Each flower head, held well above the palmate leaves, features a center surrounded stockade-fashion by a ruff of petal-like greenish or pink bracts. They never fail to attract attention in the garden, and are also suitable for bouquets, fresh or dried.

Long popular in English perennial gardens, masterwort is now winning the affections of American gardeners. Provided it gets moist, well-drained soil, it grows well, blooms prolifically, and is trouble-free.

GOOD CHOICES: 'Buckland'; maroon 'Rubra'

Athyrium nipponicum
Japanese Painted Fern

SIZE (height × width): 1 to 2 feet × 1 to 2 feet
BLOOM DESCRIPTION: grown for its striking foliage
BLOOM PERIOD: not applicable
EXPOSURE: partial to full shade
HARDY IN ZONES: 5 to 8
SPECIAL NOTES: sensitive to cold

Shade gardeners prize Japanese painted fern because, unlike the majority of ferns, it has handsomely variegated fronds. They're pewtery-silver with a green border; the veins are plum or wine-red, as are the stems. Some gardeners believe the more light the plant receives, the more pronounced is the silvery coloration.

This gorgeous plant is sensational in almost any shady setting. It's spectacular in groupings or sweeps, but also combines beautifully with any number of other shade plants, from bold hostas to delicate epimediums. A favorite with gardeners who grow spring-blooming bulbs and wildflowers, Japanese painted fern appears in the nick of time in late spring. It is sensitive to cold and fronds can be damaged by an early freeze, but it will send up new leaves once the weather warms; covering the plants can help protect them.

GOOD CHOICES: 'Pictum' has more pronounced coloration; 'Ursula's Red', 'Silver Falls'; a related species native to the United States is *A. filix-femina*

Aurinia saxatilis
Basket-of-Gold

SIZE (height × width): 1 to 2 feet × 1 foot
BLOOM DESCRIPTION: clusters of small blooms
BLOOM PERIOD: spring
EXPOSURE: full sun
HARDY IN ZONES: 3 to 8
SPECIAL NOTES: wonderful companion for spring bulbs

A trailing, sprawling plant, basket-of-gold is covered with cheerful color every spring. It looks wonderful spilling over walls or the edges of containers, windowboxes, or raised beds, and weaving among your spring-blooming bulbs. The densely packed, tiny flowers are usually bright, buttery yellow, though a few other colors are available.

Beneath this color are fuzzy, gray-green leaves and a tough, drought-tolerant plant. However, after blooming is over, the hummock form can get a bit rangy and bedraggled-looking, so it's best to trim the plants back by about a third at that point. They'll return in full glory next spring.

GOOD CHOICE: peachy-hued 'Sunny Border Apricot'

Baptisia australis
False Indigo, False Blue Indigo
SIZE (height × width): 3 to 4 feet × 2 to 3 feet
BLOOM DESCRIPTION: blue spikes
BLOOM PERIOD: early summer
EXPOSURE: full sun to partial shade
HARDY IN ZONES: 3 to 9
SPECIAL NOTES: deer resistant

Bergenia cordifolia
Bergenia
SIZE (height × width): 1 to 1¹/₂ feet × 1 foot
BLOOM DESCRIPTION: clusters of rosy bells
BLOOM PERIOD: spring
EXPOSURE: partial shade
HARDY IN ZONES: 3 to 8
SPECIAL NOTES: deer resistant

An easy and pretty choice for poor-to-average soil, false indigo soon forms a nice, shrubby profile that is adorned with blue flower spires early every summer. These remain on the plant for weeks on end, and also make a nice, airy addition to home-grown bouquets. *Baptisia* is a member of the pea family, so the flowers somewhat resemble related flowers, including sweet peas and lupines. When they fade, they're replaced by intriguing, pendulous brown seedpods.

Once established, false indigo is quite durable, self-sufficient, and tolerant of dry spells. The drought tolerance is due to the plant's deep tap-root. So be sure to site it where you want it to stay, because digging up and successfully moving a mature plant is tricky.

GOOD CHOICES: the species or its white-flowered relative *B. alba;* 'Purple Smoke' is a hybrid between the two species

Big, bold, shiny cabbage-like leaves make this tough plant stand out. In fall, as cooler weather arrives, it often turns handsome shades of bronze, russet, or purple. And in mild climates, the foliage remains all winter. Overexposure to hot sun or too-dry soil can make the edges brown, so site appropriately and keep the plants moist during dry spells. Bergenia looks terrific as a tall ground-cover on a slope (provided it receives adequate moisture), or as part of a shade display.

The flowers, which appear in spring, are gorgeous, if fleeting. Arising on reddish stalks above the clump of leaves, they are topped with lush trusses of small, bell-shaped flowers. Particularly dramatic are the crimson flowers of 'Evening Glow' and the pink-blushed white ones of 'Silver Light'.

GOOD CHOICES: 'Evening Glow' ('Abenglut'); 'Silver Light' ('Silberlicht')

Boltonia asteroides
Boltonia

SIZE (height × width): 4 to 6 feet × 2 to 4 feet
BLOOM DESCRIPTION: small white daisies
BLOOM PERIOD: late summer into fall
EXPOSURE: full sun
HARDY IN ZONES: 4 to 9
SPECIAL NOTES: deer resistant

For lots of bright, billowing color late in the season, boltonia is unbeatable. All summer long it develops into a substantial, somewhat sprawling plant of willowy, gray-green foliage. Then, in August, it leaps into the spotlight with an extravagant flower show when small yellow-centered white daisies completely cover the plant.

Its only requirement is lots of sunshine. If your garden soil is naturally moist and fertile, boltonia will thrive for years with little attention. It even does well in drier soils, though it may not grow as tall or lush.

Boltonia is a natural in combination with other late-blooming perennials, especially asters. The combination is also fun in bouquets. For best flowering and color, grow the popular cultivar 'Snowbank'.

GOOD CHOICES: 'Snowbank'; 'Pink Beauty'

Brunnera macrophylla
Perennial Forget-Me-Not

SIZE (height × width): 1 to 2 feet × 1 to 2 feet
BLOOM DESCRIPTION: sprays of tiny blue flowers
BLOOM PERIOD: late spring to early summer
EXPOSURE: morning sun to partial shade
HARDY IN ZONES: 3 to 8
SPECIAL NOTES: deer resistant

Everyone loves this charmer's flowers, which are produced in sprays of dainty little electric-blue blossoms with yellow-centers. It will grow well in partial shade in most soils (provided it remains evenly moist).

The foliage is also attractive. Large and heart-shaped, the leaves spread out to form a handsome clump. For a bit more sparkle in shadier settings, try the silver-leaved cultivar 'Jack Frost'.

Perennial forget-me-not is a splendid plant to include in your woodland garden. The delicate bright blue flowers look lovely with grape hyacinths and small-flowered daffodils, and the foliage provides an attractive, bold texture for the rest of the season, contrasting with delicate-leaved plants such as ferns and astilbes.

GOOD CHOICES: 'Jack Frost'; 'Langtrees'

Campanula species
Bellflower

SIZE (height × width): varies
BLOOM DESCRIPTION: cup-shaped or tubular bells
BLOOM PERIOD: late spring to summer
EXPOSURE: full sun to partial shade
HARDY IN ZONES: 3 to 9
SPECIAL NOTES: sensitive to hot, humid weather

Lovers of full sun or light shade, campanulas are easy to grow in cooler climates. The bell-shaped flowers are pretty and confer a cottage-garden feel to any flowerbed. Most are in the china-blue, purple, and white range, colors that fit in well almost anywhere. They also make nice cut flowers.

Low-growing *Campanula carpatica* forms 6- to 8-inch-high mounds that are studded with cup-shaped blossoms for weeks on end. For the most consistent and long-lasting color, seek out the superb duo, 'Blue Clips' and 'White Clips'. These are great in the front of a perennial border, but they will also thrive in a container or windowbox.

Taller campanulas are naturals for mid- or rear-border settings. These send up spires several feet high that are adorned with more elongated bells on all sides of the stem. *Campanula persicifolia* has larger flowers and blooms till midsummer in most areas, making it a splendid companion for peonies and irises.

GOOD CHOICES: low-growers 'Blue Clips' and
 'White Clips'; taller *C. persicifolia*

Centranthus ruber
Valerian, Jupiter's Beard

SIZE (height × width): 1 to 3 feet × 1 to 2 feet
BLOOM DESCRIPTION: loose clusters
BLOOM PERIOD: all summer
EXPOSURE: full sun to partial shade
HARDY IN ZONES: 5 to 8
SPECIAL NOTES: best in cooler climates

Few other perennials can match valerian's long-lasting bloom and easy nature. The branching stems are strong and sturdy, and clothed in smooth, bluish-green leaves. Tiered flower stalks rise above, bearing plenty of lightly fragrant flower clusters. The typical color is raspberry-red (look for the excellent cultivar 'Coccineus'), though you can also find white ('Albus'). They remain in bloom for practically the entire summer, making them a great source of dependable color in a mixed perennial bed.

Valerian is at its best in average to sandy soil in full sun. It may flag in hot, humid weather. If your plants become floppy, it's safe to cut back the entire plant in the middle of the summer—it will rebound.

Be advised that valerian self-sows. So you sometimes find new plants popping up in surprising places, such as wedged among paving stones or in a rock wall. If you don't want it to wander, simply cut off the flowers before they go to seed.

GOOD CHOICES: raspberry-red 'Coccineus'; white 'Albus'

Ceratostigma plumbaginoides
Leadwort, Plumbago

SIZE (height × width): 6 to 12 inches × 1 to 2 feet
BLOOM DESCRIPTION: clusters of small electric blue flowers
BLOOM PERIOD: midsummer to fall
EXPOSURE: full sun to partial shade
HARDY IN ZONES: 6 to 9
SPECIAL NOTES: evergreen in milder climates

Chrysanthemum hybrids
Hardy Chrysanthemum, Hardy Mum

SIZE (height × width): 2 to 3 feet × 2 to 3 feet
BLOOM DESCRIPTION: "button" or daisy flowers
BLOOM PERIOD: late summer into late fall
EXPOSURE: full sun
HARDY IN ZONES: 4 to 9
SPECIAL NOTES: very cold hardy and durable

A pretty and reliable groundcover, leadwort is a superb choice for the front of a border, a difficult-to-landscape bank, a rock garden, or between rocks in a wall. It does well in full sun and partial shade alike, performing best in ground that is somewhat moist. The dark-green, diamond-shaped leaves are always attractive, and the clusters of 1-inch bright blue flowers are most welcome when they finally appear later in the summer.

The perky gentian-blue flowers continue well into fall and when they start to flag with the colder weather, the leaves return to the stage. Rather than turning brown or fading away, they turn bright red or orange—a welcome sight! So this is a good plant for any area where you want color later in the growing season.

In milder climates, Zone 8 and southward generally, leadwort maintains its green leaves right through the winter months. In any event, it's a good idea to cut back the plants when spring returns so it will produce fresh foliage.

GOOD CHOICE: There are no cultivars, so plant the species.

Good old hardy mums have seen an exciting explosion of new cultivars. Your local garden center (which may carry plants under the botanical name *Dendranthema*) will always have a handful of choices, but bigger nurseries and mail-order catalogs are capitalizing on the trend and offer dozens of fantastic new choices. Some look like plush daisies, and others are full and fluffy. There are solid colors and ones with contrasting centers. All are extraordinarily durable, standing up to fall rains, cold nights, and windy days.

To get the most out of your mum displays: Buy field-grown or potted plants early and get them in the ground early, so they can become established and generate strong root growth to carry them through the rest of the season—and so you can enjoy a longer show. Aficionados take care never to let the plants dry out as the summer progresses and pinch back or remove buds for bigger fall blooms (for exact details, ask someone who already does this, but the general rule is to remove unwanted side buds until midsummer, then stop pinching).

GOOD CHOICES: *C.* × 'Ryan's Yellow'; *C.* × *rubellum* 'Clara Curtis'; 'Rosetta'

Cimicifuga racemosa
Bugbane, Fairy Candles
SIZE (height × width): 3 to 6 feet × 3 feet
BLOOM DESCRIPTION: white spires
BLOOM PERIOD: mid- to late summer
EXPOSURE: full sun to partial shade
HARDY IN ZONES: 3 to 8
SPECIAL NOTES: not tolerant of hot, humid weather

In the middle of an island bed or against a backdrop such as a wall, fence, or evergreen shrub, this imposing plant is spectacular. It is also trouble-free and long-lived, requiring little more than moist soil, especially when in bloom.

It begins the season by forming a dense cluster of very dark green, much-divided foliage that can be up to 3 feet tall and wide. Then, in midsummer, leafless stalks rise up an additional 2 or 3 feet and wave dramatic white candelabra flower spires that last for many weeks. If you can't find it as *Cimicifuga racemosa*, try looking for *Actaea racemosa*, which is synonymous.

GOOD CHOICES: shorter versions include *C. ramosa* or
  C. simplex 'White Pearl'

Convallaria majalis
Lily-of-the-Valley
SIZE (height × width): 6 to 12 inches × infinite
BLOOM DESCRIPTION: dainty white bells
BLOOM PERIOD: spring
EXPOSURE: partial to full shade
HARDY IN ZONES: 2 to 8
SPECIAL NOTES: deer resistant, sensitive to heat and humidity

A sweep or carpet of lily-of-the-valley in a shady spot in your yard makes an excellent groundcover— an established stand of it is lustrous and beautiful and excludes weeds. It works well under trees or in north-facing locations where few other plants will thrive.

Or you may grow lily-of-the-valley for sentimental reasons, because it reminds you of childhood memories or a favorite aunt. Every spring, little stems rise up level with the leaves, adorned with dainty white bells that waft one of the sweetest scents imaginable. Some gardeners even pick these for small but charming bouquets. (You might even be able to find the pink-flowered version, called 'Rosea'.)

Moist, organically rich soil is best for this plant. There are rarely any pest or disease problems. This is truly a trouble-free groundcover.

GOOD CHOICE: 'Rosea'

Coreopsis species
Coreopsis, Tickseed

SIZE (height × width): 1 to 3 feet × 2 to 3 feet
BLOOM DESCRIPTION: small yellow daisies
BLOOM PERIOD: summer
EXPOSURE: full sun
HARDY IN ZONES: 5 to 9
SPECIAL NOTES: drought tolerant, deer resistant

No perennial garden should be without this deservedly popular perennial. Not only is it especially long blooming—established plants bloom generously for months on end—but it is also tough and durable. Coreopsis will provide plenty of color for very little effort.

Best of all, easygoing coreopsis combines so well with other plants. Its airy, weaving habit allows it to fit in and among all sorts of other perennials, giving a garden a lush, casual look that is very appealing. And the colors of coreopsis look good with other flowers. There are bright yellow ones like the fluffy-petaled 'Sunray', versatile lemon-yellow ones like 'Moonbeam', and, in recent years, some welcome pink-hued newcomers, notably 'Sweet Dreams'.

GOOD CHOICES: *C. verticillata* 'Moonbeam'
and 'Zagreb'; *C. grandiflora* 'Sunray'; *C. rosea*
'Sweet Dreams'; *C. lanceolata* 'Tequila Sunrise'

Crocosmia hybrids
Crocosmia, Montbretia

SIZE (height × width): 2 to 3 feet × 1 to 2 feet
BLOOM DESCRIPTION: panicles of many small flowers
BLOOM PERIOD: mid- to late summer
EXPOSURE: full sun to partial shade
HARDY IN ZONES: 5 to 9
SPECIAL NOTES: superb late-season color

For a vibrant dash of late-season color, few plants can equal crocosmia. Erect grass-like clumps of foliage are a nice contribution to any perennial display throughout the season, but are finally joined in mid- to late summer by spectacular flowers, vaguely reminiscent of miniature gladiolus blooms. Ranging from soft lemon yellow to hot orange to scarlet, they generate a lot of excitement. If you have the room, it's a great idea to grow several different cultivars together to get a fiery show. Or, for a show-stopping combination, mix them with purple-hued flowers, either in the garden or a vase.

The plants arise from small corms and perform best in milder climates. Any site in full sun with humus-rich soil will do. Gardeners in colder climates can still grow them; simply dig up the corms in fall and store them over the winter as you would gladiolus.

GOOD CHOICES: scarlet 'Lucifer'; yellow 'George
Davidson'; orange-red 'Star of the East'; brilliant
reddish-orange 'Severn Seas'

Delphinium elatum
Delphinium, Larkspur

SIZE (height × width): 3 to 8 feet × 2 to 3 feet
BLOOM DESCRIPTION: tall, dense spires
BLOOM PERIOD: spring into summer
EXPOSURE: full sun
HARDY IN ZONES: 3 to 9
SPECIAL NOTES: may need staking, doesn't like heat and humidity

Success with this perennial garden classic eludes some gardeners, but it shouldn't. First, choose wisely. If you cannot plant your delphiniums in an area sheltered by a fence, wall, or shrubbery, select stockier, lower-growing types. Generally speaking, newer varieties are your best choice because hybridizers have been concentrating on creating ones that stand up better, have denser flower spires, and are better able to handle hot and humid weather.

The other secret to wonderful delphiniums is the right soil. Organically rich soil that is moist yet drains well is ideal. Replenish the area's organic matter every spring and every fall, and maintain a layer of good organic mulch at all times. For best results, also feed your plants monthly during the growing season with a balanced fertilizer.

The classic blue-purple ones, sometimes with contrasting white center "bees," are widely available. Mixes, such as 'New Heights' and 'Round Table', deliver a color-balanced show. If you have a pastel-themed bed, seek out the pink selections, such as 'Astolat' or 'Magic Cherry Blossom'. Pure white 'Galahad' is sensational.

GOOD CHOICES: 'Magic Fountain'; 'Pepe'

Dianthus cultivars
Pinks, Dianthus

SIZE (height × width): 6 to 12 inches × 12 inches
BLOOM DESCRIPTION: like a mini carnation
BLOOM PERIOD: spring to midsummer
EXPOSURE: full sun
HARDY IN ZONES: 3 to 8
SPECIAL NOTES: likes a slightly alkaline soil, deer resistant

Plush mounds of grassy foliage are studded with adorable old-fashioned flowers in late spring and on into summer. These resemble miniature carnations (to which they are related), and some radiate that signature spicy-sweet clove scent. They last a long time in the garden, and are suitable for small bouquets. Pinks are terrific for edging, placing in pots, or tucking in here and there near the front of a perennial border for perky, dependable blooms and attractive foliage.

Pinks get their common name not from their color—though you find them in varying hues of pink as well as red and white—but from the fringed or "pinked" petal edges. This feature adds fluffiness to their already abundant charm.

Rarely troubled by any pests or diseases, pinks are a cinch to grow well. All they really require is quick-draining soil (sandy loam is perfect) that's a little on the alkaline side. Gravel mulch is beneficial.

GOOD CHOICES: *D. caryophyllus* 'Cotillion'; *D. deltoides* 'Zing Rose'; *D. plumarius* 'Pink Spray'; 'Raspberry Crush'; 'Royal Velvet'; red-eyed white 'Side Kick'; *D. gratianopolitanus* cultivars, especially 'Bath's Pink'

Dicentra spectabilis
Bleeding Heart

SIZE (height × width): 2 to 3 feet × 2 feet
BLOOM DESCRIPTION: pink and white "lockets"
BLOOM PERIOD: spring
EXPOSURE: full to partial shade
HARDY IN ZONES: 2 to 8
SPECIAL NOTES: may go dormant in summer

Bleeding heart's ferny, much-divided foliage forms a beautiful, loose mound about as wide as it is tall. Every spring, the endearing little (1 inch or so) locket-shaped flowers line the arching stems. They come in pink and white or pure white ('Alba') and last an amazingly long time—up to six weeks— while other spring bloomers come and go. Pure pink flowers adorn the closely related but slightly smaller species of *D. formosa* and *D. eximia*; a good cultivar is 'Luxuriant'.

Because of its larger size and loose but graceful profile, bleeding heart is a dramatic addition to any shady perennial garden. It is also often employed in early spring bulb displays because it effectively covers over and distracts from those flowers when they fade and while you wait for their foliage to die down. If your summers get hot or your shade garden's soil tends to dry out as the season progresses, your bleeding heart plants will yellow and die back, becoming dormant until next spring.

GOOD CHOICES: 'Alba'; 'Luxuriant'

Digitalis purpurea
Foxglove

SIZE (height × width): 3 to 5 feet × 2 to 3 feet
BLOOM DESCRIPTION: tubular bells on tall spires
BLOOM PERIOD: early to midsummer
EXPOSURE: full sun to partial shade
HARDY IN ZONES: 4 to 8
SPECIAL NOTES: deer resistant

So easy, and so enchanting! Tall spires of foxglove rise up in the spring and show off their numerous lovely tubular bell flowers. Newer, improved varieties abound, including large-flowered ones that remain in bloom for many weeks and ones with especially vivid or unusual coloration. Look for the aptly named 'Apricot' or glowing white 'Alba'. Or get a range of lovely hues for little effort by growing a good mix such as Excelsior Hybrids or 'Giant Shirley'. If a shorter, smaller foxglove is your wish, strawberry-pink *D. × mertonensis*, at 2 to 3 feet, is an excellent choice.

Technically, most foxgloves are biennial, meaning they have a two-year life cycle: The first year is spent in root and rosette (plant) development, and blooms arise in the second season. But foxgloves love to self-sow, so once you a have a few growing in your displays, there will always be more.

GOOD CHOICES: 'Apricot'; Excelsior Hybrids Mix; 'Giant Shirley' Mix

Echinacea purpurea
Purple Coneflower
SIZE (height × width): 2 to 4 feet × 1 to 2 feet
BLOOM DESCRIPTION: orange centers and dark pink petals
BLOOM PERIOD: summer
EXPOSURE: full sun
HARDY IN ZONES: 3 to 9
SPECIAL NOTES: deer resistant, heat tolerant

Purple coneflower's remarkable popularity with perennial gardeners is a real Cinderella story. Originally an ordinary prairie and meadow wildflower, it soon was brought into the garden and improved. The shuttlecock-shaped blooms come in wonderfully vibrant hues, are larger than ever (up to 6 inches across), and the plants are more compact and sturdy. Yet the plant retains all the virtues of its wild ancestors: long-lasting blooms that look great in bouquets, fresh or dried; strong stems that never need staking; and robust, drought-tolerant growth.

The orange-to-bronze cone or seedhead that appears so prominently in the middle of each flower is an irresistible landing pad for butterflies in summer and migrating songbirds in fall—two more good reasons to invite this outstanding plant into your perennial borders.

This perennial is gaining even more popularity with new varieties being introduced that are fragrant and have new colors such as orange.

GOOD CHOICES: white 'Alba'; two-tiered 'Doppelganger'™; purple-pink 'Magnus'; 'Orange Meadowbrite'™ ('Art's Pride')

Echinops ritro
Globe Thistle
SIZE (height × width): 2 to 4 feet × 1 to 2 feet
BLOOM DESCRIPTION: spiky, blue balls
BLOOM PERIOD: summer
EXPOSURE: full sun
HARDY IN ZONES: 3 to 8
SPECIAL NOTES: deer resistant, needs good drainage

The 1- to 2-inch, globe-shaped flower heads, topping strong stems, are composed of many tiny florets. They come in blue hues—the best are silvery blue 'Taplow Blue' and deeper, darker 'Veitch's Blue'. The color holds up very well in the garden but also lasts in a vase and is great for dried-flower arrangements. Globe thistle combines well with yellow flowers, including daylilies and coreopsis. It's also wonderful with upright blue bloomers such as verbena.

Because of its medium height and the fact that its lower leaves tend to dry up and fade away, not to mention its somewhat coarse foliage, globe thistle is ideally sited towards the middle or back of a perennial garden. Its handsome blooms will rise up and deliver dependable color for practically the whole summer.

GOOD CHOICE: 'Taplow Blue'; 'Veitch's Blue'

Epimedium cultivars and hybrids
Epimedium, Barrenwort

SIZE (height × width): 6 to 12 inches × 12 to 18 inches
BLOOM DESCRIPTION: small, spurred
BLOOM PERIOD: spring
EXPOSURE: partial to full shade
HARDY IN ZONES: 5 to 8
SPECIAL NOTES: especially pretty as a groundcover

An outstanding groundcover that deserves wider use, epimedium combines natural toughness with delicate beauty. The pretty, oblong, heart-shaped leaves are carried on wiry stems. They're reddish when they first emerge in spring, and change to red-tinged green over the summer. A flurry of small, spurred flowers join the show briefly in spring—*E. × rubrum* has red ones, while *E. versicolor* 'Sulphureum' has yellow flowers.

Epimedium prefers damp shade but will also do well in traditionally difficult sites such as under a tree or in a dry shade area.

GOOD CHOICES: *E. × rubrum*; *E. versicolor* 'Sulphureum'

Erigeron cultivars and hybrids
Seaside Daisy, Fleabane

SIZE (height × width): 1 to 2 feet × 2 feet
BLOOM DESCRIPTION: small daisies
BLOOM PERIOD: all summer
EXPOSURE: full sun to partial shade
HARDY IN ZONES: 5 to 8
SPECIAL NOTES: deer resistant

For a full summer of perky, colorful daisies, this carefree plant is hard to beat. The centers always boast a big boss of golden stamens, and the dense fringe of "ray flowers" (petals) comes in bright colors. One species is violet-blue; look for a terrific newer cultivar called 'Sea Breeze', which is pink. A robust plant, clothed with gray-green foliage, seaside daisy blooms from early summer till fall. For best performance, cut the plant back between flowering cycles.

Because seaside daisy is such a reliable bloomer, it's ideal for borders where you want continuous color, or as an edging plant. It is tolerant of well-drained, moderately fertile soil, and loves full sun.

GOOD CHOICE: 'Sea Breeze'

Eryngium alpinum
Sea Holly

SIZE (height × width): 3 to 5 feet × 1 to 3 feet
BLOOM DESCRIPTION: prickly flower heads
BLOOM PERIOD: summer to early fall
EXPOSURE: full sun
HARDY IN ZONES: 4 to 8
SPECIAL NOTES: excellent as a dried flower, deer resistant

A ruff of spiny bracts surrounds fascinating teasel-shaped flower heads; a multibranched plant full of these is a dramatic sight. Stiff stems, usually blue or silver-blue, that don't require staking hold them aloft. The deepest-colored one to date is the gorgeous 'Blue Star'. One plant, or a trio, looks terrific among other blue-hued perennials or in a bed of mixed primary colors. Sea holly also makes an excellent dried flower.

The foliage and stems are not as thistlelike as you might expect from the appearance of the flowers. The basal leaves tend to be smooth and rounded. Sea holly is drought tolerant once established, because it sends down a deep, carrotlike taproot. So you should plant it where you want it to stay and refrain from dividing it—successfully digging up a full-grown plant is tricky.

GOOD CHOICE: 'Blue Star'

Erysimum species
Wallflower

SIZE (height × width): 2 to 3 feet × 1 to 2 feet
BLOOM DESCRIPTION: stalks of small clustered blooms
BLOOM PERIOD: mid-spring to early summer; repeats
EXPOSURE: full sun
HARDY IN ZONES: 3 to 8
SPECIAL NOTES: not tolerant of heat and humidity

For a flush of early color, wallflower is splendid. Bright flowers—purple, mauve, lavender, yellow or orange, depending on species—are borne in terminal racemes. These are not densely packed, but rather loose, pretty clusters, each individual flower with only four petals. They waft a sweet delightful fragrance over the garden, especially when grown in groups or massed in sweeps.

A resilient plant of lance-shaped, gray-green foliage, wallflower tolerates even poor soil and grows to medium height. So it's a good citizen in a mixed border, especially in front of taller perennials that come into bloom later. Some gardeners enjoy wallflower among spring-blooming bulbs, where it brings refreshing, ongoing color throughout the spring months.

The British have long valued wallflower in their gardens, and adding some to yours confers an instant British cottage garden feel. The Brits have also worked to extend the color range of this excellent, reliable plant. One of the finest is purple-flowered 'Bowles Mauve'.

GOOD CHOICES: 'Bowles Mauve'; 'Variegatum'

Eupatorium maculatum
Joe-Pye Weed

SIZE (height × width): 4 to 6 feet × 2 to 4 feet
BLOOM DESCRIPTION: large, loose terminal clusters
BLOOM PERIOD: summer into early fall
EXPOSURE: full sun to partial shade
HARDY IN ZONES: 3 to 10
SPECIAL NOTES: deer resistant

With little more than damp soil and full sun, Joe-Pye weed can be counted on to deliver a fabulous performance. The strong, erect stems are wine red and tall, and clothed in handsome, toothed leaves that may grow as long as a foot. Atop the imposing stems in late summer, you get dazzling flowers—usually pinkish-purple, they draw butterflies like a magnet. The cultivar 'Gateway' is a bit shorter, and has darker colored flowers and darker stems.

Because it is such a big, spectacular plant, Joe-Pye weed is best sited to the back of a border, where it will provide a nice backdrop for other perennials throughout the summer—and then deliver plentiful color later in the season. Essentially trouble-free, it is one of the easiest, most exciting tall perennials.

GOOD CHOICE: 'Gateway'

Euphorbia species
Spurge

SIZE (height × width): varies with the species or cultivar
BLOOM DESCRIPTION: umbels or globe-shaped clusters
BLOOM PERIOD: spring into early summer
EXPOSURE: full sun to partial shade
HARDY IN ZONES: 5 to 9
SPECIAL NOTES: deer resistant

"Green-on-green" is the best way to describe this unique flowering perennial. Prized by many gardeners for its handsome, usually mounding form, the dense foliage is typically dark green or blue green and arranged along the stem like a bottlebrush. Extra drama may be provided by purple-leaved forms such as *E. amygdaloides* 'Purpurea', and those with red-tinted leaves, such as *E. griffithii* 'Fireglow' or 'Dixter'.

The flowers, which technically are colored "bracts," are borne terminally on the stems and are typically vivid chartreuse green. They make a noble contribution to any flowering border.

You can get the most out of the green-on-green show with cushion spurge (*E. polychroma*), which grows 12 to 18 inches high. Enjoy its citrus-yellow flowers in spring, lime-green foliage by summer, and russet or red leaves in the fall. *Euphorbia* species have a milky sap that is poisonous and may cause skin irritations similar to poison oak on some people. It's best to wear gloves when handling the plants.

GOOD CHOICES: *E. amygdaloides* 'Purpurea'; *E. robbiae*;
   E. griffithii 'Fireglow'; *E. polychroma*

Filipendula rubra
Queen-of-the-Prairie, Meadowsweet

SIZE (height × width): 6 to 8 feet × 3 to 4 feet
BLOOM DESCRIPTION: large plumes
BLOOM PERIOD: early to midsummer
EXPOSURE: full sun to partial shade
HARDY IN ZONES: 3 to 9
SPECIAL NOTES: requires damp soil

If you have an area of damp soil on your property that you would like to fill with exuberant, low-maintenance color, this is your plant. It's a towering, bushy plant (up to 8 feet high when mature) that bursts forth early every summer with gorgeous plumes atop strong stems. They're pink or lavender-pink. Deep rose-pink ones are available on the cultivar 'Venusta'. The plumes are composed of myriad tiny flowers, but so many that the plume itself can be up to 9 inches long.

The jagged foliage is dark green and plentiful. In or out of bloom, queen-of-the-prairie is terrific in clumps, in front of a wall or fence, or along the back of a moist-soil border. If your garden is smaller or your plans less ambitious, try the dwarf version, pink-flowered 'Kahome'.

GOOD CHOICES: 'Venusta'; 'Kahome'

Gaillardia × *grandiflora*
Blanket Flower

Back

SIZE (height × width): 2 to 3 feet × 1 to 2 feet
BLOOM DESCRIPTION: large red and yellow daisies
BLOOM PERIOD: summer
EXPOSURE: full sun
HARDY IN ZONES: 3 to 9
SPECIAL NOTES: deer resistant

Constantly covered with vivacious red-and-yellow blooms, blanket flower is as vivid as an Indian blanket. The plant forms tidy clumps of somewhat fuzzy, trouble-free foliage. Once established, it performs very consistently.

It's also an undemanding plant, thriving easily in poor soil, drought conditions, and long, hot summers. A natural for low-maintenance borders, this cheerful plant looks great with other bright colors, including yellow daisies or coreopsis, or red salvia. Solid-color versions are also available; one of the best is wine-red 'Burgundy', which combines beautifully with blue perennials such as veronica. For the front of a border or container display, try the dwarf cultivar, 'Goblin'.

GOOD CHOICES: 'Burgundy'; 'Fanfare'; 'Goblin'

Galium odoratum
Sweet Woodruff
SIZE (height × width): 6 to 12 inches × 12 inches
BLOOM DESCRIPTION: tiny white stars
BLOOM PERIOD: spring
EXPOSURE: partial to full shade
HARDY IN ZONES: 4 to 8
SPECIAL NOTES: both leaves and flowers have a sweet scent

Gaura lindheimeri
Gaura, Wandflower *hillside*
SIZE (height × width): 2 to 3 feet × 1 to 3 feet
BLOOM DESCRIPTION: small delicate blooms, pink or white
BLOOM PERIOD: summer
EXPOSURE: full sun
HARDY IN ZONES: 5 to 10
SPECIAL NOTES: deer resistant, performs best in hot summers

An enchanting groundcover for woodland or other shady settings, sweet woodruff is easy to grow and full of charm. Try it on an embankment, along walkways, under trees, or weaving throughout your shade displays. It tolerates both wet and dry soil and is very durable. It doesn't, however, like heat and humidity.

Its long, thin, apple-green leaves occur in whorls and spread slowly but surely over the years to densely cover large areas. Each spring, the plants are studded with tiny, dainty, white flowers (just 1/4 inch across).

The name refers to the fact that both the leaves and those tiny flowers are scented when dried. Some craftspeople like to add sweet woodruff to the stuffing in pillows. Sprigs are also used to flavor a traditional German homemade wine, known as May wine.

GOOD CHOICE: there are no cultivars, so plant
the species.

A lovely wildflower for sunny areas, gaura's easy-going grace has captured the attention of plant breeders in recent years. One result is less straggly, more compact versions, notably 'Siskiyou Pink' and 'Sunny Butterflies'. New and better colors, and more flowers per plant, are also now available, including the vivid hues of 'Siskiyou Pink', as well as hot pink 'Crimson Butterflies'. There's even a version with gold-margined foliage called 'Corrie's Gold'.

Common to all of these is the wonderful durability of the species. Established plants have a sturdy, fleshy taproot and are quite drought tolerant as a result, though well-drained soil is still important. Gardeners in the hot, humid South are especially enthusiastic about gaura, because it thrives despite scorching heat and high humidity.

Gaura's arching wands of sweet little flowers weave naturally into any sunny perennial display and also make a nice accent in homegrown bouquets. Gaura plants are also fabulous among rosebushes, especially ones with complementary flowers of pink, white, or red.

GOOD CHOICES: 'Corrie's Gold'; 'Crimson Butterflies';
'Siskiyou Pink'; 'Sunny Butterflies'; 'Passionate Pink'

Geranium cultivars and hybrids
Hardy Geranium, Cranesbill

SIZE (height × width): 1 to 2 feet × 1 to 2 feet
BLOOM DESCRIPTION: saucer shaped
BLOOM PERIOD: varies; spring or summer
EXPOSURE: full sun to partial shade
HARDY IN ZONES: 5 to 9
SPECIAL NOTES: prefers well-drained soil

Geum cultivars
Geum, Avens

SIZE (height × width): 1 to 2 feet × 1 to 2 feet
BLOOM DESCRIPTION: small, buttercup-like
BLOOM PERIOD: late spring to early summer
EXPOSURE: full sun to partial shade
HARDY IN ZONES: 3 to 7
SPECIAL NOTES: best performance in cooler areas

Among the prettiest and most trouble-free of all perennials, hardy geraniums are valuable not only for their pretty, saucer-shaped blooms, but for their ability to create an attractive groundcover. The leaves of most species are palm-shaped or deeply lobed or cut; some turn red or orange in autumn, adding a nice unexpected splash of late color.

If you mass your hardy geraniums—all of a kind, or mix-and-match—you get an especially handsome groundcover. Otherwise, individual plants may be used in the front of a border or along pathways, where they can be relied upon for their informal charm.

One of the most popular ones is a bright-blue bloomer called 'Johnson's Blue', which is especially wonderful as a "weaver" among other perennials. Many lovely pink-hued ones are also available, such as the superb *G. endressi* 'Wargrave Pink' and the electric magenta blooms (with chartreuse foliage) of 'Ann Folkard'. For groundcover use, try dwarf *G. cinereum* 'Purple Pillow', which is studded with small, deep purple flowers, or *G. sanguineum*, which comes in magenta, white, or white with pink veins.

GOOD CHOICES: 'Brookside', 'Boone'; 'Johnson's Blue'

This very showy bloomer gets a lot of mileage out of its relatively small 1-inch flowers, thanks to their profusion and their bright colors. In the red-yellow-orange range, they bring welcome vibrancy to late spring and early summer. They're especially splendid in combination with the small blue flowers of *Brunnera*. The most popular cultivar is the fiery orange-red 'Mrs. Bradshaw', but a red as pure as scarlet 'Red Wings' is hard to come by. Geums also make excellent cut flowers.

Full sun and well-drained soil guarantee a great show. Soggy ground is fatal, so take care not to site in a low spot or in poorly drained ground; never overwater the plants.

GOOD CHOICES: *G. chiloense* 'Mrs. Bradshaw';
   G. coccineum 'Red Wings'; *G. hybrid* 'Mangolassi'

Gypsophila paniculata
Baby's Breath
SIZE (height × width): 1¹/₂ to 4 feet × 3 to 4 feet
BLOOM DESCRIPTION: masses of tiny little button blooms
BLOOM PERIOD: summer
EXPOSURE: full sun
HARDY IN ZONES: 3 to 9
SPECIAL NOTES: likes slightly alkaline soil

Helenium autumnale
Sneezeweed
SIZE (height × width): 3 to 4 feet × 1 to 2 feet
BLOOM DESCRIPTION: small daisies with prominent centers
BLOOM PERIOD: late summer
EXPOSURE: full sun
HARDY IN ZONES: 3 to 10
SPECIAL NOTES: it does not trigger allergic reactions

So familiar as a bouquet accent from the florist, baby's breath is also quite easy to grow yourself for your own flower arrangements. The plant is full and billowing, so allow it sufficient elbowroom. It also does best in slightly alkaline soil and is known for thriving in lean, rocky, well-drained soils.

Once established, baby's breath is an incredibly abundant bloomer. Those adorable little button flowers literally cover the plant. It's certainly safe to snip off stems even when the plant is in full bloom because it will continue to produce more. Improved versions with plusher, double flowers are now common; 'Bristol Fairy' is the best. For something different and equally pretty, try 'Pink Fairy'.

GOOD CHOICES: 'Bristol Fairy'; 'Pink Fairy'

Late every summer, branched stems arise from a medium-size clump of dark green leaves. These are topped by 2-inch daisylike flowers, each with a plush, prominent center surrounded by notched petals. The species is all yellow, a bright and lively sight. Several cultivars are also worthwhile, including bronze-red 'Moerheim Beauty' and aptly named 'Brilliant', which is a rich orange with a darker center.

Sneezeweed is not really a fair name, for this perky bloomer doesn't generate offensive pollen. Most likely it got its unfortunate moniker from its tendency to bloom at the same time as the real culprit, the far less attractive ragweed. The origin of the name "sneezeweed" could come from the old practice of using the dried leaves to make snuff.

For best results, grow this plant in moist ground. If it becomes rangy, it's safe to cut it back to about a foot high in midsummer. You'll still get your late-season flower display.

GOOD CHOICES: 'Brilliant'; 'Ruby Dwarf'; 'Wyndley';
  'Red Army'

Helianthus × *multiflorus*
Perennial Sunflower
SIZE (height × width): 4 to 6 feet × 2 to 3 feet
BLOOM DESCRIPTION: yellow daisies
BLOOM PERIOD: midsummer into fall
EXPOSURE: full sun
HARDY IN ZONES: 5 to 9
SPECIAL NOTES: a large plant, so allow plenty of space

These hybrid sunflowers are a wonderful perennial alternative to the huge annual sunflowers. True, they're not as big—the flowers are generally 3 to 5 inches across—but the plants are more manageable, growing up to 5 feet tall with a lesser spread. Space permitting, allow one or two a spot towards the back of your sunny perennial garden, and they'll thrill you every year with their generous, exuberant show.

Among the cultivated varieties are a number of doubles, meaning that the flowers have a double load of petals. It makes them look almost like chrysanthemum or dahlia blooms (with which they share a bloom time and look splendid with, in the garden or in a vase). Double 'Flore Pleno' is excellent.

GOOD CHOICE: 'Flore Pleno'

Helleborus orientalis
Hellebore, Lenten Rose
SIZE (height × width): 1$\frac{1}{2}$ feet × 2 feet
BLOOM DESCRIPTION: nodding, slightly cup-shaped
BLOOM PERIOD: early spring
EXPOSURE: partial to full shade
HARDY IN ZONES: 4 to 8
SPECIAL NOTES: deer resistant

Once the province of expert perennial gardeners, the hellebore secret is now out and being trumpeted by ordinary gardeners. Hellebores are easy and they're gorgeous, and bring wonderful color to early spring. For best results, plant your hellebores in moist ground in partial shade, and protect their roots with a light mulch.

Hellebores are now offered with flowers in lime green to royal purple, sometimes with subtle shadings or accenting freckles. Fluffy-petaled, speckled double white 'Betty Ranicar' is breathtaking; dark purple 'Blue Lady' stands out against melting patches of snow. Best of all may be the mixes, which give you a chance to sample the variety this unusually beautiful plant has to offer. The Royal Heritage™ Mix is widely available; these often remain in bloom for an astounding three months.

GOOD CHOICES: Royal Heritage™ Hybrids; 'Betty Ranicar'; 'Blue Lady'

Hemerocallis cultivars and hybrids
Daylily

SIZE (height × width): 1 to 3 feet × 1 to 3 feet
BLOOM DESCRIPTION: trumpet-shaped to spidery blooms
BLOOM PERIOD: all summer
EXPOSURE: full sun to partial shade
HARDY IN ZONES: 3 to 10
SPECIAL NOTES: individual blossoms really do only last a day

Heuchera cultivars and hybrids
Coral Bells, Alumroot

SIZE (height × width): 1 to 2 feet (blooming) × 1 to 2 feet
BLOOM DESCRIPTION: tiny bells arrayed along slender stems
BLOOM PERIOD: late spring into early summer
EXPOSURE: partial shade
HARDY IN ZONES: 3 to 9
SPECIAL NOTES: many gorgeous foliage colors available

No perennial garden should be without at least a few daylilies, if not an entire bed or band of them somewhere prominent. Daylilies are so colorful, so dependable, so long blooming, and so easy to grow that few other plants can even begin to rival them. Just give them fertile, well-drained soil. Remove flowers as they fade to keep the plant looking neat—yes, individual flowers really do only last a single day.

Recent years have brought an explosion of outstanding cultivars. There are literally hundreds, so don't settle for plain old orange or yellow if you want something more exciting. Browse specialty catalogs and feast your eyes on the amazing range of choices. Among the more appealing hues are gorgeous peach-colored ones with lavender throats, nonfading crimsons with golden throats, and even chartreuse selections. Grow your daylilies with other perennials, or devote an entire display to them. For a stouter plant and a fuller flower, choose a "tetraploid" variety. The best dwarf daylily for smaller spaces remains the popular, golden-hued 'Stella d'Oro'.

GOOD CHOICES: 'Stella d'Oro'; lemon yellow
 'Moon Traveler'; 'Happy Returns'

Despite the fact that one common name calls attention to its darling flowers, coral bells is extremely valuable as a foliage plant. Indeed, the recent flurry of hybridization has capitalized on the plant's leaf variations, resulting in the introduction of several beautiful plants. One of the first was big-leaved, bronzy-purple 'Palace Purple'. Dark purple leaves with lighter veining and splashes of silver make 'Cathedral Windows' irresistible, and 'Pewter Veil' starts out copper-pink but fades to pewter as the summer progresses (all the while retaining royal purple undersides). The handsome foliage is an asset to the front of a shady border among colorful flowers, ferns, and hostas, and traffic-stopping when planted in sweeps.

In spring, tall graceful stalks arch above the magnificent foliage, lined with tiny bells. They may be red, pink, or white, and while they don't last very long, they are pretty. A patch of coral bells in bloom has an enchanting, fairyland quality.

GOOD CHOICES: 'Palace Purple'; 'Cathedral Windows';
 'Pewter Veil'

Hibiscus moscheutos
Rose Mallow

SIZE (height × width): 4 to 6 feet × 3 to 4 feet
BLOOM DESCRIPTION: classic hibiscus flowers
BLOOM PERIOD: mid- to late summer
EXPOSURE: full sun
HARDY IN ZONES: 5 to 9
SPECIAL NOTES: fast growing

Related to the tropical tree hibiscus but cold hardy enough to be grown in most areas, rose mallow is a dramatic plant, providing big, bold color for late summer. The flowers are amazingly large, up to 10 inches across, complete with those distinctive five broad, silky petals and bottlebrush center. The plant generates numerous flowers and they last for many weeks. Red and pink are the most common colors (for best quality, seek out any of the Disco Belle Series), but a glowing white one called 'Blue River II' is sensational.

Because it grows quickly and gets bushy, rose mallow is sometimes mistaken for a flowering shrub. It is certainly large enough. But it dies back in winter and returns every spring, just like other perennials. Because it's one of the last perennials to sprout in spring, be careful not to mistake it when weeding. Just site it somewhere where it has enough space and organically rich soil, and let it dazzle.

GOOD CHOICES: Disco Belle Series; 'Blue River II'

Hosta cultivars
Hosta, Plantain Lily

SIZE (height × width): 1 to 2 feet × 1 to 5 feet; varies
BLOOM DESCRIPTION: wands of small tubular flowers
BLOOM PERIOD: varies, depending on species and cultivar
EXPOSURE: partial to full shade
HARDY IN ZONES: 4 to 9
SPECIAL NOTES: some hosta flowers are sweetly fragrant

A "must" for shade displays, hosta is a great favorite for many good reasons. It's easy to grow, requiring little care. The clumps fill in their allotted space and stay put. And there is tremendous variety, from white-splashed mint green ones to puckered, textured powder-blue ones, to golden-leaved beauties that glow in dim spots.

Hosta flowers line arching wands above the mounding foliage in the summer, bringing welcome color (usually lavender or white), sometimes a sweet fragrance, and always a lovely grace. They can be quite a show in their own right, especially if you've planted a grouping.

Borders, rock gardens, and massed plantings are all great ways to explore hosta's many possibilities. Plant size should be your first consideration, however. Keep your hostas in scale with one another and with other shade plants you may be growing.

GOOD CHOICES: rich green leaves, white flowers on *H. plantaginea* 'Royal Standard'; white-rimmed, green-leaved, with lavender flowers on *H. undulata* 'Albo-Marginata'; quilted blue leaves and white flowers on *H. sieboldiana* 'Elegans'; huge chartreuse leaves, lavender flowers on 'Sum 'n' Substance'

Iberis sempervirens
Candytuft
SIZE (height × width): 6 to 12 inches × 1 to 2 feet
BLOOM DESCRIPTION: clusters of small white flowers
BLOOM PERIOD: late spring
EXPOSURE: full sun to partial shade
HARDY IN ZONES: 3 to 8
SPECIAL NOTES: deer resistant

Tidy mounds or mats of slender, glossy leaves look good before, during, and after flowering. But candytuft's glory is its lengthy springtime show, when it covers itself in 1- to 2-inch lacy white flower clusters—a refreshing sight after a long winter. Aptly named 'Snowflake' has slightly larger blooms and stays around 10 inches high, making it ideal as a groundcover. 'Little Gem' is a perky dwarf version.

Versatile candytuft is a great edging plant, tucks well into spring bulb displays, forms handsome masses along walls and walkways, and also looks great at the base of ornamental trees and shrubs. The plant performs best in full sun, and needs well-drained soil. Deer shun it and pests never nibble it. So once you get it growing, you'll delight in it year after year.

GOOD CHOICES: 'Little Gem'; 'Snowflake'

Inula hirta
Inula Daisy
SIZE (height × width): 1 to 2 feet × 1¹/₂ feet
BLOOM DESCRIPTION: large, thin-petaled yellow daisies
BLOOM PERIOD: early summer
EXPOSURE: full sun or partial shade
HARDY IN ZONES: 3 to 8
SPECIAL NOTES: crowding can lead to mildew

Borne singly or in clusters, the bright yellow daisies of inula make quite a splash early every summer. And they last—the show continues for up to six weeks. Not a very tall or imposing plant, it is therefore best sited towards the front of a perennial flowerbed. The foliage is gray-green and somewhat fuzzy. *I. hirta* has brilliant yellow, finely cut ray petals and keeps blooming for the entire summer. (If you like the plant but want low, compact growth, try the groundcovering *I. candida* var. *verbascifolia*, which remains under 8 inches high.)

For best results, grow your inula daisy in moist but well-drained soil. It is fairly heat tolerant and will keep blooming in the South. Because the blooms are so abundant, feel free to snip some stems for bright, informal bouquets.

GOOD CHOICE: *I. candida* var. *verbascifolia*

Iris hybrids
Tall Bearded Iris

SIZE (height × width): 3 to 4 feet × 2 to 3 feet
BLOOM DESCRIPTION: large papery blooms
BLOOM PERIOD: late spring
EXPOSURE: full sun
HARDY IN ZONES: 4 to 9
SPECIAL NOTES: plant the rhizomes shallowly

"Every color of the rainbow" is scarcely an exaggeration when describing bearded irises. Hybridizers have produced, and continue to generate, an astounding array of ravishingly beautiful choices. Traditionally, bearded irises have been grown in groups or sweeps, but with all these colors to choose from, mix-and-match combinations are also attractive. Large blooms consist of upper "standards" and lower "falls," with a tuft of "beard" in the middle.

It is very important, however, to plant these irises properly. Never bury the rhizomes completely; they should be set shallowly, buried about halfway up the sides, into moderately fertile, well-drained soil. And always keep your plants well groomed, so pests and diseases are not harbored in dead leaves or other garden debris. Don't mulch. Tall bearded irises are vulnerable to a small pink grub called the "iris borer," which feeds on the rhizomes until they become hollow shells—so be neat and vigilant.

GOOD CHOICES: 'Beverly Sills'; 'Crater Lake Blue'; 'Edith Wolford'; 'Immortality'; 'Pixie Dust'; 'Raspberry Kiss'; 'Velvet Ballerina'

Iris sibirica
Siberian Iris

SIZE (height × width): 2 to 4 feet × 2 to 3 feet
BLOOM DESCRIPTION: elegant, narrow petals
BLOOM PERIOD: early summer
EXPOSURE: full sun to partial shade
HARDY IN ZONES: 4 to 9
SPECIAL NOTES: fertile, moist, slightly acidic soil is ideal

Flocks of pretty, 2- to 4-inch flowers appear dependably early every summer. Among irises, none are easier and more trouble free; all they need to thrive is fertile, moist, slightly acidic soil. Pests and diseases are rare, division is rarely needed, and the flowers hold up admirably in the garden and in a vase.

Siberian irises have been extensively hybridized. There are dozens to choose from, most in the blue-purple-white range. Soft blue 'Summer Sky' is especially pretty, while 'Orville Fay' has delphinium-blue flowers with darker veining. Other colors exist, however. 'Ewen' has wine-red blooms, and the whimsically named 'Butter and Eggs' is a white-and-yellow bicolor.

After the flowers pass, clumps of strappy green foliage remain and are an asset in any perennial display. The leaves remain handsome and unmarred for the rest of the season, contributing what landscapers like to call "vertical interest."

GOOD CHOICES: 'Butter and Eggs'; 'Ewen'; 'Orville Fay'; 'Summer Sky'

Kniphofia uvaria
Red Hot Poker, Torch Lily

SIZE (height × width): 2 to 4 feet × 1 to 2 feet
BLOOM DESCRIPTION: dense spires of small tubular flowers
BLOOM PERIOD: late summer into fall
EXPOSURE: full sun
HARDY IN ZONES: 6 to 9
SPECIAL NOTES: well-drained soil is a must

Tapering spires rise above a grassy-leaved clump and put on one of the most dramatic shows you can get in mid- to late summer. The colors are traditionally fiery, in the red-orange-yellow range. A bicolor effect occurs when the tubular blooms that make up each spire open from the bottom up. Red hot pokers look great grown in a row along a fence or wall.

Admittedly the hot colors are not easy to incorporate into a traditional perennial border, but hybridizers have addressed that issue. You can now get a pastel-hued mix called Newest English Hybrids. Or even the pretty vanilla-white 'Little Maid', which is also shorter, topping out at 20 inches.

Grow the plants in full sun and well-drained soil. Soggy ground, especially over the winter, causes the roots to rot.

GOOD CHOICES: 'Little Maid'; hot-color mix 'Flamenco'; pastel-hued mix Newest English Hybrids

Lamium maculatum
Lamium, Spotted Nettle

SIZE (height × width): 8 to 12 inches × 12 to 18 inches
BLOOM DESCRIPTION: small hooded blooms in pink or white
BLOOM PERIOD: early summer
EXPOSURE: partial to full shade
HARDY IN ZONES: 4 to 8
SPECIAL NOTES: needs moist soil to thrive

One of the finest and easiest groundcovers for shady areas, lamium's main feature is its especially attractive variegated foliage. The oval leaves are a fresh mint green, spotted, ribbed, or marked with white, light green, or silver. 'Beacon Silver' and 'White Nancy', the best cultivars, have green-rimmed foliage that is otherwise entirely silver. In moist, well-drained soil, the plant forms a carpet that excludes weeds and looks splendid.

In spring, small but appealing flowers burst on the scene; they're hooded, less than an inch across, and appear in small clusters just above the foliage. Those of 'Beacon Silver' are pink; those of 'White Nancy' are white. The white-with-white show of 'White Nancy' really creates a bright spot in dim areas.

GOOD CHOICES: 'Beacon Silver'; 'White Nancy'

Lavandula angustifolia
Lavender

SIZE (height × width): 2 to 3 feet × 2 to 3 feet
BLOOM DESCRIPTION: fragrant spikes of lavender blue
BLOOM PERIOD: late spring into summer
EXPOSURE: full sun
HARDY IN ZONES: 5 to 9
SPECIAL NOTES: deer resistant, needs superior drainage

Lavatera thuringiaca
Mallow, Tree Mallow

SIZE (height × width): 3 to 6 feet × 3 to 5 feet
BLOOM DESCRIPTION: 2- to 3-inch flowers resemble hollyhocks
BLOOM PERIOD: summer
EXPOSURE: full sun
HARDY IN ZONES: 5 to 8
SPECIAL NOTES: sometimes troubled by Japanese beetles

No longer confined to the herb garden, easygoing, fragrant lavender is more than welcome in the sunny perennial bed. Hybridizers have accordingly developed varieties with showier flower spikes and tidier growth habits. One of the best is deep violet-blue 'Hidcote Superior', which is especially compact and floriferous. Old favorite 'Munstead' sets the standard with a neat profile and lavender-blue, richly scented spikes.

The plants grow best in light, very well-drained soil with a higher pH. (If your soil is acidic, try adding lime dust or chips to the planting area.)

Lavender is a wonderful, dependably colorful contributor to sunny beds, among pastel-hued perennials or roses. It's equally pretty with yellow coreopsis. Some gardeners prefer to grow it as an edging plant or low hedge around a flowerbed, uses that suit it very well. Even when it matures and develops a somewhat woody base, lavender retains a tidy profile. Shearing or clipping is a pleasant chore and one from which the plant recovers quickly.

GOOD CHOICES: 'Hidcote Superior'; 'Munstead';
'Kew Red', 'Provence'

An easy-to-grow, long-blooming old favorite, mallow brings exuberant color to your sunny summer garden. A tall, bushy plant, it is best placed to the back of a border where it won't overwhelm smaller perennials. Any well-drained soil of average fertility is fine.

The flowers, which strongly resemble single hollyhocks, come in appealing colors and keep blooming for virtually the entire summer. The species is rose pink, but 'Burgundy Wine' has lilac-hued flowers. Best of all is 'Barnsley Baby', a perky British import that sports white flowers with contrasting ruby-red centers—and a shorter stature that allows it to be grown midborder if you wish.

GOOD CHOICES: 'Barnsley Baby'; 'Burgundy Wine'

Leucanthemum × superbum
Shasta Daisy

SIZE (height × width): 1 to 3$^{1}/_{2}$ feet × 2 to 3 feet
BLOOM DESCRIPTION: large 5-inch daisies
BLOOM PERIOD: summer
EXPOSURE: full sun to partial shade
HARDY IN ZONES: 5 to 9
SPECIAL NOTES: best in well-drained soil

Liatris spicata
Spike Gayfeather, Blazing Star

SIZE (height × width): 2 to 3 feet × 1 foot
BLOOM DESCRIPTION: tall, fringed spires
BLOOM PERIOD: summer
EXPOSURE: full sun
HARDY IN ZONES: 3 to 9
SPECIAL NOTES: attracts butterflies

Classic daisies cover a somewhat rounded bush of strong stems, loosely lined with slender, toothed leaves. Don't hesitate to pick plenty of bouquets—this inspires the plant to continue producing more flowers all summer long. In fact, few perennials are as long blooming as this stalwart.

Shasta daisy is easy to grow well. All it requires is moderately fertile, well-drained soil. It performs somewhat better in cooler summers, so if you live where summers are hot and steamy, provide some afternoon shade and keep them well watered.

Not surprisingly, a perennial this pretty and carefree has captured the attention of plant breeders. Nowadays there are many excellent cultivars to choose from. 'Becky' is outstanding—long blooming, and able to stand up to heat and humidity; it won the Perennial Plant Association's top award for 2003. Somewhat shorter at 30 to 36 inches, 'Alaska' is also excellent. Shorter still, at 24 inches, is 'Esther Read'. For a totally different, refreshing look, try the heavily fringed 'Aglaia', which is especially long blooming.

GOOD CHOICES: 'Aglaia'; 'Alaska'; 'Becky'; 'Esther Read';
  'Little Princess'

Prized by bouquet lovers, spike gayfeather bears dense, beautiful spires of small purple flowers. They last a long time in a vase and retain their color well when dried. If you can resist picking them, however, your garden will soon be hosting lots of butterflies, which find the blooms irresistible.

This is a tough plant, thanks to its origins on the American prairie. It does fine in somewhat sandy, fertile soil and, in time, develops a strong tuberous rootstock that stores water for survival during dry spells.

Other colors are available. Rich lavender flowers can be found on 'Kobold', which is also a shorter plant, no more than 2 feet tall. Those of 3-foot-tall 'Floristan Violet' are rosy purple, and 'Floristan White' (2 to 3 feet tall) is bright and lively.

GOOD CHOICES: 'Floristan Violet'; 'Floristan White';
  'Kobold'

Lilium hybrids
Asiatic Lily, Oriental Lily

SIZE (height × width): 2 to 5 feet (varies) × 8 to 12 inches
BLOOM DESCRIPTION: 5- to 8-inch-wide trumpets
BLOOM PERIOD: summer, depends on type and cultivar
EXPOSURE: full sun to partial shade
HARDY IN ZONES: 3 to 9
SPECIAL NOTES: keep roots cool

No wonder these magnificent flowers are so beloved by gardeners. They're easy to grow and vigorous, and they do well everywhere from full sun to light shade. And the flowers are big, bright, and abundant. The Oriental hybrids are also richly fragrant.

Lilies are indeed perennials; once their bulbs are properly planted, they return faithfully year after year. Because their plant profile is tall and narrow, they are best sited towards the middle or back of a bed or border. Mixing them with colorful perennials benefits them—it hides their lower stems, and it keeps their roots cool while their flowers enjoy the sunshine.

If you choose from an array of different types, you're guaranteed a summer-long lily show. Asiatic lilies (hardy in zones 3 to 9) bloom in early summer in bold hues: red, orange, purple, yellow, cream, pink, and white. Fragrant, bigger-flowered Oriental lilies (hardy in zones 4 to 8) burst on the scene in mid- to late summer and are pink, rose-red, maroon-red, or white, sometimes with speckles.

GOOD CHOICES: Asiatic lilies: deep yellow 'Connecticut King'; rose-pink 'Montreaux'; Oriental lilies: pure white 'Casablanca'; pink-red 'Stargazer'

Lobelia cardinalis
Cardinal Flower

SIZE (height × width): 3 to 5 feet × 1 foot
BLOOM DESCRIPTION: spikes of small, fan-shaped flowers
BLOOM PERIOD: summer
EXPOSURE: full sun to partial shade
HARDY IN ZONES: 3 to 8
SPECIAL NOTES: best in moist soil, attracts hummingbirds

One of the very best wildflowers for garden use, thanks to its agreeable disposition and beautiful flowers. In nature, cardinal flower appears in damp meadows and along streams, so you can grow it in a damp spot in your yard. Lacking a damp spot, however, it will be happy with regular watering and a moisture-conserving mulch at its feet.

A robust plant, yet not rangy or invasive, cardinal flower has striking flower spires for most or all of the summer. If you look closely, you'll see that they are composed of myriad small, fan-shaped blossoms. The species is red, but several cultivars have other lovely colors. 'Ruby Slippers' has flowers of dark, velvety ruby-red. A soft pink one is called 'Heather Pink' and a good white is 'Alba'.

A recent introduction is 'Queen Victoria', whose profuse scarlet flowers are complemented by dark, bronzy leaves and stems. It's a knockout in groupings, and also attracts hummingbirds.

GOOD CHOICES: 'Alba'; *L.* × *speciosa* 'Queen Victoria'; 'Heather Pink'; 'Ruby Slippers'

Lupinus hybrids
Lupine

SIZE (height × width): 3 to 4 feet × 1¹/₂ to 2 feet
BLOOM DESCRIPTION: tall, dense stalks
BLOOM PERIOD: late spring into early summer
EXPOSURE: full sun to partial shade
HARDY IN ZONES: 4 to 8
SPECIAL NOTES: deer resistant, not tolerant of hot weather

Gracious and stately, lupines are a mainstay of the classic perennial border. The tall, dense flower stalks range from creamy white to lemon yellow to peppermint pink to scarlet to royal blue to deep purple—sometimes in bicolor forms as well. Get a mix and revel in this wonderful range of hues. The Russell Hybrids, which include bicolors, are an old favorite. For a dazzling array of solid colors on especially stout stems, try the 'New Generations Hybrids' Mix, which have won numerous gold medals at England's prestigious Chelsea Flower Show.

Even the foliage of lupines is lance-shaped, between 6 and 12 inches long, and gathered in palmate leaflets. The leaves have a light coating of silky hairs that capture water droplets.

For best results, grow your lupines in moist, organically rich, well-drained soil that is slightly acidic. They're sensitive to hot, dry weather, so apply a protective mulch around their bases and provide some shade. In hot, humid climates, lupines can be grown as annuals by planting in fall for bloom the following spring.

GOOD CHOICES: New Generation Hybrids Mix;
  Russell Hybrids Mix

Malva alcea
Hollyhock Mallow

SIZE (height × width): 3 to 4 feet × 1 to 2 feet
BLOOM DESCRIPTION: 2-inch saucers
BLOOM PERIOD: midsummer into fall
EXPOSURE: full sun
HARDY IN ZONES: 4 to 9
SPECIAL NOTES: heat and drought tolerant

An easygoing, bushy, long-blooming beauty, this plant is not really a hollyhock at all, though it deserves to be grown as widely. It is incredibly generous with its small, jaunty, saucer-shaped blooms, usually a sweet rose pink with dark veining and a cream-colored center. (*M. moschata* 'Alba' is a prolific white version.) Needing only average soil and full sun, the plant blooms for months on end. It's a great choice for the middle of a sunny border or even a big container on a deck or porch.

The billowing plant is laden with rather dainty, lobed palmate leaves. The sometimes-lax stems mean you will either have to enjoy the plant in an informal, cottage-garden setting or stake them. A neater, more upright plant is the pretty 'Fastigiata'.

Hollyhock mallow owes its tough constitution to a thick, fibrous root system. And if that doesn't assure its survival in your garden, its propensity to self-sow will if it's not cut back after blooming.

GOOD CHOICES: 'Fastigiata'; *M. moschata* 'Alba';
  M. sylvestris 'Zebrina'

Mertensia virginica
Virginia Bluebells

SIZE (height × width): 1 to 2 feet × 1½ feet
BLOOM DESCRIPTION: clusters of blue tubular bells
BLOOM PERIOD: spring
EXPOSURE: partial to full shade
HARDY IN ZONES: 3 to 8
SPECIAL NOTES: goes dormant in summer

Such a pretty plant! Large, rounded leaves are mainly at ground level, though a few ascend the stems on short, succulent stalks. At the top of these stalks are clusters of the most charming little tubular bells. They begin as pink buds, but open to lilac-blue flowers (they're darker blue in deeper shade). A plant in the process of blooming displays both pink and blue at once.

Bluebells is often touted as an ideal companion for spring-flowering bulbs, with good reason. This plant likes similar growing conditions, namely organically rich soil in cool shade. Plus, the colors seem to go with everything, though they are especially fetching combined with small-flowered white or yellow narcissus.

Like the bulbs, bluebells' show ends as summer arrives. The stems die down after bloom and the plant gradually goes dormant and disappears from view. So mark its spot so you don't accidentally plant something over it.

GOOD CHOICE: the species is beautiful

Miscanthus sinensis
Miscanthus, Eulalia Grass

SIZE (height × width): 3 to 8 feet × 3 to 5 feet
BLOOM DESCRIPTION: arching plumes
BLOOM PERIOD: late summer into fall
EXPOSURE: full sun
HARDY IN ZONES: 5 to 8
SPECIAL NOTES: thrives in moist but well-drained soil

Of all the ornamental grasses to capture the affections of perennial gardeners in the past decade or two, no other has been quite as popular as the excellent, easy-to-grow, boldly architectural miscanthus. Tough and attractive in all seasons, it now comes in a tantalizing array of foliage colors and plant sizes to fit every landscape. It shows off best as a freestanding specimen, though some of the more modestly sized ones are also good in mixed borders. Moist but well-drained ground is ideal.

Of the taller versions, 'Cabaret' is big and splashy, reaching between 6 and 8 feet. Its broad green leaves are brushed with a wide cream stripe. 'Gracillimus' (commonly known as maiden grass) has an especially graceful, fountainlike profile. The leaves are green, ribbed with a slender white-to-silver stripe; the lovely late-season plumes are silvery. The leaves of 'Purpurascens' turn wine-red as summer progresses, and segue to vivid orange-red by fall. The plumes are creamy white.

For smaller gardens, borders, or more restricted spaces, there are a number of dwarf versions.

GOOD CHOICES: 'Cabaret'; 'Gracillimus'; 'Morning Light'; 'Purpurascens'; dwarf 'Yaku Jima'

Monarda didyma
Bee Balm

SIZE (height × width): 2 to 3 feet × 1 to 2 feet
BLOOM DESCRIPTION: up to 4-inch flower heads
BLOOM PERIOD: mid- to late summer
EXPOSURE: full sun to partial shade
HARDY IN ZONES: 4 to 9
SPECIAL NOTES: deer resistant

This showy perennial is easy to grow, provided your garden has the moist, rich soil it needs to thrive. It has dark green aromatic leaves (it's related to mint) and big, showy flower heads that are a knockout in full bloom. Hummingbirds find them irresistible, and bees and butterflies also visit.

The species is red and many of the cultivars are an improvement upon it, with bigger flowers and sturdier growth. 'Cambridge Scarlet' and 'Gardenview Scarlet' are spectacular. Some pastels have debuted in recent years, making it possible to add bee balm to a pastel-themed display; best among these are pink 'Marshall's Delight' and mauve 'Aquarius'. Rose-lavender 'Petite Wonder' is under a foot tall, ideal for smaller garden settings. There's even white; look for the ravishing 'Snow Queen'.

Bee balm has traditionally been victim to leaf-damaging mildew, which disfigures the plant late in the season. All the cultivars mentioned here, and many others, are billed as resistant. You can also do your part by allowing plants sufficient air circulation by not planting them too close together.

GOOD CHOICES: 'Aquarius'; 'Cambridge Scarlet';
   'Gardenview Scarlet'; 'Marshall's Delight';
   'Petite Wonder'; 'Snow Queen'

Nepeta × faassenii
Catmint

SIZE (height × width): 1 to 1¹/₂ feet × 1¹/₂ feet
BLOOM DESCRIPTION: long, plush spires
BLOOM PERIOD: early to midsummer
EXPOSURE: full sun
HARDY IN ZONES: 4 to 9
SPECIAL NOTES: deer resistant

Easy to grow and very generous with its flower spires, catmint is a superb addition to any sunny border in need of early summer color. It generates so many spires that the plant looks solid light purple. For plusher, darker-purple flowers, you can try the excellent cultivar 'Dropmore'. After catmint has finished flowering, you can cut it back about halfway and inspire a second round of blooms later in the summer.

Catmint leaves are gray-green and fragrant. Unlike some herblike plants, however, it is not at all rangy. The plant has a natural grace and remains compact and tidy looking. You can certainly use it as an edging or along the front of a border or along a path. If you have the space, 'Six Hills Giant' gets large enough (2 to 3 feet tall) to hold its own among rosebushes and other flowering shrubs.

GOOD CHOICES: 'Six Hills Giant'; 'Dropmore'; 'Little Titch'

Oenothera fruticosa
Evening Primrose, Sundrops
SIZE (height × width): 2 to 3 feet × 1 to 2 feet
BLOOM DESCRIPTION: small to medium saucers
BLOOM PERIOD: spring into summer
EXPOSURE: full sun
HARDY IN ZONES: 4 to 9
SPECIAL NOTES: deer resistant

Paeonia lactiflora
Peony
SIZE (height × width): 1 to 3 feet × 2 to 3 feet
BLOOM DESCRIPTION: large, double- or single-petaled
BLOOM PERIOD: spring
EXPOSURE: full sun
HARDY IN ZONES: 3 to 8
SPECIAL NOTES: best given a head start with fall planting

One of the longest-blooming perennials available, evening primrose is also a cinch to grow well. Not fussy about soil, the plant may actually become a bit floppy in fertile ground. It is happiest in well-drained soil. Rather than stake the bloom-laden stems, try interplanting with supportive, color-harmonious companions such as penstemons or bellflowers.

As the main attraction, the perky flowers are saucer-shaped and softly fragrant. The common name comes from the fact that the scent attracts night-pollinating moths. Traditionally sundrops is sunny yellow—look for the large-flowered, radiant *O. fruticosa* 'Fireworks' or 'Highlights'. *O. speciosa* 'Alba' has pure-white flowers that seem to fit in anywhere—and, because they remain open late, will be a highlight in your garden at dusk.

GOOD CHOICES: 'Fireworks'; 'Highlights';
  O. speciosa 'Alba'

As tough as they are gorgeous, peonies are very cold hardy and utterly dependable. All they really need is organically rich, well-drained soil (for a head start on the following spring's show, plant your peonies the previous fall). Every spring, you can look forward to the shrubby, handsome, much-divided foliage, soon upstaged by luscious flowers. Big, plush with petals, and radiating a sweet, haunting fragrance, peonies are beautiful in your spring garden and in big bouquets.

The most widely grown peonies are double-flowered, white, pink, or red selections; within that range are many spectacular choices. The early-blooming, crimson-flecked, double white 'Festiva Maxima' is an old favorite. For soft, romantic pink blooms, try 'Sorbet'. For ruby red ones, try 'Karl Rosenfeld'. Pure white 'Avalanche' is a beauty.

Recent trends in hybridizing have produced single peony flowers with extra tufts of petals in the middle. Light pink within dark pink 'Pink Cameo' may be the best of these.

GOOD CHOICES: 'Avalanche'; 'Festiva Maxima';
  'Karl Rosenfeld'; 'Pink Cameo'; 'Sorbet'

Papaver orientale
Oriental Poppy
SIZE (height × width): 2 to 4 feet × 2 to 3 feet
BLOOM DESCRIPTION: 4 to 6 inches, goblet-shaped
BLOOM PERIOD: early summer
EXPOSURE: full sun
HARDY IN ZONES: 3 to 8
SPECIAL NOTES: deer resistant, goes dormant by midsummer

It's amazing but true that flowers this exquisite are very easy to grow. Just plant them in full sun in well-drained soil. Oriental poppy has light green, rather downy foliage and big, crepe-paper-textured blossoms, which open to a graceful goblet shape. Then their black accent markings towards the center become visible, as well as a fat, distinctive center mound of stamens. The effect is sensational, especially in the fiery red- and orange-flowered cultivars. But the drama is not lost on the pink-flowered ones either.

Oriental poppies put on a brief but exciting show in early summer, blooming around the same time as peonies and lupines—a border of all three is thrilling to behold. Some gardeners also like to grow poppies alongside baby's breath, which peaks just as the poppies are beginning to fade and quickly billows over the gaps they leave behind.

Summer bloomers such as daylilies or coneflowers also fill the void as poppies go dormant.

GOOD CHOICES: red-orange 'Glowing Embers'; salmon-pink 'Helen Elizabeth'; purple-red 'Patty's Plum'

Pennisetum alopecuroides
Fountain Grass
SIZE (height × width): 1 to 3 feet × 1 to 3 feet
BLOOM DESCRIPTION: fluffy plumes
BLOOM PERIOD: late summer into fall
EXPOSURE: full sun
HARDY IN ZONES: 5 to 8
SPECIAL NOTES: four seasons of interest

As the common name indicates, these clump-forming perennial grasses make a graceful fountain shape in any sunny spot with decent, well-drained soil. The flowers are fluffy little plumes that rise above the plant in summer and continue well into autumn. Where you want a compact, four-season ornamental grass, this one really shines.

Compact and tidy enough to qualify as a mound, 'Hameln' sports slender, dark green foliage. Fuzzy greenish-white flower spikes adorn taller, arching stems starting in midsummer; later, they turn a gorgeous shade of mauve. Smaller still is the excellent cultivar 'Little Bunny'. Its light-colored flower heads are especially fluffy. 'Little Bunny' looks great planted in masses.

For a stylish contribution to a sunny border display, seek out 'Moudry', also called black fountain grass. The glossy green leaves are joined a little later in summer by dark brown to black flower spikes (flower arrangers adore them). However, don't let 'Moudry' go to seed since it can be quite invasive.

GOOD CHOICES: 'Hameln'; 'Little Bunny'; 'Moudry'

Penstemon cultivars
Penstemon, Beard-tongue
SIZE (height × width): 2 to 4 feet × 1 to 3 feet
BLOOM DESCRIPTION: tubular flowers in spires
BLOOM PERIOD: summer
EXPOSURE: full sun
HARDY IN ZONES: 4 to 8
SPECIAL NOTES: well-drained soil is a must

Perovskia atriplicifolia
Russian Sage
SIZE (height × width): 3 to 4 feet × 2 to 3 feet
BLOOM DESCRIPTION: tall, downy spires of blue
BLOOM PERIOD: midsummer into fall
EXPOSURE: full sun
HARDY IN ZONES: 4 to 9
SPECIAL NOTES: deer resistant, cut back low yearly

Penstemons are handsome, shrubby-looking plants of arching stems loosely decorated with showy, tubular flowers that attract hummingbirds. Many are native to the mountains of the West, but may be grown successfully in other areas, that is if similar conditions are provided: full sun and lean, well-drained soil (damp or rich soil causes them to rot). Though they are not always long-lived, they often self-sow.

Numerous cultivars are available to gardeners and are often superior to the wild species in terms of flower size, flower color, and density of flowers. One of the most splendid is the award-winning (Perennial Plant Association, 1996) 'Husker Red', a cultivar of *P. digitalis,* owing its name to its reddish foliage and stems; the flowers are white, though sometimes they develop a pink cast. 'Donna' sports a flurry of vibrant pink, nonfading flower clusters. Other selections are lavender, violet, blue, rose, true red, and orange-red.

GOOD CHOICES: 'Donna'; 'Husker Red'

The combination of silvery-gray foliage and fuzzy, soft lavender flowers is enchanting. And Russian sage, growing broad and bushy, makes a big show. The flower spires are long and last for many weeks. It's fun to snip a few for homegrown bouquets. When you do, you'll notice that the foliage has a pleasant, sagelike fragrance that only adds to the plant's appeal.

Few perennials are easier. All Russian sage seems to want is sunshine, well-drained soil, and room to show off. (The cultivar 'Little Spires' reaches only about 2 feet in height, so is appropriate for smaller spaces.) It is immune to pests and diseases, and never nibbled by deer. It's a good idea, though, to step in and cut it back to the ground after flowering is over in the fall or first thing the following spring, so the plant can generate a fresh new show each summer.

GOOD CHOICES: 'Filagran'; 'Longin'; 'Blue Spire'; 'Little Spires'

Phlox divaricata
Blue Phlox, Wild Sweet William
SIZE (height × width): 1 to 1¹/₂ feet × 1 foot
BLOOM DESCRIPTION: 1 inch or less; scented
BLOOM PERIOD: late spring into early summer
EXPOSURE: partial to full shade
HARDY IN ZONES: 4 to 9
SPECIAL NOTES: beloved by nibbling rabbits

Phlox paniculata
Summer Phlox
SIZE (height × width): 2 to 5 feet × 2 feet
BLOOM DESCRIPTION: terminal clusters of small florets
BLOOM PERIOD: summer
EXPOSURE: full sun to partial shade
HARDY IN ZONES: 3 to 9
SPECIAL NOTES: seek out mildew-resistant cultivars

For the front of a shade border, wildflower garden, or as a woodland groundcover, blue phlox is perfect. In return for humus-rich soil, and perhaps a mulch to protect its somewhat shallow roots, it will deliver handsome leaves and numerous pretty little flowers. The five-petaled flowers have fringed edges, and are normally light blue and sweetly fragrant. Two excellent forms are 'Chattahoochee' (actually a hybrid), lavender blue with dark purple centers, and 'Fuller's White', which is so prolific that it looks like countless white butterflies hovering in your shade garden.

The setting is important for best performance. Too much sun, heat, or humidity, and blue phlox may flag or develop mildew. Also, wild rabbits find the plants irresistibly tasty.

GOOD CHOICES: 'Fuller's White'; 'Dirigo Ice';
P. × 'Chattahoochee'

Summer phlox has been extensively hybridized and there are many enticing choices, from snowy white to pink, red, lavender, and purple. Many have a contrasting center eye that adds extra sparkle, helping your phlox display stand out even at a distance.

The plants bloom heavily for weeks every summer, provided they're growing in organically rich soil and they get the moisture they need. Though not a problem everywhere, a long-standing challenge for some gardeners has been powdery mildew on their phlox leaves. The good news is that many excellent new cultivars are billed as mildew-resistant. You can also help your plants by not crowding them, which increases air circulation.

GOOD CHOICES: pink with crimson eye 'Bright Eyes'; mildew-resistant, white 'David'; mildew-resistant, pink with a white eye 'Laura'

Platycodon grandiflorus
Balloon Flower
SIZE (height × width): 1¹/₂ to 2¹/₂ feet × 1 foot
BLOOM DESCRIPTION: 2-inch saucers
BLOOM PERIOD: summer
EXPOSURE: full sun to partial shade
HARDY IN ZONES: 3 to 9
SPECIAL NOTES: distinctive "balloons" at the bud stage

Polygonatum odoratum
Solomon's Seal
SIZE (height × width): 1 to 2 feet × 1 to 2 feet
BLOOM DESCRIPTION: tiny greenish-white bells
BLOOM PERIOD: spring
EXPOSURE: partial to full shade
HARDY IN ZONES: 4 to 8
SPECIAL NOTES: grows from a stout rhizome

The unusual flower buds give the plant its common name—they puff out like tiny balloons before opening. Then they assume a saucer shape reminiscent of bellflowers, to which they are closely related. A balloon flower plant often has both the puffy buds and the perky flowers at the same time.

Balloon flower is usually blue ('Fuji Blue' is especially vivid). But other hues are available, notably white ('Alba' or double 'Hakone White') and pink ('Fuji Pink' and 'Shell Pink'). They look wonderful in combination with one another and also make a valuable contribution to a perennial border in need of easy, continual color. Keep the plants deadheaded to encourage continued flowering.

Balloon flower is valuable in the low-maintenance garden because it is a tough customer. It is very cold hardy and tolerates summer dry spells. While sandy, well-drained soil is best, it adapts to most sites well. It flowers in full sun and partial shade alike.

GOOD CHOICES: 'Alba'; 'Hakone White'; 'Fuji Blue'; 'Fuji Pink'; 'Shell Pink'

Grown mainly for its foliage, this elegant plant has a wonderful presence in the shade garden. Grow it in cool, moist soil. Strong, graceful stalks will spread outward, bearing along their length oval-shaped, parallel-veined leaves. Dangling along the underside of the stems in spring, you'll spy a jaunty row of tiny, pale-green, lightly perfumed, bell-shaped flowers. These become blue-black berries by late summer.

The cultivar 'Variegatum' is superb. Its leaf edges and tips are splashed with white markings, which helps the plant stand out. It looks especially stunning in the company of hostas, white-variegated ones or others.

GOOD CHOICE: 'Variegatum'

Potentilla species
Cinquefoil

SIZE (height × width): 1 to 2 feet × 1 to 2 feet
BLOOM DESCRIPTION: loose panicles of small 1-inch saucers
BLOOM PERIOD: early summer
EXPOSURE: full sun
HARDY IN ZONES: 5 to 8
SPECIAL NOTES: deer resistant

Shrubby cinquefoil (*Potentilla fruticosa*) is a mounding, woody-stemmed plant. *Potentilla atrosanguinea*, a terrific perennial version, is a low-mound-former or groundcover. You get attractive, dense, weed-excluding foliage all season long—medium green, underlain with silver, in compact rosettes of five-fingered leaflets. It's good for a sunny rock garden, or sprawling in the front of a perennial border.

Early summer brings a splashy flower show. Small but bright flowers completely blanket the plants, eliciting admiration. 'Gibson's Scarlet' has single ruby-red flowers, while those of 'William Rollinson' are semidouble and deep orange to yellow.

Best of all, it is easy to grow in moderate climates and ordinary conditions of fertile soil and full sun. Pests and diseases never trouble it.

GOOD CHOICES: 'Gibson's Scarlet'; 'William Rollinson'

Pulmonaria cultivars
Lungwort, Bethlehem Sage

SIZE (height × width): 9 to 18 inches × 12 to 24 inches
BLOOM DESCRIPTION: clusters of small bells
BLOOM PERIOD: spring
EXPOSURE: partial to full shade
HARDY IN ZONES: 3 to 8
SPECIAL NOTES: deer resistant

Among shade perennials, lungwort is surely one of the prettiest and most carefree. Large clumps of lance-shaped leaves dappled with silvery spots and blotches make the plant sparkle in dim areas—when you plant it *en masse*, you get an elegant, luminous carpet. It's also glorious lining a wooded pathway. And it mixes well with other shade-lovers, especially the white-flowered bleeding heart (*Dicentra spectabilis* 'Alba').

Lungwort is a true shade-lover and indeed can tolerate deeper shade than many other plants. It appreciates the shelter of deciduous trees and thrives in moist, organically rich soil.

Springtime brings a lovely flower display. Bare stems rise out of the clump of leaves, topped with clusters of little bells; these start out as pink buds but soon open to sweet, violet-blue bells. 'Mrs. Moon' has pink flowers that age to blue and more prominently spotted leaves. 'Sissinghurst White' has white flowers that glow. Lungwort is at its showiest as spring bulbs are starting to fade.

GOOD CHOICES: *P. officinalis* 'Sissinghurst White';
    P. saccharata 'Mrs. Moon'

Ratibida species
Mexican Hat, Prairie Coneflower

SIZE (height × width): 3 to 5 feet × 1 to 2 feet
BLOOM DESCRIPTION: small shuttlecock daisies
BLOOM PERIOD: summer
EXPOSURE: full sun
HARDY IN ZONES: 4 to 8
SPECIAL NOTES: very drought tolerant

Rudbeckia species
Black-Eyed Susan

SIZE (height × width): 2 to 3 feet × 2 feet
BLOOM DESCRIPTION: 4- to 6-inch daisies
BLOOM PERIOD: midsummer into fall
EXPOSURE: full sun
HARDY IN ZONES: 3 to 8
SPECIAL NOTES: outstanding for bouquets

These carefree wildflowers bloom from spring to fall. The flowers look like little shuttlecocks, with 1- or 2-inch petals ("ray flowers") swooping back from the prominent center cone. The cone is gray-green to start, but gradually darkens. The flowers are wonderful in flower arrangements—they keep for many days, and they also dry well.

For golden yellow flowers, look for prairie coneflower, *R. pinnata*. For dramatic two-tone flowers, yellow on the tips and mahogany towards the center, you want Mexican hat, *R. columnifera*. Either or both look splendid with purple cone-flower and black-eyed susan.

Native to the prairies, this sun-lover is not fussy about soil, tolerating everything from damp to dry situations. Because of its height and informal profile, it would be ideal along a fence, towards the back of a wildflower border, or in a meadow. As with other prairie natives, moving it later becomes difficult because the plant develops a ranging, fibrous root system, so site it where you want it to stay.

GOOD CHOICES: *R. columnifera; R. pinnata*

This plant is amazingly long blooming, starting in midsummer and continuing right up until the first frost of fall. The flowers are uniform, never straggly, always bright and perky. They're set off well against handsome, dark-green leaves. The plants don't get leggy, don't flop, and are blessed with strong, rigid stems, so staking is not usually necessary, as long as the plants are in full sun and lean soil. Pests and diseases rarely trouble it. Heat and drought don't bother it. In short, black-eyed susan is a superstar.

Within the genus, there are a number of variations, all with the same excellent qualities of the species. Everyone's favorite, and the PPA Plant of the Year winner in 1999, is *R. fulgida* var. *sullivantii* 'Goldsturm', which has larger flowers, up to 4 inches across. *R. laciniata* 'Goldquelle' is much taller and has shaggy double yellow flowers. *R. hirta* 'Irish Eyes', which is best classed as a short-lived perennial, has green centers.

Black-eyed susan is a great mixer in perennial displays. It's grand with bee balm (especially red), daylilies, ornamental grasses, lavender, and roses.

GOOD CHOICES: *R. fulgida* var. *sullivantii* 'Goldsturm'; *R. laciniata* 'Goldquelle'; 'Prairie Sun'

Salvia × *sylvestris*
Perennial Sage

SIZE (height × width): varies with species and cultivar
BLOOM DESCRIPTION: loose spires of flowers
BLOOM PERIOD: summer
EXPOSURE: full sun
HARDY IN ZONES: 4 to 8
SPECIAL NOTES: deer resistant

Scabiosa columbaria
Pincushion Flower

SIZE (height × width): 1 to 2 feet × 1 to 2 feet
BLOOM DESCRIPTION: 1- to 2-inch lacy umbels
BLOOM PERIOD: summer
EXPOSURE: full sun
HARDY IN ZONES: 5 to 9
SPECIAL NOTES: prefers slightly alkaline soil

Perennial sage has moved out of the herb garden and into the flower borders and hearts of gardeners in all regions. The plants are long blooming and thrive in heat, which makes them quite valuable in sunny summer displays.

These sages tend to be clump-formers that develop woody bases. They have gray-green to green foliage, often deliciously scented. The flower spires appear in profusion above the leaves. Some spires are sturdy and erect, better for more formal settings, while others have arching wands that are perfect for casual plantings.

Some standout sages include *S. verticillata* 'Purple Rain', which sports smoky-purple flowers on long, 20-inch stems all summer. PPA Plant of the Year award-winner (in 1997) was 'May Night', a beauty with 12- to 14-inch violet spikes. Other great *S.* × *sylvestris* cultivars include 'Carradonna', a knockout with 24- to 30-inch stalks of bluish-purple flowers and glowing purple stems; and 'Rose Queen', with rosy-pink blooms on 24-inch stems. And there are many more.

GOOD CHOICES: 'Caradonna'; 'May Night'; 'Rose Queen';
    S. verticillata 'Purple Rain'

So enthusiastic and dependably long blooming is pincushion flower that many perennial gardeners would never be without it. It produces clouds of small, lacy blooms for practically the entire summer, especially if you deadhead or pick bouquets. The plants maintain themselves as tidy clumps and have slightly fuzzy stems and small, cut leaflets of sage green. 'Butterfly Blue' (PPA Plant of the Year for 2000) is widely available and is actually more lavender than blue. 'Pink Mist' is a sweet shade of pink. Use them together to bring an instant cottage garden feel to your garden.

Grow pincushion flower in full sun in a light, loamy soil on the alkaline side. Keep deadheading to inspire continuous bloom. Although pincushion flower tolerates excessive heat and humidity, Southern gardeners should place it where there's a little afternoon shade.

GOOD CHOICES: 'Butterfly Blue'; 'Pink Mist'

Sedum cultivars and hybrids
Sedum, Stonecrop

SIZE (height × width): 1 to 2 feet × 1 to 2 feet
BLOOM DESCRIPTION: dense umbels or clusters
BLOOM PERIOD: late summer
EXPOSURE: full sun to partial shade
HARDY IN ZONES: 4 to 9
SPECIAL NOTES: watch for aphids in early spring

Autumn's rich, earthy tones signal cooling temperatures and the winding down of the gardening year. Many of us grow the classic 'Autumn Joy' especially for this time of year. Actually 'Autumn Joy' and others like it (mauve-pink 'Brilliant' and smoky pink 'Matrona') have a seasonal metamorphosis of hue—the flower heads start summer light green, and change to raspberry red and then to garnet in fall. In all but the harshest climates, tenacious border sedums continue to delight as the foliage turns russet, copper, and bronze; come winter, they often wear a jaunty cap of snow.

Groundcover types of sedum, sometimes called stonecrop, are closely related but creep, spread, and sprawl. They have succulent, drought-resistant foliage that changes color in the fall, and their bright, starry flowers are carried in clusters.

All sedums are easy to grow. Full sun is ideal, but partial shade is tolerated in hot climates. Average, well-drained soil is just fine. Pests or diseases rarely trouble them.

GOOD CHOICES: 'Autumn Joy'; *S. spurium* 'Dragon's Blood'

Solidago cultivars
Goldenrod

SIZE (height × width): varies with species and cultivar
BLOOM DESCRIPTION: spires composed of tiny golden flowers
BLOOM PERIOD: midsummer into fall
EXPOSURE: full sun
HARDY IN ZONES: 3 to 9
SPECIAL NOTES: best in lean soil

Goldenrod is a real Cinderella story. Long scorned or overlooked as a weed, or avoided because it was falsely thought to cause hay fever (the real culprit is the much less showy ragweed, which blooms at the same time), it is now enjoying praise and popularity. And it's no wonder. In full bloom, it is a glorious sight, and the sunny color complements many other late-season bloomers—it's especially beautiful with the golden-center, blue-petaled New England aster. Poor to average, well-drained soil suits goldenrods just fine.

There are some terrific cultivars. The best ones are well behaved enough to stay in bounds in your perennial borders, and feature plush plumes of tiny golden flowers. Like their wild cousins, these improved goldenrods are easy to care for. The aptly named *S. rugosa* 'Fireworks' is a compact, dome-shaped, clump-forming plant, 3 to 4 feet tall, that cascades with bright yellow color. *S. sphacelata* 'Golden Fleece' is a dwarf selection, under 2 feet high, that carries its cheery sprays in a tidy, pyramidal fashion. It's ideal for smaller garden spaces.

GOOD CHOICES: *S. rugosa* 'Fireworks';
   S. sphacelata 'Golden Fleece'

Stachys byzantina
Lamb's Ears

SIZE (height × width): 8 to 12 inches × 2 to 3 feet

BLOOM DESCRIPTION: stout, woolly spikes

BLOOM PERIOD: late spring

EXPOSURE: full sun to partial shade

HARDY IN ZONES: 4 to 9

SPECIAL NOTES: does fine in lean soil

Stokesia laevis
Stokes' Aster

SIZE (height × width): 1 to 2 feet × 1 to 2 feet

BLOOM DESCRIPTION: fluffy 4-inch flower heads

BLOOM PERIOD: summer

EXPOSURE: full sun

HARDY IN ZONES: 5 to 9

SPECIAL NOTES: great for bouquets; untroubled by pests

As an attractive foliage plant for perennial displays, lamb's ears is without peer. So long as it is growing in poor to average soil, it will produce plenty of oblong leaves in a consistently lovely shade of silvery gray. The sweet name comes from the texture, which is as soft as felt . . . or a lamb's ear.

Because the plant likes to sprawl, it is ideal for a soft edging along a path or at the front of a mixed flower border. It goes great with pink, lavender, purple, or red-flowered perennials or roses. It is also lovely interwoven with irises—it seems to go with all types and colors.

The flowers appear each spring and are stout, woolly spikes studded with small magenta flowers. Some gardeners cut them off as soon as they appear, preferring to keep the foliage in the spotlight. 'Silver Carpet' is a nonflowering cultivar, while 'Helene von Stein' has large, felty leaves and a high degree of heat tolerance.

GOOD CHOICES: 'Silver Carpet'; 'Helene von Stein'

The flowers of Stokes' aster are big, 4 inches or so across, and very full and fluffy. The effect is created by the many thin petals (ray flowers) and a flurry of stamens in the middle. Two of the best cultivars are lavender-blue 'Blue Danube' and powder blue 'Klaus Jelitto'. 'Alba' is white and 'Mary Gregory' is yellow.

Stokes' aster forms a mound, covered in spear-shaped leaves that make a fine contrast to the interesting flowers. It is no trouble to grow, and happiest in soil that is neither too fertile nor too poor.

For the front of the border or container displays, there is an exciting new dwarf introduction. Only 8 to 12 inches high, 'Peachie's Pick' has a very tidy, compact growth habit. The name refers not to the color but to the plantswoman who found it, Peachie Saxon of Mississippi; from midsummer on, it's covered in proportionately smaller blue flowers.

GOOD CHOICES: 'Alba'; 'Blue Danube'; 'Klaus Jelitto'; 'Mary Gregory'; 'Peachie's Pick'

Thalictrum aquilegifolium
Meadow Rue
SIZE (height × width): 2 to 3 feet × 1 foot
BLOOM DESCRIPTION: clusters of fluffy little puffballs
BLOOM PERIOD: spring
EXPOSURE: partial shade
HARDY IN ZONES: 5 to 8
SPECIAL NOTES: no pests or diseases

Every spring, tiny lavender "beads" sway atop slender stalks, opening to enchanting little lavender powder-puff blooms. The cultivar 'Album' has the same buds but they open white. Carried in stem-top clusters, the blooming flowers give the plant a sweet but lively look.

The plants themselves are clothed in delicate green leaves that look very much like those of columbine (hence the species name *aquilegifolium*). Usually between 2 and 3 feet tall, meadow rue is a nice companion for irises, purple coneflower, and globe thistle, bringing a softness and daintiness to the scene. It thrives in full sun if it receives ample moisture. For best performance, grow meadow rue in part shade and moist, well-drained soil.

GOOD CHOICES: 'Album'; 'Thundercloud'

Tiarella cordifolia
Foamflower
SIZE (height × width): 6 to 12 inches × 6 to 12 inches
BLOOM DESCRIPTION: starry spires
BLOOM PERIOD: spring
EXPOSURE: partial to full shade
HARDY IN ZONES: 4 to 8
SPECIAL NOTES: best massed or as a groundcover

The white flowers of the aptly named foamflower are profuse and beautiful, but they are gone by summer. They leave behind exceptionally handsome foliage that will make your shade garden distinctive and fabulous. Each leaf is about 4 inches across and reminiscent of a coral bell's leaf or perhaps even a maple leaf. It is leaf color that makes the display so appealing. In the cultivar 'Mint Chocolate', the leaves are mint green with a chocolate overlay (and the flowers have a soft chocolate cast). 'Cygnet' leaves are beige but infused with tints of green and purple. One gorgeous cultivar has leaves so like those of an oak tree that it's named 'Oakleaf'.

Foamflower spreads by underground stems, which allows the plants to fill in an area nicely. A mat of foamflower will exclude weeds and shade its own roots, making the beautiful carpet virtually maintenance free.

The flowers are carried above the leaves every spring, to a height of 6 to 9 inches. The stems are studded along their length in tiny white blooms. A patch in full bloom is sensational.

GOOD CHOICES: 'Cygnet'; 'Mint Chocolate'; 'Oakleaf'

Tradescantia virginiana
Spiderwort

SIZE (height × width): 1 to 2 feet × 3 feet
BLOOM DESCRIPTION: 1 to 2 inches across, three-petaled
BLOOM PERIOD: summer
EXPOSURE: full sun to partial shade
HARDY IN ZONES: 5 to 8
SPECIAL NOTES: may be invasive in moist ground

Because this grassy-leaved, long-blooming, spreading plant tends to grow in large, thick drifts, it is ideal for a low-maintenance underplanting for trees and shrubs. Individual leaves can be as long as a foot, and they interweave and overlap, effectively excluding weeds. The distinctive, three-petaled flowers, about $1^1/2$ inches across, look a bit like tri-cornered colonial hats. In the species, they are purple or blue, but several good cultivars have different colors.

Spiderwort will grow in full sun, but it really fares best in partial or light shade. There it looks neater and seems to stay in bloom even longer. It's not fussy about soil quality, but appreciates some moisture. If need be, cut back flowering stems after their show is over, both to prevent self-sowing and perhaps to inspire a second round of bloom before the season is through.

GOOD CHOICES: maroon-flowered 'Hawaiian Punch'; large blue flowered 'Zwanenburg Blue'; white 'Snowcap'; golden-leaved 'Sweet Kate'

Tricyrtis formosana
Toad Lily

SIZE (height × width): 2 to 3 feet × 1 to 2 feet
BLOOM DESCRIPTION: small 1-inch funnels
BLOOM PERIOD: late summer into fall
EXPOSURE: partial to full shade
HARDY IN ZONES: 5 to 9
SPECIAL NOTES: spreads via its creeping roots

At the end of the summer and on into early autumn, this elegant plant generates an incredible flower show. The funnel-shaped blooms have flaring or outwardly curving petals that are usually creamy white, speckled or dabbed in violet, curiously evocative of an orchid. These appear in great numbers, singly and in clusters, bringing abundant color and interest to your shady beds at a time when color is very welcome. *T. hirta* 'Miyazaki' has purple-spotted white flowers; it's hardy in Zones 3 to 8. *T. formosana,* for Zones 5 to 9, has pale pink blooms with yellow throats and wine-purple markings.

The foliage, as is typical of true lilies, is lance-shaped and parallel-veined. The plant is a clump-former, but its creeping rootstock will expand the show in the seasons to come.

To get a good performance out of your toad lilies, grow them in slightly acidic soil that is evenly moist and well drained. Try them among ferns, or with purple-leaved alumroot.

GOOD CHOICES: 'Gilt Edge'; 'Amethystina'; 'Dark Beauty'; *T. hirta* 'Miyazaki'

Trollius × *cultorum*
Globeflower

SIZE (height × width): 2 to 3 feet × 1 foot
BLOOM DESCRIPTION: 1 to 2 inches, globe-shaped
BLOOM PERIOD: late spring
EXPOSURE: full sun to partial shade
HARDY IN ZONES: 3 to 8
SPECIAL NOTES: moist soil is a must, not tolerant of heat

With the twin virtues of great beauty and exceptional toughness, globeflower is irresistible. All the plant needs to thrive is moist soil. Late every spring, globeflower will delight you with long weeks of dazzling little blooms. These begin as round, fat buds and soon burst open to petal-packed, 1- to 2-inch, globe-shaped flowers that look a bit like tiny lotus blossoms (though they are actually related to buttercups).

The attractive foliage is dark green, palmate, deeply divided, and lines the stems at intervals. The plants tend to form rather loose, open clumps, yet stay within bounds.

Traditionally golden yellow or orange, globeflower is available in improved cultivars. 'Etna' is a fiery dark orange, while 'Lemon Queen' is lemon yellow. Because the flowers are usually borne on single, strong stems, globeflowers are a natural for sweet, cheerful bouquets.

GOOD CHOICES: 'Etna'; 'Lemon Queen'

Verbascum species and hybrids
Mullein

SIZE (height × width): 4 to 8 feet × 2 to 3 feet
BLOOM DESCRIPTION: spires of numerous tiny flowers
BLOOM PERIOD: summer
EXPOSURE: full sun
HARDY IN ZONES: 5 to 9
SPECIAL NOTES: best in well-drained soil

Thanks to its stately profile and easygoing nature, mullein is a dramatic candidate for a low-maintenance garden. Once considered nothing more than a roadside weed, in recent years it has seen splendid improvements in flower quality and color range. The usual primrose-yellow blooms are now joined by the red-and-white spectacle of *V. chaixii* var. *album,* the creamy pink, raspberry-red-centered 'Raspberry Ripple', and the 'Southern Charm' hybrids, which come in pastels from apricot to soft pink to light purple.

Some cultivars are tall plants, best placed to the back of a sunny border or shown off along a wall or fence. *V. chaixii* and *V.* 'Southern Charm' are smaller, usually 2 to 3 feet tall, and should be sited accordingly. Most are technically biennials, so all you see during their first summer is large, felted, silvery-gray leaves in a low, ground-hugging rosette. Their second summer, though, is worth waiting for, when substantial spires rise up and display their beautiful blooms for weeks on end.

GOOD CHOICES: white or yellow flowered *V. chaixii;* 'Raspberry Ripple'; pastel-hued 'Southern Charm' hybrids; 'Cherry Helen'

Verbena bonariensis
Verbena, Vervain

SIZE (height × width): 2 to 4 feet × 2 to 3 feet
BLOOM DESCRIPTION: small, somewhat loose clusters
BLOOM PERIOD: summer
EXPOSURE: full sun to partial shade
HARDY IN ZONES: 6 to 9
SPECIAL NOTES: makes a good "see-through" plant

Few other perennials can rival verbenas for their tireless summer-long show. Literally in bloom from early summer until the first frost of fall, you can count on these tough plants to keep their perky flowers coming—all you need to do is pinch off spent flowers from time to time. Usually purple, verbenas weave in and mix well with many other perennials. The airy profile of *V. bonariensis* means you can place it near the front a border, where it won't block your view of plants behind.

Well-drained soil seems to be their key requirement. There, verbenas will grow easily and quickly and tolerate periods of drought or neglect.

Trailing or creeping species may be used as groundcovers, in planter boxes, or even in hanging baskets—look for varieties of *V. canadensis* and *V. tenuisecta*. They're just as tough and floriferous.

GOOD CHOICES: *V. tenuisecta* cultivars; *V. canadensis* cultivars (which vary in hardiness and are often used as annuals in colder regions); Temari 'Patio Blue', 'Patio Red', and 'Patio Salmon'

Veronica spicata
Spike Speedwell, Veronica

SIZE (height × width): 1 to 2 feet × 1 to 2 feet
BLOOM DESCRIPTION: dense spires, usually about 10 inches tall
BLOOM PERIOD: summer
EXPOSURE: full sun to partial shade
HARDY IN ZONES: 4 to 9
SPECIAL NOTES: deer resistant

Thanks to its full, showy flower spikes, veronica is a terrific choice for any sunny or partially sunny perennial display. You can count on it to be in bloom for most of the summer—a performance few other flowers can equal. Usually blue-purple, its most famous edition is the sensational, 18- to 20-inch-high 'Sunny Border Blue', which won top Perennial Plant Association honors in 1993 and continues to be phenomenally popular. This versatile plant mixes well with many other mid-border perennials. Rosy red 'Red Fox' is an exciting color variation.

A good edging veronica, at 8 inches tall, is the closely related *V. peduncularis* 'Georgia Blue'. Its flowers are true blue and it forms low, spreading mounds. Silvery-gray leaves consort with 10-inch blue spikes in lovely *V. incana*.

No matter which veronica you choose, give this easy perennial moderate soil that is neither too damp nor too dry; it adapts well to full sun or partial shade. Pests and diseases are unheard of, and deer never nibble it.

GOOD CHOICES: 'Sunny Border Blue'; 'Red Fox'; *V. peduncularis* 'Georgia Blue'; *V. incana*

GROWING PERENNIALS IN THE MIDWEST

Melinda Myers

Introduction

Perennials have escaped the back yard garden and moved to the front yard, to shrub beds, and to any available planting space. In fact many perennials are taking over the front yard replacing large lawns and foundation plantings. You can see all types of perennial gardens, including English cottage gardens filled with a collection of colorful blossoms. The New American Gardens are composed of masses of ornamental grasses and perennials, and mixed borders fill our landscapes. This trend has brought color, birds, butterflies, and winter interest to many Midwestern homes.

No matter the garden style, everyone seems to want season-long bloom with no maintenance. While many perennials require less maintenance, they do require some yearly care. Always select perennials suited to the growing location, and the time and effort you are willing and able to expend.

Very few perennials bloom from spring through fall. But a well-planned garden can provide year-round interest from foliage, flowers, and seedpods. Some gardeners, myself included, mix a few annuals in with their perennials. Annuals can fill in voids left by winter damage, between new plantings, and

created by planning mistakes. An added challenge is the often harsh growing conditions of the Midwest. Our weather is often described as variable, extreme, and unpredictable. Frequent cool, wet springs are often followed by hot and humid summers and cold winters, making gardening a challenge. Though the weather varies throughout this region we do share one thing in common—extremes and variability.

Much of the Midwest experiences freezing temperatures followed by a January or February thaw that includes a week of temperatures in the 60s. Many perennials will appear just in time for a sudden temperature plunge below zero. This constant fluctuation can damage—even kill—perennials and leave gardeners struggling to help their gardens survive.

Springs tend to be cool and moist with fluctuating temperatures and unexpected late spring snow showers or ice storms. May snow storms have taken down hundreds of mature trees, and ice storms that coat spring bulbs make you wonder if the planting season will ever arrive. Besides being frustrating, the lingering snow or cool, wet spring weather can increase the risk of disease.

Then there is the heat and humidity of summer. Summers are usually warm with temperatures reaching 80, 90, and even 100 degrees Fahrenheit. These hot spells are often interrupted by a weather front that brings summer showers or thunderstorms and cooler temperatures. But those in the southern Midwest suffer longer, hotter, more humid and often drier summers. This can be hard on perennials and the gardener. The summer extremes can halt flowering and increase pest problems.

Those around Lake Michigan may have to wait a little longer for warm summer temperatures. On a positive side the lake moderates both summer and winter temperature extremes and extends the season by increasing the number of frost-free days. But move just a few miles away and you will feel the difference.

Fortunately there are many beautiful perennials that will tolerate or even thrive in these less-than-ideal conditions. And if you're like me, you like the perennials that give you the greatest beauty with the least amount of care. Many old favorites and new introductions will do just that.

Cold and Heat Hardiness

Hardiness is usually associated with cold tolerance but now it also includes the plants ability to withstand extreme heat. See the USDA Cold Hardiness map on page 214 to determine your cold hardy zones. Cold hardiness is based upon the average annual minimum temperature. Each zone represents an area within a ten degree range. The "a" and "b" ratings further break down the area into 5-degree differences. The Midwest includes cold hardiness Zone 7a in the south through Zone 3a in the north. There are even a few hardy gardeners tackling this job in a small area of 2b in northern Minnesota.

Heat Hardiness is a relatively new rating for the country and our plants. This hardiness rating is based on maximum summer temperatures. The country was divided into regions based on the number of eighty-six degree (or higher) days that occur during the growing season. Eighty-six degrees was selected since it is the temperature at which some plants can suffer injury. Different parts of the plants may be affected at different times and in different ways. The plant may fail to bloom, or be stunted or wither.

A Heat Zone map is available for reference from the American Horticultural Society.

Selecting the Location

Take a little time to evaluate garden views and growing conditions. If you are adding a new garden or expanding an existing bed check out the view from inside and outside your home. Make sure the garden is in an area where it can be enjoyed and easily maintained.

Consider the sunlight both for the plants and your enjoyment. Record how much light the garden gets throughout the day and throughout the growing season. Then select plants that will thrive in these light conditions. Also evaluate how the sunlight plays upon the plants and surrounding structures. Lighting can change the look of your garden.

Check the soil and drainage. Try to correct problem areas before planting and always match the plant to the soil conditions.

Drought tolerant plants will survive the rigors of sandy soil and hot summers better than moisture loving plants that will require mulch, water and constant care just to survive.

Find or create microclimates in the landscape. Sheltered areas, warming stones, and windbreaks can result in warmer or cooler areas within your own landscape. These warm and cool spots allow you to push the hardiness zone, growing plants just beyond it.

Designing the Garden

Once you have a list of potential plants for the garden check out their bloom time. You can design your landscape so something is always blooming in every part of the yard. Or you may prefer peak areas of interest that change throughout the season. You may have one garden or a section of a garden that looks great for a short period of time. As it fades another area comes into full bloom and becomes the new focal point. Place the gardens in the areas where you will get the most enjoyment when they are at their peak.

If you get stuck, try first designing your garden in a vase. Collect flowers that bloom at the same time. If they look good together in a vase they will probably make good-looking garden partners. Design gardens that fit your lifestyle and your desire to have cut flowers, attract wildlife, or grow fragrant flowers.

Don't forget to plan for year-round interest. Use a mixture of spring, summer, and fall blooming perennials in each garden. Or design individual gardens for display at a specific time of the season. Perhaps you place the spring garden outside the kitchen window, the summer garden next to the deck, and fall

garden outside the family room. Select the design that best fits your family's likes and habits.

Consider the foliage as well as the flowers when planning the garden. Some plants like coralbells have attractive foliage all season long. Brighten the winter garden by including some perennials that provide winter interest and food for wildlife. Add ornamental grasses, coneflowers, and other plants that make a great self-serve bird feeder. Plus a few seed pods, swaying grasses, and evergreen leaves can add motion, interest and beauty to the landscape during our longest season—winter.

Soil Preparation

The more time and energy you invest in improving the soil the healthier and more beautiful your perennials will be. Add several inches of peat moss, aged manure or other organic matter to the top 12 inches of soil. This amazing material will improve drainage in heavy soils and increase the water-holding capacity of sandy and gravelly soils.

Consider taking a soil test to find out how much and what type of fertilizer is needed. Follow the soil test results to save money and increase your gardening success by adding only the nutrients and lime your soil needs. Contact your local Extension Office or check the yellow pages for certified soil testing labs.

Only add fertilizer if recommended by your soil test report. Recent research found that organic matter usually provides sufficient nutrients for perennials growing in properly prepared soil. Avoid excess fertilizer that can cause poor flowering, leggy growth and stunted root systems. Overdoing fertilizer can cause some plants to topple. Incorporate no more than 1 pound of a 10 percent, or 2 pounds of a 5 percent nitrogen fertilizer per 100 square feet if soil test results are not available and you feel your garden soil needs a nutrient boost.

Planting Perennials in the Midwest

Perennials are sold as bare root, container grown, and field-potted. You can buy them through a garden catalogue, on-line, at a garden center or perennial nursery. Check with friends, local botanical gardens and the Extension Service for your county for sources of quality plants. No one needs to buy problems—most gardens come with enough of their own.

Bare root perennials are plants sold without any growing media on the roots. Plant bareroot perennials as soon as they arrive in spring and the ground can be worked. If the weather is bad, store the plants in a cool (frost free) location, such as a root cellar or refrigerator, until they can be planted outdoors.

Container-grown plants are grown and sold in pots. They are available in 4-inch, 1-gallon or 2-gallon pots. The smaller plants may look a little sparse at first, but leave sufficient room for these to reach full size.

Plant container-grown perennials spring through fall. Do the majority of planting in spring and late summer. This allows plants to become established before the heat of summer and cold of winter make establishment difficult. However most perennials are tough and can be planted just about anytime that proper post-planting care can be provided.

Field-potted plants are grown in the field and potted for delivery as they are dug. Transplant with care since their root system is not established.

Care and Maintenance

Proper soil preparation, plant selection, and planting will help reduce future maintenance. Water is critical for establishing and growing plants. Give special attention to new plantings. Check them every other day for the first weeks.

Water early in the day to reduce the risk of disease and the amount of water lost to evaporation. Consider using a watering wand or drip irrigation system to keep the water off the plants and on the soil where it is needed.

Reduce the need to water and improve your plant's health with mulch. Spread a 1- to 2-inch layer of organic material such as cocoa bean shells, twice shredded bark, shredded leaves, or pine needles over the soil surface surrounding the perennials. Mulch conserves moisture and reduces watering frequency. Established, mulched, and drought tolerant plants can tolerate longer periods between watering. It's time to water when the top 4 inches of soil is cool and crumbly. When needed, water thoroughly so the top 8 inches of soil is moist. This encourages deep roots that are more drought tolerant which is better for the plant and less work for you.

Mulch also reduces weed problems by preventing many weed seeds from germinating.

Some gardeners resort to chemicals to keep troublesome weeds under control. Spot-treat quack grass, ground ivy and other hard-to-control perennial weeds with a total vegetation killer. Be sure to protect the nearby plants or they can be killed. A master gardener taught me a useful trick: Remove the bottom of a plastic milk jug. Cover the weed and spray with the total vegetation killer. This concentrates the spray where it is needed and protects desirable plants from damage.

Pre-emergents can be worked into the soil to prevent weed seeds from sprouting. They can also prevent perennial seeds from sprouting, or damage desirable plants. Be sure to read and follow all label directions before purchasing and using any chemical in your garden.

If your perennial garden is a weed patch it may be easier to start over. Remove the plants you want to keep. Make sure to remove all the roots and rhizomes of unwanted weeds. Then treat the area as described below. Amend the soil, plant, and keep on top of the weeds to avoid this problem in the future.

Avoid many difficult weeds by controlling them before planting the garden. Eliminate quack grass, ground ivy, and other perennial weeds prior to planting. Spray the actively growing weeds with a total vegetation killer. Wait four to fourteen days (check label) before tilling and preparing the soil. Badly infested areas may benefit from a second treatment as soon as new weed growth appears (again waiting an appropriate length of time to prepare soil and plant).

Alternatively, you can cover the area with newspaper and woodchips. Edge the garden and cover the soil to block out the sunlight and kill many of the weeds. The newspaper and woodchips decompose, improving the soil while reducing the weed population.

Deadheading and Pruning

Some plants require a lot of work and others perform fine on their own. Some cultivars have been bred to reduce maintenance and decrease problems. Select the perennial and its cultivars that best fit your growing conditions and maintenance schedule.

Control plant height, reduce floppiness, and delay flowering with proper pruning. Cut back sedum, coneflower, asters, and mums early in the season. This encourages shorter, stiffer branches. Stop pruning by July to avoid delaying bloom until frost.

Thin out $1/4$ to $1/3$ of the stems on garden phlox, monarda and other powdery mildew susceptible plants. Thinning improves light penetration and air flow to encourage stiffer stems and reduce disease problems.

Remove faded flowers, (deadhead) to lengthen bloom time and improve the appearance of some perennials. Deadheading allows the plant to put energy into forming new flowers instead of setting seed. Stop deadheading at the end of the bloom time to encourage the plants to harden off and form seeds for the birds and winter interest for you.

Use a garden scissors or hand pruner to make the cuts. Remove the flower stem just above the first set of leaves or side shoots. Prune back further on the stem after the second flush of flowers or when floppy growth appears. This encourages fuller, more compact growth and more attractive foliage.

Divide perennials to improve their health and appearance or to start new plants. Start with plants that are too big for the location, flower poorly, flop over, or are open in the center. Dig out the clump and set it next to the hole. Use a knife or shovel to divide the clump into several pieces. Prepare the old and all the new locations by adding compost, peat moss, or other organic matter. What you don't plant you can give to friends.

Pest Control

Perennials are fairly pest free. Always use the most pest-resistant species and varieties available. Match the plant to the growing conditions, provide proper care and keep weeds under control to further reduce insect and disease problems.

Check plants frequently. Removing a few insects or a diseased leaf is often enough to keep the pest from taking over and destroying your garden. When problems arise don't just reach for the spray can. Consult with your Extension Service, garden center staff, or other professionals. They can help you identify the problem, decide if treatment is needed, and plot the best course of action.

Winter Care

Remove all disease and insect infested plant debris in fall to reduce the source of infection. I like to leave the seedheads and healthy foliage for winter interest and improved plant health. Research has revealed that letting plants stand for the winter increases hardiness. Plus, they provide a great habitat for beneficial insects, attract some beautiful butterflies, and supply food for the birds. In this case, your major cleanup comes in late winter or early spring before new growth begins.

Reduce winter care by selecting hardy plants that are tolerant of Midwest winters. Proper soil preparation will also improve the health and hardiness of plants. However, sometimes all of us break the rules and plant a little late in the season, or plant something that is not reliably hardy for our area because we have to have that plant. Winter mulch can help these tender plants and new plantings survive Midwest winters. Cover the plants with evergreen branches, straw or marsh hay after the ground surface freezes. This is usually done after a week of freezing temperatures. I usually wait until after Christmas. I gather all the discarded trees in the neighborhood, remove the branches and mulch any tender plantings. It is free mulch and a great way to recycle trees.

Remove the mulch in spring as new growth begins. Winter mulching keeps the soil temperature consistently cold. This eliminates frost heaving caused by the freezing and thawing of soil throughout the winter. Frost heaving damages plant roots and can even push perennials right out of the soil.

And what about those unplanted perennials—you know, the ones you didn't get into the garden before winter? Or maybe you are growing a few perennials in above-ground planters. Both need special care to get through the winter. The small amount of soil in the container is not enough to protect the roots from the cold winters found throughout most of the Midwest. You can bury the container in an unused but protected spot in the landscape near the house. Or move the container garden into an unheated garage. In the far north, you may want to increase the insulation by placing the pot in a box or larger container filled with foam peanuts or other insulating material. Check the soil and water anytime the soil is dry and not frozen.

TASK LIST
for Perennial Growers in the Midwest

Every living thing needs some care and attention, and perennials are no exception. Fortunately we can keep this to a minimum by selecting the right perennial for the growing conditions. Look for the most pest resistant species and cultivars, then make sure their maintenance needs match the time and effort you want to dedicate to gardening. I find a little weeding, some digging and dividing, and a bit of deadheading is therapeutic. More than that becomes a chore in my busy schedule. Now spread these minor tasks throughout the year and perennial gardening is fun!

Since the weather can vary from year to year and throughout the Midwest, we will look at seasonal care and take our maintenance cue from nature. Use your calendar as a guideline but follow the weather patterns for best results. And always read and follow all label directions whenever purchasing and using any pesticide.

Late Winter to Early Spring

- Remove winter protection as the temperatures consistently hover near freezing.
- Cut back grasses and perennials left standing for the winter. Compost the debris.
- Plant bare-root perennials as soon as they arrive. Heel plants in the garden or store them in a cool dark location if they can't be planted right away. Store in a spare refrigerator, root cellar, or other location where temperatures remain above freezing. Keep the roots moist and covered with peat moss or sawdust.
- Plant sprouted bare root perennials and grow in a sunny frost-free location. Move these outdoors after the danger of frost has passed.
- As growth begins, start digging and dividing summer and fall blooming perennials that have outgrown their location, become floppy, failed to bloom, or need to be moved to a new location.
- Be careful not to disturb late emerging perennials like butterfly weed and balloon flower.

Spring

- Continue with tasks of late winter and early spring.
- Finish digging and dividing summer and fall blooming perennials.
- Field-grown and dormant potted or bare-root perennials can be added to the garden as soon as the soil can be worked.
- Harden off and plant greenhouse-raised perennials outdoors after the danger of frost has passed.
- Spread a 1- to 2-inch layer of compost over the soil in established perennial gardens. This provides all the nutrients and amendments most perennials need.
- Fertilize only if needed. Follow soil test recommendations (see Midwest introduction for more details).

- Take a soil test for new planting beds or those experiencing problems.

- New beds can be developed any time the ground is workable and you have time. Work the soil when it is moist. Working wet soil results in clods. Grab a handful of soil and gently squeeze. Now tap with your finger. If it breaks into smaller pieces it is ready to work. Work several inches of organic matter into the top 8 to 12 inches of soil. Rake smooth and allow the soil to settle for a week or gently sprinkle before planting.

- Thin powdery mildew-prone plants such as bee balm and garden phlox. Remove $1/4$ to $1/3$ of the stems, increasing light and air penetration and reducing disease problems.

- Cut back summer and fall blooming plants subject to flopping.

- Keep asters and mums pinched back to 6 inches to encourage short compact growth.

Summer

- Replace any dead plants and fill any voids in the garden.

- Continue planting perennials through-out the season. Limit new plantings during the hot, dry part of summer. This minimizes the stress on young plants and workload on your part. Plant tender perennials early in the season so they can become established before winter.

- Finish pinching and pruning fall bloomers by the end of June.

- Deadhead spring and early summer bloomers to encourage a second flush of flowers.

- Cut back early bloomers that have finished flowering and need a little rejuvenation.

- Mulch with shredded leaves, cocoa bean shells or other organic material to help conserve moisture and reduce weeds. Avoid burying the crowns of the plants.

- Water as needed. New plants should be checked several times a week. Keep their roots cool and moist. Established plants can tolerate longer periods of drought. Water thoroughly when the top 4 to 6 inches of soil feels cool and crumbly. Check perennials growing in containers daily and water thoroughly allowing excess to run out the bottom of the pot.

- Monitor and control pests as needed. Remove weeds that can harbor disease, and pest-infected leaves and stems. (See the section on common pest problems and their controls.)

- Look for signs of animal and rodent damage. Apply repellents, use scare tactics, or install a decorative fence to keep animals out.

Late Summer/Early Fall

- Continue to pull weeds and control pest and animal damage.

- Dig and divide early blooming perennials that have outgrown their location, become floppy, failed to bloom, or need to be moved to a new location.

- Dig and divide peonies if needed.

- Finish all planting and transplanting by late September to mid October for the greatest overwintering success.

- Take advantage of the good weather and get a jump on spring by preparing new perennial garden beds now.

- Evaluate the health, beauty and vigor of your plants. This will help in planning for replacements and new additions to the garden.

Fall

- Plant bulbs throughout the perennial garden for added spring interest.

- Leave the stems or mark the location of late emerging perennials such as butterfly weed, balloon flower and hardy hibiscus.

- Sink unplanted perennials into a vacant garden area for winter. The top of the container should be level with the surrounding soil.

- Gather materials needed for winter protection.

- Look for tracks, droppings, and other signs that animals are present and waiting to make a meal of your perennials. Start using repellents, scare tactics, or barriers before they start feeding.

- Mulch new plantings, tender perennials, or those subject to frost heaving after the ground freezes. Straw or evergreen branches make a suitable winter mulch.

- Remove any insect or disease infested plant material.

- Consider letting the stems and seedpods of healthy perennials stand for winter. Doing this increases winter hardiness, provides a habitat for beneficial insects, and invites birds to the winter landscape.

Winter

- Store pesticides securely in a dark frost-free location.

- Start your wish list of tools, gloves, books, and perennials you need or want for your gardening efforts. Add them to your holiday gift list.

- Start planning your garden for the upcoming season.

- Review the notes in your garden journal. If you don't have one, now's the time to start. Record information on the names, place of purchase, planting location, and care of each rose you plant.

- Scour catalogues for long-time favorites and new introductions.

- Place your order for bare-root perennials you will be purchasing through the mail or on-line.

- Attend local plant society meetings, garden shows and lectures for fresh ideas and new resources.

- Relax and enjoy the winter beauty of your well-planned garden.

LOW-MAINTENANCE PERENNIALS
for the Midwest

Each of us may have a different idea of what constitutes low maintenance; some don't mind deadheading, others don't mind weeding a few stray seedlings, while some dutifully place support structures near the plants as needed. I like to minimize all maintenance activities so here are the criteria I use when selecting low maintenance long blooming perennials:

- Needs infrequent division—every 4 years or longer
- Is self supporting—no staking required
- Is not weedy in the garden or invasive in natural areas
- Faded flowers do not detract from the plant's overall appearance
- Is pest free
- Is hardy

This list is by no means complete, just a foundation for you to build upon. And a few of the plants I included may be lacking in one of the categories but their overall benefits outweighed the one weakness. I will be sure to point these out so you can decide if they are worth that little bit of extra effort.

Spring through early Summer

Peony (*Paeonia lactiflora*)
An old fashioned favorite that provides fragrant spring blooms, nice summer foliage, and fall color. Select cultivars with strong stems so no staking is required.

Use peonies as a backdrop for other flowers, mixed with shrubs for a foundation planting, or bring a few in for your favorite flower vase. I have stumbled across peonies that have been growing in the same garden for over 75 years. Though they do not need frequent division gardeners often like to share a piece with a friend.

Fringed Bleeding Heart (*Dicentra eximia* and *Dicentra formosa*)
The fine ferny foliage provides a nice backdrop for the rosy-pink or white flowers. Watch for the peak display in late spring through early summer and with some minor deadheading you will have continuous bloom throughout the season. A small plant—only 12 to 18 inches tall and wide—it's perfect for the edge of a perennial garden or in a shady spot in a rock garden. The ferny foliage makes a nice ground cover and the flowers are attractive in the garden or a vase indoors.

Bleeding Heart (*Dicentra spectabilis*)
Perhaps you know the story that lies within the flowers. Pull apart a flower and see if you can find the princess, slipper, and sailboat then create a fairy tale of your own. This spring bloomer puts on a shorter lived, but bigger display in spring. Reaching 2 to 3 feet tall and wide, this beauty covered with heart shaped flowers adds appeal to any spring landscape. The plants die back in midsummer so grow them where their absence won't be noticed. Or try cutting them back as the flowers fade to encourage new foliage that will last all summer.

Coral Bells (*Heuchera* spp.)
Add this plant to your landscape for interesting foliage and flowers that attract hummingbirds and make great cut flowers.

Common coralbells (*Heuchera sanguinea*) forms a mass of foliage about 8 to 15 inches high. In late spring through early summer wiry stems filled with bell-shaped flowers will rise above the foliage and continue sporadically throughout the summer. Don't be afraid to use this low grower in a rock garden, as a ground cover, or at the edge of a perennial garden. You can see right through the airy bloom to the plants behind. The foliage looks good all summer and is evergreen in mild winters even in northern regions of the Midwest. Palace purple (*Heuchera micrantha* 'Palace Purple') is a purple-leafed *Heuchera* that helped spark the interest in breeding and buying of fancy-leaved coralbells. Watch for all the new cultivars that keep popping up in the garden center. This is one of the few perennials small-space gardeners can collect and still have room for other plants.

This flexible plant tolerates full sun to fairly heavy shade and a wide range of soils. Avoid scorch on the purple-leafed varieties by keeping them out of the direct, hot afternoon sun. Divide the plants every few years to avoid woody stems and watch for frost heaving. Plant the crowns an inch below the soil surface and reset frost heaved plants in early spring.

Cranesbill Geranium (*Geranium sanguineum*)

Add this perennial to shrub beds and perennial gardens for several seasons of interest. In late spring through early summer the lobed green leaves are covered with pink, lavender or white blooms. Many will continue to bloom sporadically throughout the summer.

Cut back the plant to 4 inches after the main bloom to encourage new growth as needed. In fall watch for the reddish purple foliage that often lasts through mild winters.

Geranium varieties vary in size from 8 to 15 inches tall and 24 inches or more wide. Some are fast growing and need room to spread or need an occasional dividing to contain in smaller spaces. This plant tolerates full sun to part shade and prefers moist, well-drained soil.

Try bigroot geranium (*Geranium maccrorrhizum)* for hotter and dryer locations. This geranium maintains good looking leaves all season long. It grows about 12 to 18 inches tall and reseeds allowing it to fill in large areas quickly. The wonderful red-purple fall color makes a colorful end to the growing season.

Summer Bloomers

Clump Verbena (*Verbena canadensis*)

This plant almost fits the bill as the perfect perennial. Mine blooms from late May/early June through frost. The rose-pink flowers are fragrant and attract hummingbirds and butterflies. The deeply lobed leaves hug the ground making this 6- to 9-inch by 18-inch plant an excellent edger and ground cover. I first used mine trailing over the wall by my back alley and it planted itself throughout my garden. This can be a downside for some. You may need to do some light weeding to keep this plant in its place, though I like to let mine wander through the garden. Though rated hardy in Zones 4 through 7, I find hardiness varies with the source. A hard winter may kill the parent plant but there is usually enough seed in the ground to make up for the loss. This plant prefers full sun and well-drained soil.

Hosta (*Hosta* spp.)

Be careful—you too may become a hosta-holic. It starts with a few free plants from a friend, then you buy a couple with interesting variegation in the leaves or with fragrant flowers. The next thing you know you are ripping out grass and growing trees just to create the right environment for your hosta collection.

Whether you need a little variegated foliage to brighten the shade or bold textured leaves to contrast with the ferns and astilbe in the garden—hostas are a sure winner. The easy care and wide variety of choices (6 inches to 4 feet tall and wide) make it easy to add to any shade garden.

Grow hosta in full to part shade. Though some cultivars like 'Sum and Substance', 'Royal Standard', and 'Gold Edger' tolerate sun, most hosta leaves will scorch (brown) when grown in too much sun. And yes slugs are a problem. Avoid damage by growing slug-resistant hosta like 'Blue Angel' and 'Krossa Regal', 'Francis Williams', and *Hosta sieboldiana* 'Elegans'. These snails without shells eat holes in the leaves of hostas and other shade-loving plants. A little beer in a shallow dish works great as a trap. Or try Sluggo® or other environmentally friendly slug products that use iron phosphate as the active ingredient. This product kills the slugs but does not harm the slug eating toads and birds or other wildlife.

If deer have you swearing off hostas try lungwort (*Pulmonaria*). This plant seems to be less appealing to deer and has a similar appearance to hostas. Or treat hostas with a repellent as soon as the leaves emerge in spring and throughout the season. The bitter taste may drive deer elsewhere to dine.

Daylily (*Hemerocallis* spp.)

Get your mind out of the ditch and into the garden center. Orange daylilies seen growing in the roadside ditches demonstrate this plant's hardiness but the numerous varieties provide superb beauty and longer lasting bloom. Try some of the repeat bloomers such as 'Stella de Oro', 'Happy Returns', or 'Rosy Returns' for summer-long flowers and good looking foliage. Divide repeat bloomers every three or four years to keep them blooming all summer long. Or mix a few varieties of one-time blooming daylilies (with different bloom times) for a summer full of flowers. Though each flower only lasts a day the flower spikes contain many blooms providing a month of color.

Daylily flowers are great for cutting and attracting butterflies and hummingbirds to the garden. Select varieties with nice foliage or remove declining leaves to encourage new growth. Daylilies prefer full to part sun and tolerate a wide range of soil types.

Threadleaf Coreopsis (*Coreopsis verticillata*)

A near perfect perennial, with fine foliage covered with small yellow daisy-like flowers from June through October—and no dead-heading needed. The straight species is reliably hardy and grows 2 to 3 feet tall by 2 feet wide. Threadleaf coreopsis performs best in full sun with moist well-drained soil, and will tolerate droughty conditions once established. Divide plants every four years to keep them free-flowering and avoid the need to deadhead. 'Moonbeam' is 18 to 24 inches with clear yellow flowers. I find it's not reliably hardy in northern gardens with clay soils. 'Zagreb' is shorter, only 12 inches, and hardier.

This is one perennial that can blend well in a formal, informal, or more natural garden. The fine foliage looks good all season and the flowers attract butterflies and can be used for cutting. Let the airy plants and seedheads stand for added winter interest. Though I think you have to be a diehard fan, like me, to appreciate its subtle winter beauty.

Snakeroot, Bugbane (*Cimicifuga* spp.)

Add a low maintenance towering beauty to your shade garden. Snakeroot (*Cimicifuga racemosa*) produces spikes of fragrant white flowers on plants 4 to 6 feet tall. The fern-like foliage looks good all season and mixes well with hostas, astilbe, ferns, ginger, and other shade loving perennials. The white flowers help brighten up the shade and add vertical interest in the garden. The white flowers occur on dark stems that blend into the shade. I prefer the common name fairy candle that so aptly describes this plant. It appears as if the candle-like flowers are floating, with the help of fairies, in the air. Mix in a few Autumn snakeroot (*Cimicifuga simplex*) for a fall floral display. Consider adding some additional color to the garden by using 'Brunette' or other purple-leafed varieties.

Garden Phlox (*Phlox paniculata*)

Yes, I am talking about the summer blooming phlox that seems to be synonymous with

powdery mildew. Fortunately you can have the long season of bloom without the mildew. Start by selecting mildew resistant varieties such as 'David' (white) and 'Katherine'(rose). Or grow the garden phlox look-a-like *Phlox maculata* that resists mildew.

Reduce mildew problems on susceptible species by growing the plants in full sun with plenty of space. Remove $1/3$ of the emerging stems in spring to provide better air flow and reduce the risk of mildew.

Pinch back the plants in early June to reduce the height and delay bloom. Deadhead for even better reflowering and to prevent reseeding. Use these 2- to 4-foot-tall plants in sunny perennial borders for vertical accent, for cut flowers, and for attracting butterflies. The white, pink, lavender, or bicolor flowers provide fragrant summer-long bloom from July through September.

Russian Sage (*Perovskia atriplicifolia*)

This perennial has won the hearts of many gardeners. The fragrant gray-green foliage provides a nice base for the pale blue flowers that appear from July through September. The large, 4- to 5-foot plant is a nice backdrop for perennials and combines nicely with shrub roses and purple coneflower.

Grow it in full sun and well-drained soil. Prune the plant back to 3 to 4 inches in late winter. The fragrance will provide a little "aromatherapy" as you clean up the perennial garden in late winter. An additional trim by $1/2$ when the plants reach 12 inches will encourage denser and sturdier growth that may be needed for older plants. Or try

'Longin' that is narrowly upright, or the shorter 'Little Spire' to avoid staking chores.

Fall Bloomers

Sedum 'Autumn Joy'

The outstanding show and long season of interest explain why this is such a popular perennial. Pink flowers top the succulent foliage in August. These deepen and turn to rusty red after a frost. The seedheads persist for winter and add a little needed plant relief from the long Midwest winters. Grow sedum in full sun and well-drained soils for best results. Use low growers in rock gardens and walls or as ground covers and edging plants. More upright types can also be used in mixed perennial borders. 'Autumn Joy' sedum grows about 24 inches tall and 18 inches wide. Plants may flop open when grown in shade or rich moist soils. Eliminate this problem by cutting the plants back to 4 inches in early June.

Consider adding other sedums to your perennial and rock gardens. Try the Orange stonecrop (*Sedum kamtschaticum*) for orange or yellow summer bloom and outstanding fall color. Or include the 8- to 12-inch-tall 'Vera Jameson' with interesting purple-pink leaves, or the improved 'Purple Emperor' for a little different look.

Goldenrod (*Solidago* spp.)

Often mistakenly blamed for hay fever, this beautiful native makes a nice addition to the fall garden. Its less noticeable weedy neighbor, ragweed, is the cause of hay fever. Goldenrod's yellow flowers mix nicely with asters and ornamental grasses and are great for cutting, attracting butterflies, and adding interest to the winter garden. Look for their beautiful yellow flowers from July through October.

Plants vary in size from 3 to 4 feet tall by 2 feet wide. 'Fireworks' is one of my favorites. The flower stems shoot out in all directions like a fireworks display. 'Fireworks' and other goldenrods need little care when grown in a natural setting. Use a compact type such as 'Golden Fleece' or 'Crown of Rays', or do a little pruning to encourage compact fuller growth in the flower border. Pinch plants back in May or cut the plants back by half in early June. This tough plant prefers full sun and tolerates dry soils.

Ornamental Grasses

For the ultimate in low maintenance and a long season of interest, consider adding ornamental grasses to the flower border. Select non-invasive clump formers to avoid creating lots of work and problems with the environment. Cut the plants back at the end of winter and you have done your yearly maintenance.

Most grasses prefer full sun and well-drained soils. Allow the plants to stand for winter interest. Many have fall color and some attract birds to the garden. I incorporate ornamental grasses in my small lot to provide vertical accents and screening in small spaces. Those with larger landscapes can mass grasses for a grander effect.

Feather Reed Grass (*Calamagrostis* × *acutiflora* 'Karl Foerster')

This tough grass tolerates difficult growing conditions including heavy clay soils, salt, cold, and reflected heat. It blooms in early summer and reaches a size of 4 to 5 feet tall and about 2 feet wide. Use this mixed with other perennials, next to a water feature, or as a low screen for hiding the compost pile or dog house. Try the variegated and slightly shorter (24 to 30 inches) cultivar 'Overdam'. The green and white leaves easily blend with the flowers and foliage of other plants while brightening any garden. Or try the later blooming Korean feather reed grass—*Calamagrostis arundinacea*. It is a little shorter and blooms later than feather reed, making it a great partner for purple coneflower.

Grow feather reed grass in full sun or light shade. It prefers moist well-drained soils, but will tolerate moist soils and even heavy clay, or wet soils with drainage. Plant this grass in spring or early summer to get it established before winter.

Blue Oat Grass (*Helictotrichon sempervirens*)

This is my favorite among the blue foliage grasses. It tolerates clay soils much better than blue fescue and provides good winter interest. The rosette of blue leaves grows about 2 feet tall and wide. It blooms in late summer though some gardeners choose to remove the beige seedheads and just enjoy the foliage.

Try using this as a focal point, filler with bolder texture plants, or massed in a New American Garden design. Don't worry if you forget to cut the plants back in late winter. The new growth will mask these older leaves. Or run your fingers through the fresh new leaves removing the old leaves with each pass.

Hakone Grass (*Hakonechloa macra* 'Aureola')

This is one of the few ornamental grasses that will tolerate shade. The green and yellow variegated bamboo-like leaves make a nice contrast to the bold texture of blue or green hostas. The pink flowers and fall color, though subtle, create a bit of surprise and whimsy in the shade garden.

Grow this plant in partial shade and moist well-drained soils. Add organic matter to improve drainage in clay soils and water-holding ability in sandy soils. Be patient. It takes a few years for this plant to get established. Make sure the plant receives sufficient moisture during establishment. It is rated hardy to Zone 5 though I have seen plants thriving in Zone 4. A winter mulch of evergreen boughs applied after the ground freezes may help northern gardeners get this plant through cold open winters.

Ornamental and Native Sedges (*Carex* spp.)

Many of our native sedges can provide light airy texture in moist or shady locations. Some of the ornamental types add variegated or chartreuse foliage that help brighten up a shady spot in the landscape. Look for those that are hardy to your area, non-invasive, and fit the available space and landscape design.

'Ice Dance' (*Carex morrowii*)

This plant has really caught my attention. Its variegated leaves contrast with hosta and other greens in the shade garden. It tolerates our cold winters, moist soil, and shade. Consider adding one or two to your favorite shady spot.

PERENNIAL RESOURCES
for the Midwest

A landscape architect once told me that as gardeners and professionals we are always borrowing and improving on each other's designs. I would agree. I find my best garden designs are a combination of luck, borrowed ideas, and experimentation. Increase your luck by visiting private and public gardens in your area. They are great places to see which perennials will thrive in your area, plant combinations that provide great impact, and other design ideas that work or don't fit your gardening style.

And don't just make one visit. You really need to see the plants throughout the year. You will be amazed at how they change. Make sure the plant you just can't resist in bloom looks just as good when the flowers fade or the snow flies. Yes, snow—stop by in winter to see if you and the birds will enjoy these plants in your garden. And don't be shy about asking other visitors, volunteers, and staff about their favorite plants or combinations. There is a wealth of information growing in and walking through the gardens.

Here are a few of the Midwest perennial gardens that are open to the public. If I have left one out, sorry, but please let me know so we can try to include it in the next edition. For more information on some of these and other perennial gardens around the country visit the Perennial Plant Association website at www.perennialplant.org. Or purchase a copy of the 5th edition of *A Guide to Herbaceous Perennial Gardens in the United States and Canada*, available through the Perennial Plant Association, 3383 Schirtzinger Road, Hilliard, Ohio 43026, (614) 771-8431 or **www.perennialplant.org**.

Perennial Gardens by State

Illinois

Ball Seed Company
622 Town Road
W. Chicago, IL 60185
Call for an appointment
(630) 231-3500

Cantigny
15151 Winfield Road
Wheaton, IL 60187
(312) 668-5161

Chicago Botanic Garden
P.O. Box 400
Glencoe, IL 60022
(847) 835-5440

Craig Bergmann's Country Garden
700 Kenosha Road
Winthrop Harbor, IL 60096
(847) 746-0311

Earthman Nursery
5201 Monclair Avenue
Peoria Heights, IL 61614
Appointment required
(Phone number not available)

Fantasy Trail of Bald Eagle Nursery, Inc.
18510 Sand Road
Fulton, IL 61252
(815) 589-4121

George L. Luthy Memorial Botanical Garden
Glen Oak Park
2218 N. Prospect Road
Peoria, IL 61603
(309) 686-3362

Grinsteads Garden
204 Creek Street
Edwardsville, IL 62025
(618) 656-2181

Illinois Central College Arboretum
1 College Drive
East Peoria, IL 61635
(309) 694-5-ICC

Lake of the Woods Botanical Garden
P.O. Box 336
Mahomet, IL 61853
(217) 586-2612

Morton Arboretum
4100 Route 53
Lisle, IL 60532
(630) 968-0074

The Planter's Palette
28 W. 571 Roosevelt Road
Winfield, IL 60190
(708) 293-1040

Indiana

Indianapolis Museum of Art and the Oldfields Estate
1200 West 38th Street
Indianapolis, IN 46208
(317) 923-1331
www.ima-art.org

Purdue University
Dept. of Horticulture
West Lafayette, IN 47907
(317) 494-1296

Iowa

Bickelhaupt Arboretum
340 South 14th Street
Clinton, IA 52732
(563) 242-4771
www.bickarb.org

Des Moines Botanical Center
909 East River Drive
Des Moines, IA 50310
(515) 242-2934

Living History Farms
2600 N.W. 111th
Des Moines, IA 50310
(515) 278-5286

Reiman Gardens
Iowa State University
1407 Elwood Drive
Ames, IA 50011
(515) 294-2710
www.hort.iastate.edu

Kentucky

Akin' Back Farm
2501 Hwy. 53 S
LaGrange, KY 40031
(502) 222-5791

Locust Grove Historic Home
561 Blankenbaker Lane
Louisville, KY 40207
Appointment required
(502) 897-9845
www.locustgrove.org

University of Kentucky
Horticulture and Landscape Architecture Dept.
Lexington, KY 40506
(859) 257-6955

Michigan

Beal Botanical Garden at Michigan State University
Michigan State University
East Lansing, MI 48824-1112
(517) 432-9182 - garden use
(517) 355-9582 - curator
www.cpp.msu.edu/beal

Braeloch Farm
9124 N 35th Street
Richland, MI 49083
(616) 629-9884

The Bryer Patch Nursery
10206 West Q Avenue
Mattawan, MI 49071
(616) 668-3429

Cranbrook Gardens
380 Lone Pine Road
Bloomfield Hills, MI 48013
(248) 645-3147 or 877-GO-CRANBrook
http://www.cranbrook.edu

Dow Gardens
1018 W. Main Street
Midland, MI 48640
(517) 631-2677

Englerth Gardens
2461 22nd Street
Hopkins, MI 49328
(616) 793-7196

Fernwood Botanic Gardens
1720 Rangeline Road
Niles, MI 49120
(616) 695-6491

Fertile Crescent Nursery and Display Gardens
8110 M L Avenue
Kalamazoo, MI 49009
Appointment required
(616) 372-1598

Fox Hill Farm
444 W. Michigan Avenue
Parma, MI 49269
Appointment required
(517) 531-3179

Hunter's Creek Perennial Gardens
2555 South Lapeer Road
Lapeer, MI 48446
(313) 667-3891 or (313) 667-0635

Matthaei Botanical Gardens at the University of Michigan
1800 North Dixboro Road
Ann Arbor, MI 48105
(734) 998-7061
http://www.lsa.umich.edu/mbg

Michigan State University
Dept. of Horticulture
East Lansing, MI 48824-1112
(517) 355-0348

Nichols Arboretum,University of Michigan
610 Washington Heights
Ann Arbor, MI 48109
(734) 998-9540
http://www.umich.edu/~wwwarb

Willard's Weigh Herbs & Heirlooms
4579 West E Avenue
Kalamazoo, MI 49007
Appointment needed for off-season visits
(616) 342-5636

Minnesota

Borkeleta Gardens
15980 Canby Avenue
Faribault, MN 55021
(507) 334-2807

Busse Gardens
5873 Oliver Avenue
S.W. Cokato, MN 55321
http://www.bussegardens.com

Lyndale Park Perennial/Annual Garden
NE shore of Lake Harriet on Roseway Road
between King's Highway and Lake Harriet Parkway
Lyndale, MN 55359

Rice Creek Gardens, Inc.
11506 Highway 65
Blaine, MN 55434
Appointment required
(763) 754-8090
www.ricecreekgardens.com/

University of Minnesota Landscape Arboretum
PO Box 39, 3675 Arboretum Drive
Chanhassen, MN 55317
(952) 443-2460
www.arboretum.umn.edu/

Missouri

Gilberg Perennial Farms
2906 Ossenfort Road
Glencoe, MO 63038
Appointment required for tour
(636) 458-2033
http://www.gilbergperennials.com

Missouri Botanical Garden
4344 Shaw Boulevard
P.O. Box 299
St. Louis, MO 63166
(314) 577-5100
(314) 577-9400
(800) 642-8842
www.mobot.org

Powell Gardens
1609 NW US Highway 50
Kingsville, MO 64061
(816) 697-2600 Ext. 241
www.powellgardens.org

Woodland and Floral Garden University of Missouri
Columbia, MO 62511

Ohio

Chadwick Arboretum
The Ohio State University
Columbus, OH 43210
http://chadwickarboretum.osu.edu

Cincinnati Zoo and Botanical Garden
3400 Vine Street
Cincinnati, OH 45220
(513) 281-4701 Ext. 8307
www.cincyzoo.org (Revised!)

Cleveland Botanical Garden
11030 East Boulevard
Cleveland, OH 44106
(216) 721-1600

Columbus Zoological Gardens
9990 Riverside Drive
P.O. Box 400, Powell, OH 43065

Dawes Arboretum
7770 Jacksontown Road SE
Newark, OH 43055
(800) 44-DAWES or (740) 323-2355
www.dawesarb.org

Fellows Riverside Gardens of Mill Creek Park
816 Glenwood Avenue
Youngstown, OH 44502
Appointment required

Gardenview Horticultural Park
16711 Pearl Road (Route 42)
Strongsville, OH 44136-6048
(216) 238-6653

Gateway Gardens and Nursery
8079 Ferguson Road
Streetsboro, OH 44240

Hillview Idea Gardens
10923 Lamb's Lane N.E.
Newark, OH 43055
(740) 763-2873

Holden Arboretum
9500 Sperry Road
Mentor, OH 44060
(216) 256-1110

Homestead Division
8448 Mayfield Road
Chesterland, OH 44026
(440) 729-9838 (New!)

Inniswood Metro Gardens
940 South Hempstead Road
Westerville, OH 43081
(614) 895-6216
http://metroparks.co.franklin.oh.us

Kingwood Center
900 Park Avenue
West, Mansfield, OH 44906
(419) 522-0211

Lantern Court
9203 Kirtland-Chardon Road
Kirtland, OH 44060
Appointment required

Spring Hill Nurseries
110 W. Elm Street
Tipp City, OH 45371

Stan Hywet Hall Foundation, Inc.
714 N Portage Path
Akron, OH 44303

Sunnybrook Farms, Homestead Garden
9448 Mayfield Road
Chesterland, OH 44023
(216) 729-7232

The Ohio State University Agricultural Technical Institute
1328 Dover Road
Wooster, OH 44691
(330) 264-3911

Toledo Botanical Gardens
5403 Elmer Drive
Toledo, OH 43615
(419) 936-2986
http://www.toledogarden.org

Wisconsin

Allen Centennial Gardens
University of Wisconsin Campus
620 Babcock Drive
Madison, WI 53706
(608) 262-1549
www.hort.wisc.edu/acg

Boerner Botanical Gardens
5879 South 92nd Street
Hales Corners, WI 53130
(414) 525-5600

Green Bay Botanic Gardens
2600 Larsen Road
Green Bay, WI 54305
(920) 490-9457

Hanson's Rhinelander Floral & Garden
2660 Highway G
Rhinelander, WI 54501
Appointment required
(715) 365-2929

Olbrich Botanical Gardens
3330 Atwood Avenue
Madison, WI 53704
(608) 246-4551

Prairie Ridge Nursery
9738 Overland Road
Mt. Horeb, WI 53572-2832
Appointment required
(608) 437-5245
www.prairieridgenursery.com

UW-Stout Campus Grounds
Corner of Main Street and Broadway
Menomonie, WI 54751

Winter Greenhouse
W 7041 Olmstead Road
Winter, WI 54896
(715) 266-4963

Gardening References

No one person can know it all or one book provide all the information that every gardener wants to know. Gardening is the best way to learn about growing plants successfully. But none of us have enough time to learn all we want about all the plants there are to grow. Increase your knowledge by talking with other gardeners and professionals, reading books and magazines, attending workshops and surfing the internet. Here are just a few societies, websites and books you may find helpful. Be sure to keep adding your favorites to this list.

Plant Societies

Alpine Garden Society
AGS Centre
Avon Bank
Pershore, Worcestershire. WR10 3JP
United Kingdom
http://www.alpinegardensociety.org

American Daylily Society
American Hemerocallis Society
http://www.daylilies.org

American Fern Society
http://www.amerfernsoc.org

American Horticultural Society
http://www.ahs.org

American Hosta Society
http://www.hosta.org/ahsgeneral.htm

American Iris Society
http://www.irises.org

American Penstemon Society
http://www.biosci.ohio-state.edu/~awolfe/Penstemon/Penstemon.html#links

American Penstemon Society: Dale Lindgren, West Central Research Center
Route 4, Box 46A
North Platte, NE 69101

American Peony Society
http://www.americanpeonysociety.org

American Primrose Society
www.americanprimrosesoc.org

Gardening Organizations Directory
http://www.backyardgardener.com/soc.html

National Chrysanthemum Society
http://www.mums.org

North American Rock Garden Society
http://www.nargs.org
NARGS
PO Box 67
Millwood, NY 10546

Perennial Plant Association
3383 Schirtzinger Road
Hilliard, Ohio 43026
(614) 771-8431
(614) 876-5238 Fax
www.perennialplant.org

The Sedum Society
http://www.cactus-mall.com/sedum

Websites

Chicago Botanic Garden
http://www.chicagobotanic.org/plantinfo

Iowa State University Extension publications, on-line
at http://www.extension.iastate.edu/pubs

Jackson and Perkins
www.jacksonandperkins.com

Michigan State University Extension publications
www.msue.msu.edu

Missouri Botanical Gardens
www.mobot.org

Open Days Directory: the Guide to Visiting Hundreds of America's Best Private Gardens
www.gardenconservancy.org

Perennial Plant Association website
www.perennialplant.org

Purdue University Extension Service publications
http://www.agcom.purdue.edu/AgCom/Pubs/menu.htm

The Ohio State University Extension publications
http://ohioline.osu.edu

University of Illinois Extension publications
http://www.urbanext.uiuc.edu

University of Kentucky publications
http://www.ca.uky.edu/agc/pubs/pubs.htm

University of Minnesota Extension publications
www.extension.umn.edu

University of Minnesota Landscape Arboretum website
www.arboretum.umn.edu

University of Missouri Outreach and Education publications
http://muextension.missouri.edu/xplor/agguides/hort

University of Wisconsin Extension publications
www.uwex.edu/ces/wihort

Perennial Books

Armitage, Allan, *Armitage's Garden Perennials: A Color Encyclopedia*, Portland, Oregon: Timber Press, 2000.

Cairns, Thomas. *Ortho's All About Perennials*. San Francisco, CA: Ortho Books, 1999.

Darke, Rick. *Color Encyclopedia of Ornamental Grasses*, Portland, Oregon: Timber Press, 1999.

DiSabato-Aust, Tracy. *The Well Tended Perennial Garden, Planting and Pruning Techniques*. Portland, Oregon: Timber Press, 1998.

Eddison, Sydney, Stephen Silk and Pamela Harper, *The Gardener's Palette*, McGraw-Hill, 2002

Hockenberry Meyer, Mary, *Ornamental Grasses for Cold Climates*, St. Paul Minnesota: Minnesota Extension Service, 1995.

Hudak, Joseph, *Gardening with Perennials Month by Month*. Portland, OR: Timber Press, 1994.

Myers, Melinda, *The Birds and Bloom Ultimate Gardening Guide*. Greendale, WI: Reiman Publications, 2003.

Phillips, Ellen and Colton Burrell, *Rodale's Illustrated Encyclopedia of Perennials*, Emmaus, PA: Rodale Press, 1993.

Schwartz, Bobbie, *The Design Puzzle, Putting the Pieces Together*, Shaker Heights, OH: Bobbie Schwartz, 2001.

State Specific Gardening Books

Boland, Tom, Laura Coit, Marty Hair. *Michigan Gardener's Guide Revised*, Nashville, TN: Cool Springs Press, 2002.

Fizzel, James, *Illinois Gardener's Guide Revised*, Nashville, TN: Cool Springs Press, 2002.

Fizzel, James, *Month-by-Month Gardening in Illinois*, Franklin, TN: Cool Springs Press, 1999.

Fizzel, James, *Month-by-Month Gardening in Indiana*, Franklin, TN: Cool Springs Press, 1999.

Fizzel, James, *Month-by-Month Gardening in Michigan*, Franklin, TN: Cool Springs Press, 1999.

McKeown, Denny, *Kentucky Gardener's Guide*, Franklin, TN: Cool Springs Press, 2002.

McKeown, Denny, *Ohio Gardener's Guide Revised*, Franklin, TN: Cool Springs Press, 2004.

Miller, Mike, *Missouri Gardener's Guide*, Franklin, TN: Cool Springs Press, 1998.

Myers, Melinda, *Minnesota Gardener's Guide*, Franklin, TN: Cool Springs Press, 2001.

Myers, Melinda, *Month-by-Month Gardening in Minnesota*, Franklin, TN: Cool Springs Press, 2001.

Myers, Melinda, *Month-by-Month Gardening in Wisconsin*, Franklin, TN: Cool Springs Press, 2001.

Myers, Melinda, *The Garden Book for Wisconsin Revised*, Nashville, TN: Cool Springs Press, 2004

Sharp, Jo Ellen and Tom Tyler, *Indiana Gardener's Guide*, Franklin, TN: Cool Springs Press, 1997.

USDA HARDINESS ZONES
for the Midwest

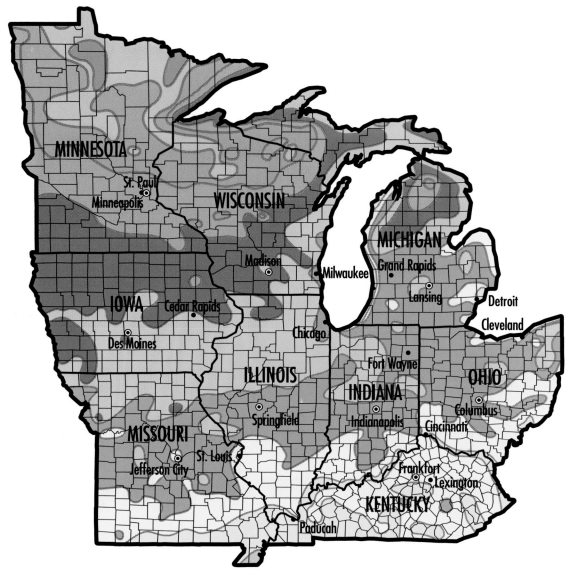

ZONE	Average Minimum Temperature °F
3a	-35 to -40
3b	-30 to -35
4a	-25 to -30
4b	-20 to -25
5a	-15 to -20
5b	-10 to -15
6a	-5 to -10
6b	0 to -5
7a	5 to 0

PRECIPITATION
for the Midwest

January 1 to December 31
Averaged from 1961 to 1990

Inches

| 2.5 | 20 | 25 | 30 | 35 | 40 | 45 | 50 | 55 |

Data from the "Midwestern Regional
Climate Center, Champaign, Illinois"

INDEX

PHOTO AND ILLUSTRATION CREDITS

Illustrations by Elayne Sears

Neil Soderstrom: 8A, 33BCD, 34, 36A, 40ABC, 42ABCDE, 43AB, 45, 47B, 48AB, 49, 50AB, 51, 52, 53, 54ABC, 55AB, 57ABCDE, 58ABCDE, 59ABC, 61AB, 62ABCDEFG, 63AB, 66ABCD, 67, 71, 72, 74AB, 76, 78, 81, 82ABC, 83, 86AB, 87ABC, 89AB, 90ABC, 91, 92AB, 93A, 100, 101AB, 103A, 104AB, 106, 107, 108B, 109AB, 118AB, 120, 121AB, 126

Thomas Eltzroth: 7, 11, 12B, 13AB, 15B, 17, 18A, 23, 26B, 27B, 28A, 32A, 33A, 37, 38, 64, 65, 79, 80B, 112, 129B, 132, 139B, 140, 142A, 143AB, 145A, 146AB, 148A, 150B, 152A, 153A, 154A, 155AB, 156B, 157B, 158B, 159B, 162A, 163B, 164A, 165AB, 166A, 167B, 168A, 169A, 170A, 171A, 172A, 173AB, 174A, 175A, 176A, 177B, 178A, 179AB, 180B, 181B, 183B, 184B, 186AB, 187AB, 189A, 190B, 191B

Jerry Pavia: 6, 8B, 10, 12C, 13C, 15A, 20, 25, 26A, 27A, 28B, 29AC, 30B, 31, 32B, 36B, 39, 41, 46, 73, 80A, 96B, 97, 105, 108A, 110, 114, 116, 117, 122B, 124B, 125, 127, 128, 129A, 130B, 131, 133AB, 136B, 139A, 141, 142B, 144B, 147A, 148B, 149A, 150A, 151A, 158A, 159A, 161A, 162B, 163A, 164B, 166B, 167A, 168B, 170B, 171B, 172B, 175B, 176B, 178B, 182AB, 185AB, 190A, 191A, 192

Charles Mann: 9, 12D, 21, 22AB, 29B, 111, 130A, 134, 135B, 137, 138, 180A, 183A, 184A

Liz Ball and Rick Ray: 44, 47C, 147B, 153B, 154B, 156A, 160B, 174B, 188B

Felder Rushing: 12A, 47A, 93B, 96A, 99, 101D, 102, 119, 122A, 123A, 157A

André Viette: 14A, 16, 24, 103B, 135A, 145B, 177A

David Winger: 30A, 115, 124A, 136A, 160A, 169B

Cathy Wilkinson Barash: 123B, 151B, 188A

Mark Turner: 144A, 161B, 181A

Michael Dirr: 149B

Erica Glasener: 18B

Pam Harper: 152B

Dency Kane: 189B

Peter Loewer: 14B

Alison Miksch, Brand X Pictures®: 35, 69, 139C

PhotoDisc® by Getty Images™: 70, 101C, 113, 118C

Key: from left to right, top to bottom of page, A=first photo, B=second, C=third, D=fourth, E=fifth, F=sixth, G=seventh

Chapter Introduction Photos: *Hemerocallis* 'Silent Entry' by Jerry Pavia (page 6), *Iris tectorum* by Jerry Pavia (10), *Hosta undulata* by Jerry Pavia (20), *Digitalis purpurea* 'Foxy' by Thomas Eltzroth (38), *Coreopsis grandiflora* 'Early Sunrise' by Thomas Eltzroth (64), *Athyrium nipponicum* 'Pictum' by Jerry Pavia (110), *Hibiscus moscheutos* 'Clown Pink' (140) by Thomas Eltzroth, *Scabiosa columbaria* 'Butterfly Blue' by Jerry Pavia (192)

Cover Photo: *Scabiosa columbaria* 'Butterfly Blue' by Jerry Pavia

Back Cover (left to right): *Hemerocallis* 'Silent Entry' by Jerry Pavia, *Coreopsis grandiflora* 'Early Sunrise' by Thomas Eltzroth, *Iris sibirica* 'Pink Haze' by Jerry Pavia

MEET THE AUTHORS

Teri Dunn

Teri Dunn is a freelance writer and editor. She is a former Senior Copy Writer for Jackson & Perkins. Her articles on roses, perennials, waterlilies, wildflowers, and other topics have appeared in *Horticulture* magazine, for which she worked for many years as an Associate Editor. Teri is the author of numerous other gardening titles, including the acclaimed *Potting Places: Creative Ideas for Practical Gardening Workplaces, Cottage Gardens, 600 Essential Plants,* and several books in the popular *100 Favorites Series* on roses, perennials, herbs, shade plants, and others. She resides on Cape Ann, Massachusetts, with her husband Shawn and sons Wes and Tristan.

Melinda Myers has authored several gardening books, including the *Minnesota State Horticultural Society's Minnesota Gardener's Guide* and *The Garden Book for Wisconsin;* has been a contributing editor and columnist for *Birds & Blooms Magazine;* and has written a bi-monthly column, "Gardener's Questions," for the *Milwaukee Journal* since 1986. Melinda is host of "The Plant Doctor Radio Show" on WTMJ and "Great Lakes Gardener," seen on PBS stations throughout the Midwest. She received the Garden Communicator's Award from the American Nursery and Landscape Association in 1998 and the Quill and Trowel award from the Garden Writers Association. In addition to writing, Melinda is also a teacher and consultant, with over twenty years of experience in the field of horticulture.

Melinda Myers